PATENTS AS PROTECTION OF TRADITIONAL MEDICAL KNOWLEDGE?

European Studies in Law and Economics Series

1. *Group Litigation in European Competition Law. A Law and Economics Perspective,* Sonja E. Keske
2. *Behavioural Economics in Consumer Policy,* Hanneke Luth
3. *Ex-Post Liability Rules in Modern Patent Law,* Rosa Castro Bernieri
4. *Competition and Innovation in the EU Regulation of Pharmaceuticals: The Case of Parallel Trade,* Claudia Desogus
5. *The Law and Economics of Organ Procurement,* Fırat Bilgel
6. *Law and Economics in the RIA World. Improving the use of economic analysis in public policy and legislation,* Andrea Renda
7. *Regulatory Competition in European Corporate and Capital Market Law,* Lars Hornuf
8. *Economic Criteria for Criminalization: Optimizing Enforcement in Case of Environmental Violations,* Katarina Svatikova

PATENTS AS PROTECTION OF TRADITIONAL MEDICAL KNOWLEDGE?

A Law and Economics Analysis

Petra Ebermann

intersentia
Cambridge – Antwerp – Portland

Intersentia Publishing Ltd.
Trinity House | Cambridge Business Park | Cowley Road
Cambridge | CB4 0WZ | United Kingdom
Tel.: +44 1223 393 753 | Email: mail@intersentia.co.uk

Distribution for the UK:
Hart Publishing Ltd.
16C Worcester Place
Oxford OX1 2JW
UK
Tel.: +44 1865 517 530
Email: mail@hartpub.co.uk

Distribution for the USA and Canada:
International Specialized Book Services
920 NE 58th Ave. Suite 300
Portland, OR 97213
USA
Tel.: +1 800 944 6190 (toll free)
Email: info@isbs.com

Distribution for Austria:
Neuer Wissenschaftlicher Verlag
Argentinierstraße 42/6
1040 Wien
Austria
Tel.: +43 1 535 61 03 24
Email: office@nwv.at

Distribution for other countries:
Intersentia Publishing nv
Groenstraat 31
2640 Mortsel
Belgium
Tel.: +32 3 680 15 50
Email: mail@intersentia.be

Patents as Protection of Traditional Medical Knowledge? A Law and Economics Analysis
Petra Ebermann

ISBN 978-1-78068-073-6
NUR 820

British Library Cataloguing in Publication Data. A catalogue record for this book is available from the British Library.

ACKNOWLEDGMENTS

This book was in large parts written while I was a research assistant at the Institute of Law and Economics at the University of Hamburg. A number of people have contributed to the final success of this project and I want to take the opportunity to thank them.

First of all, I am especially grateful to my supervisor Thomas Eger for his time, helpful comments and advice and likewise to Hans-Bernd Schäfer who kindly agreed to act as second reviewer and handled the review process very efficiently whilst offering appropriate critique. My colleagues at the Institute were supportive at all times and provided well appreciated comments and inspiration. Amongst them, I would like to mention Katharina Greczszuk and Katherine Walker explicitly who have also become good friends of mine during this time. I wish to thank the editors of the scientific series 'European Studies in Law and Economics' for giving me the opportunity to publish this book in this series: Michael G. Faure, Luigi A. Franzoni and Patrick C. Leyens. I thank the Max Planck Institute of Intellectual Property and Competition Law in Munich for allowing me to conduct parts of my research at their library. I am especially indebted to Inga Ebermann and Tanja Friedrich for their active support, valuable comments and advice and Gabor Gottlieb and Paul Stange for providing practical and technical support at all times.

Most importantly, I want to take the opportunity to thank my parents, my sister (once more) and Patrick Hauser for their support, patience, kindness and constant encouragement.

CONTENTS

INTRODUCTION

Traditional knowledge held by local and indigenous groups, often located in remote areas of the world, receives public attention more and more. Traditional knowledge applications can be found in many areas such as traditional agriculture, crafts, folklore or medical treatment. Western companies show an increasing interest in biological resources and associated traditional knowledge about their use. Especially the pharmaceutical sector has discovered the immense potential that lies in the biodiversity-rich areas of the world.

Plant resources and traditional medical knowledge provide cures for all kinds of diseases and can provide valuable clues for pharmaceutical research and development. Healers in Western Samoa, for example, use the tropical plant *Homalanthus nutans* to treat hepatitis. The National Cancer Institute has undertaken research based on this observation and developed the active agent prostratin which shows promising potential for the treatment of the 'human immunodeficiency virus' (HIV).[1] The *Rosy periwinkle* found in Madagascar provides two compounds, vinblastine and vincristine, that have been proven useful to treat Hodgkin's disease and juvenile leukemia.[2] The people of Madagascar have used the plant to treat diabetes.[3] In the Korup forest of Cameroon a vine, *Cladus korupensis*, with enormous potential for the treatment of 'acquired immune deficiency syndrome' (Aids) has been identified.[4] The Australian *Smokebush* is also discussed as a potential medication for Aids patients.[5]

The examples show that indigenous communities hold knowledge that can be of great benefit to mankind as an alternative to conventional medicine. In times of growing resistance of bacteria to antibiotics and the existence of diseases that prove to be incurable by conventional medicine, such as certain forms of cancer or HIV, these alternatives are of great interest in terms of access to cures and

---

1 www.aidsmeds.com/articles/hiv_prostratin_reservoirs_1667_17975.shtml (last visited on January 8, 2012).

2 Odek, Bio-Piracy: Creating Proprietary Rights in Plant Genetic Resources, 2 J. Intell. Prop. L. 141, 143; citing Birds and Bees, Economist May 10, 1992 at 15, 17.

3 www.livingrainforest.org/about-rainforests/anti-cancer-rosy-periwinkle/ (last visited on January 8, 2012).

4 Odek, Bio-Piracy: Creating Proprietary Rights in Plant Genetic Resources, 2 J. Intell. Prop. L. 141, 143.

5 Blakeney, The Protection of Traditional Knowledge under Intellectual Property Law, E.I.P.R. 2000, 251, 255.

medical treatment and consequently bear considerable economic and social value.

It is well-accepted practice that pharmaceutical companies attempt to secure exclusive rights in the drugs they develop in order to recoup the investments they have made during the development process. They rely on obtaining patents which allow them to market the protected substances exclusively for a certain period of time. During the protection period the patent owner can charge a monopoly price because he does not have to face competition. The system is based on the notion that investments in intellectual creations need to be stimulated in order to avoid an undersupply of intellectual creations in the market. The claim of patents for substances or applications that have been used in traditional knowledge settings, however, is controversially discussed.

The juice of the *Karela* plant, for example, has been used in India as an anti-diabetic. A patent claiming the anti-diabetic effects of *Karela* is held by a company based in the United States.[6] The development of the anti-malarial drug quinine is based on observations that chewing the bark of the South American *Cinchona* tree as practiced by the peoples of Peru prevented them from getting malaria.[7] Under US patent No. 5,401,504 a patent on *Turmeric*, a plant with wound healing properties from India, was granted to the University of Mississippi in 1994. The Indian Government challenged the patent claiming that *Turmeric* has been used in Indian traditional medicine for generations and thus lacks novelty making it unavailable for patent protection. The patent was finally revoked. However, other uses of *Turmeric* such as the treatment of skin disorders[8] or health ailments[9] are still subjects of valid patents.

Prominent examples of highly disputed patent cases are furthermore the *Neem* tree patents. The US based company W.R. Grace holds at least 40 patents in the US and 150 patents worldwide which are related to the *Neem* tree.[10] There have been two patent challenges widely spoken of. The *Neem* tree is natural to India. Its oil can, for example, be used as a pesticide. This agricultural use of the oil has been known in India for centuries. W.R. Grace received a patent for improving *Neem* tree oil. The patent claim concerns the extraction of *Neem* oil from crushed seeds in a new solvent, a storage stable azadirachtin formulation, which, unlike water which has been used before, leads to an extended shelf life.[11] Under Indian laws the substance was not eligible for patent protection because India did not provide for product patents at the time. The Indian

6 U.S. Patent No. 5,900,240.
7 Sutton, Law and Biotechnology: Cases and Materials, 237.
8 U.S. Patent No. 5,897,865.
9 U.S. Patent No. 6,048,533.
10 Dutfield, Intellectual Property, Biogenetic Resources and Traditional Knowledge, 53.
11 Patent No 5,124,349; Kadidal, Subject-Matter Imperialism? Biodiversity, Foreign Prior Art and the Neem Patent Controversy, 37 IDEA 371, 374; Dutfield, Intellectual Property, Biogenetic Resources and Traditional Knowledge, 53.

government challenged patents claiming the effects of *Neem* tree oil as a pesticide and fungicide in the United States and Europe. The European patent was revoked.[12] The challenge of the US patent, however, was unsuccessful.

These cases are often used to explain a phenomenon referred to as biopiracy defined as '*the appropriation of the knowledge and genetic resources of farming and indigenous communities by individuals or institutions seeking exclusive monopoly control over these resources and knowledge*'.[13] They indeed draw a picture of appropriation of knowledge and resources from biodiversity-rich countries in the South which are patented and commercially exploited by multinational biotechnological companies in the North.[14] The partially successful opposition to the patents for *Turmeric* or *Neem* supports the argument of unfair use. While the benefits from the developed end products to a large extent flow to the North, the inputs to a fair extent stem from biological resources and traditional knowledge frequently found in the biodiversity-rich countries of the South. It is irritating that the patent holders make high financial profits with their invention while the indigenous group that provides the knowledge and the source countries which host the plant genetic resources for new medical products and respective local groups should be left empty-handed.

This is at least a comprehensible concern when the patent concerns a substance that has been applied to treat the same disease in traditional medicine. In other cases, however, such as the development of prostratin from the *Homalanthus nutans* or vinblastine and vincristine from the *Rosy periwinkle*, it may not be an obvious case of misuse since the application differs from the one used by the indigenous peoples. In each case some kind of initial lead was provided by the original user but this link between the original remedy and the improved or modified product can be of different intensity. The contribution of the pharmaceutical companies is far more technical in nature and requires considerable financial investment. It is also valuable and crucial to the development of the final drug.

There are cases in which the providers of knowledge receive a share of the generated profits. An example worth mentioning is the case of the San people of Southern Africa who have used the *Hoodia* cactus since ancient times to suppress hunger when they went on hunting expeditions.[15] Opposition to a patent on the

---

12 Patent No. 436257 B1. The *Neem* patent proceedings will be discussed in greater detail below. See infra Part 2:2.1.2.1. and Part 2:2.1.3.2.

13 Report of the Commission on Intellectual Property Rights, 74.

14 The terms 'South' and 'North' are synonymously used to refer to the developed and underdeveloped countries in the Southern hemisphere and the developed countries in the Northern hemisphere.

15 Dolder, Traditional Knowledge and Patenting: The Experience of the Neemfungicide and the Hoodia Cases, 26 Biotechnology L. Rep. 583, 587.

use of an extract from the *Hoodia* cactus as an anti-obesity drug led to an agreement under which the San people receive royalties.[16]

Biological resources provide an array of potentially useful substances. One possible way to find effective biological remedies is to undertake a specified and targeted search for plant genetic resources and their application based on the knowledge of tribes and other communities living a traditional lifestyle. If accessible in this way, traditional medical knowledge bears a considerable market value. On the one hand there is a worldwide interest in research and development activities in this sector in order to make this knowledge available for the benefit of all. On the other hand, one must recognize the perception that traditional knowledge is exploited and marketed exclusively in order to ensure high profits without adequately compensating the providers of the knowledge. This might at one point lead to an unwillingness of the indigenous groups to grant continuing access to their resources. A tendency to restrict access can already be observed.

Different views can be found with regard to these issues. One perspective is to condemn the practice of 'biopiracy' as the appropriation and commercialization of genetic resources and associated traditional knowledge may be considered to be legally and morally wrong and to constitute unjust exploitation of the resources of the source countries. This view is based on the premise that genetic resources and associated knowledge are not in the public domain and that certain stakeholders have proprietary rights over them. As opposed to this, the importance of R&D in this area, the need to encourage investment and the great benefit to mankind that can be achieved by using these resources must not be overlooked. Supporters of this point of view acknowledge the importance of traditional knowledge and tend to allow its appropriation on the one hand, but ask for adequate compensation to those providing the knowledge and resources.

There are two distinct and obvious problems in regard to the use of genetic resources, namely access to and preservation of biological diversity. The biodiversity-rich countries in the South fear exploitation of their resources. The threat of exploitation does not only concern the exhaustion of the plant resources themselves but encompasses the extraction of the genetic information embodied in the resources. Once this information is further developed and exclusively protected in the developed countries, the source countries are deprived of the opportunity to commoditize plant genetic resources themselves. Realizing the economic value of their genetic resources to the industrialized world, governments of biodiversity-rich developing countries have started to demand a share of the profits.

---

16 http://Hoodiaoffer.com/Hoodia-uk/kalahari-Hoodia-san-royalties.html (last visited on January 8, 2012). The *Hoodia* case will be discussed in greater detail below. See infra Part 2:2.1.3.2.

Access to new plant-based remedies depends greatly on the preservation and availability of biological diversity. The ongoing depletion of the world's rainforests poses a threat as it diminishes the opportunities to find new useful remedies. The Convention on Biological Diversity (CBD) is the main international agreement that addresses the threat of biodiversity loss and aims at achieving conservation and sustainable use of biological diversity. The Convention also incorporates provisions in regard to the protection of traditional knowledge.

One institution that may be used to implement these objectives is the intellectual property regime. At first sight one deals with information – be it the genetic information embodied in a plant resource or the knowledge of the application of plant remedies to human needs. Either can be the designated subject of intellectual property rights protection.

Since the establishment of the World Trade Organization (WTO) and the implementation of the Agreement on Trade-Related Aspects of Intellectual Property Rights (TRIPS), the protection of intellectual property rights more and more becomes a global issue as Member States are required to provide minimum standards for patent protection. The interplay of the CBD and the TRIPS Agreement is an important part of the debate surrounding traditional medical knowledge and intellectual property rights. It must be discussed in order to decide whether it is possible to implement the objectives set out in the CBD in regard to the protection of traditional knowledge within contemporary patent regimes and in the context of TRIPS in a mutually supportive way. As the biological resources and the associated traditional knowledge stem from the developing countries but are used in the developed world, the international component is an important factor. The position of the developing countries is hence a vital part of the debate.

Questions of ownership and control of access to genetic resources are at the center of the discussion. While the genetic resources and the knowledge could be considered to be in the public domain it can also be argued that ownership rests with the source countries and local and indigenous groups, respectively. The pharmaceutical companies that invest in R&D might or might not be unjustly enriched if they commercialize a product that is based on traditional medical knowledge but which has, on the other hand, been modified and transformed into a product with improved characteristics as for example an increased efficiency or less side effects, which is capable of commercial exploitation or may even serve as treatment to a different disease than the original remedy.

The opinions on the question as how best to regulate traditional knowledge use are versatile. Developing countries have the intention to include traditional knowledge holders in existing intellectual property systems and establish benefit-sharing agreements. Indigenous groups claim that existing intellectual property regimes do not address the subject of traditional knowledge and lead to the destruction of biological diversity and cultural heritage.[17] Some authors hold that an entirely new system is needed[18] while others support the adaptation and incorporation in existing systems.[19]

In the context of intellectual property rights it can be noted that the topic is new and challenges existing laws. Traditional medical knowledge and biotechnology were not an issue when intellectual property laws were designed. This book provides a discussion of the applicability of intellectual property rights to traditional medical knowledge protection and asks whether intellectual property rights are suitable to promote the goals of the CBD effectively in this regard. The economic analysis of law will be used to evaluate whether the rationale of intellectual property protection applies to the problem and what effects changes of the current regimes might have on the incentives to undertake pharmaceutical R&D activities. Economic analysis can provide insights in a broad range of question such as to the benefits and costs of bioprospecting, control of access and preservation of biodiversity and the incentives that work in the respective markets. It can serve as a guidance to determine the adequateness and extent of legal intervention. This is why the economic analysis of law has been chosen to be the method to examine the issues. It will be applied to evaluate whether the implementation of the CBD objectives will result in an increase of social welfare and to analyze whether the trade-off between the implementation of the objectives in the context of intellectual property rights and the accompanying restraints in patent applications is efficient.

This book is structured as follows:

In part 1 the concepts of traditional medical knowledge and pharmaceutical biotechnological inventions, the interfaces between those concepts and the relationship with and impact of intellectual property rights are explained. The Convention on Biological Diversity with emphasis on its basic principles and objectives and its relevance to the protection of traditional medical knowledge is presented. The designated effects of the objectives are analyzed from a law and economics point of view. Furthermore, the position of traditional medical knowledge in the context of international intellectual property rights is addressed which includes a discussion on whether the protection and adequate use of traditional medical knowledge and related benefit-sharing agreements are at all an issue of intellectual property rights protection. In this context the economics of intellectual property rights, especially patents, are introduced. As the most important international agreement dealing with intellectual property

---

17 See generally: Report of the Commission on Intellectual Property Rights, 1ff.

18 Githaiga, Intellectual Property Law and the Protection of Indigenous Folklore and Knowledge, 5 Murdoch University Electronic L. J. 1998; Shiva, Global Trade and Intellectual Property: Threats to Indigenous Resources, in Krimsky/Shorett, Rights and Liberties in the Biotech Age, 98, 105.

19 Biber-Klemm/Cottier, Rights to Plant Genetic Resources and Traditional Knowledge, 245ff.

rights, the TRIPS agreements is introduced and discussed in regard to its basic objectives, the position of the developing countries to intellectual property protection and its relationship with the CBD.

In part 2 the status quo of traditional medical knowledge and biotechnological inventions protection under current patent law in the United States and the European Union is presented in order to examine whether the claimed exploitation is indeed taking place. For this purpose the patent requirements of EU and US patents law are introduced with emphasis on the rules relevant to traditional knowledge and biotechnology protection. The results are analyzed from a law and economics perspective. The patent proceedings in the *Neem* case and the *Hoodia* case are used to discuss the difficulties and contradictions involved.

In part 3 the possible different approaches to achieve fair treatment of traditional medical knowledge are examined. Possible approaches within the existing laws include the creation of traditional knowledge rights and the introduction of requirements to disclose the source of the genetic material and knowledge, provide proof of prior informed consent of the providers of traditional knowledge and conclude mandatory benefit-sharing agreements making the approval of a patent application contingent to the fulfillment of these requirements. Alternatively compensatory regimes are discussed.

This book concludes with a summary of the results and the implications for future discussion.

PART 1

TRADITIONAL MEDICAL KNOWLEDGE, BIOLOGICAL DIVERSITY AND INTELLECTUAL PROPERTY RIGHTS

CHAPTER 1

THE CONCEPT OF TRADITIONAL MEDICAL KNOWLEDGE AND THE IMPACT OF BIOTECHNOLOGY

Any discussion on adequate protection of traditional medical knowledge in the context of intellectual property rights must start with clarifying the concept of traditional medical knowledge as a subcategory of traditional and indigenous knowledge and the relevance and impact of biotechnological pharmaceutical R&D and intellectual property rights.

1.1. A DEFINITION OF TRADITIONAL MEDICAL KNOWLEDGE

Traditional peoples and communities provide a large share of the world's cultural diversity and their knowledge is quite varied in scope and application. It refers for example to agricultural methods and medical treatment. It plays an important role in the daily life of millions of people, particularly in the developing world, as it contributes to their food security and health maintenance.[20] Traditional medical knowledge is the knowledge that local and indigenous peoples hold of the healing properties of plants.

1.1.1. TRADITIONAL AND INDIGENOUS KNOWLEDGE

The only consent in regard to what traditional knowledge encompasses is that it is difficult to find a conceptual definition of traditional and indigenous knowledge.

Two basic forms of traditional knowledge can be distinguished, namely cultural expression or folklore, on the one hand, and knowledge and innovation such as plant, medical or agricultural knowledge, on the other hand.[21] Various

---

20 Report of the Commission on Intellectual Property Rights, 73.

21 Hansen/vanFleet, Traditional Knowledge and Intellectual Property, 3; Sapp, Monopolizing Medical Methods: The Debate over Patent Rights for Indigenous Peoples, 25 Temp. J. Sci. Tech. & Envtl. L. 191, 196.

approaches and attempts to define and categorize traditional knowledge can be found in the academic literature. An attempt to provide a handy short-term definition has been undertaken by Hansen and VanFleet who hold that traditional knowledge encompasses

> 'the information that people in a given community, based on experience and adaptation to a local culture and environment, have developed over time and continue to develop'.[22]

Anthropologist Martha Johnson defines traditional knowledge as

> 'a body of knowledge built by a group of people through generations living in close contact with nature' including 'a system of classifications, a set of empirical observations about the local environment, and a system of self-management that governs resource use'.[23]

Miriam Latorre Quinn relies on general characteristics to define traditional knowledge, namely the creation through a long period of time in which the knowledge has been passed down from generation to generation, the integration of new knowledge into existing knowledge as knowledge is improved, the improvement and creation of knowledge as a group effort and varying forms of ownership of indigenous knowledge between indigenous peoples.[24] The World Intellectual Property Organization (WIPO) states that no single definition would do justice to the diverse forms of knowledge held by traditional communities.[25] According to the official WIPO definition traditional knowledge comprises

> 'tradition-based literary, artistic or scientific works; performances; inventions; scientific discoveries; designs; marks, names and symbols; undisclosed information; and, all other tradition-based innovations and creations resulting from intellectual activity in the industrial, scientific, literary or artistic field. 'Tradition-based' refers to knowledge systems, creations, innovations and cultural expressions which have generally been transmitted from generation to generation; are generally regarded as pertaining to a particular group or its territory; and are constantly evolving in response to a changing environment.'[26]

---

22 Hansen/vanFleet, Traditional Knowledge and Intellectual Property, 3.

23 Johnson, Research on Traditional Environmental Knowledge: Its Development and Its Role, in Johnson, Capturing Traditional Environmental Knowledge, 3, 4.

24 Latorre Quinn, Protection for Indigenous Knowledge: An International Law Analysis, 14 St. Thomas L. Rev. 287, 292.

25 WIPO, Intellectual Property and Traditional Knowledge, 4.

26 WIPO, Intellectual Property Needs and Expectations of Traditional Knowledge Holders, Report on Fact-Finding Missions, 25.

In a conceptual sense traditional knowledge can be defined broadly or narrowly with a possible distinction between traditional and indigenous knowledge. Under a broad definition the terms indigenous and traditional knowledge are used synonymously and refer to systematic information that remains in the informal sector and is usually unwritten and preserved in oral tradition while a narrower definition includes only knowledge systems of indigenous peoples and minority cultures.[27] The term indigenous refers only to a small number of groups with specific characteristics such as having a historical continuity with pre-invasion and pre-colonial societies.[28] Such a narrow construction, however, is not satisfactory in the context of discussing the protection of traditional knowledge. As noted by Blakeney, the debate refers to traditional peoples in general who are frequently called indigenous peoples.[29] A distinction between traditional and indigenous groups appears to be rather formalistic. There is no reason to exclude traditional groups that hold traditional medical knowledge but are by definition not indigenous.

Consequently, in this book the terms traditional and indigenous are used interchangeably and always refer to a broader conceptual definition. Traditional indigenous knowledge groups in this sense are foremost native and tribal people. Specific for these groups is the close contact to nature, the development of certain lifestyles and practices over time and the cultural distinctiveness of the groups which is attributable to their lifestyle and isolation from mainstream civilisation.

1.1.2. TRADITIONAL MEDICAL KNOWLEDGE

Traditional medical and ethno-botanical knowledge is one subset of traditional indigenous knowledge. It relates specifically to the knowledge of medically effective properties of plants and their application to the needs of a traditional community. Its relevance is highlighted by the fact that up to 80% of the population in lesser developed countries relies on traditional medicine based on botanical resources for their health care.[30]

The medical knowledge of local and indigenous people is widely based on the knowledge of the biological activities of plants. However, it cannot simply be reduced to the knowledge of plants used and diseases treated. The use of traditional remedies often has an additional component peculiar to the specific groups as it is frequently based on non-scientific theories of disease and disease

27 Brush, Valuing Local Knowledge: Indigenous Peoples and Intellectual Property Rights, 4.

28 Oguamanam, International Law and Indigenous Knowledge, 21.

29 Blakeney, The Protection of Traditional Knowledge under Intellectual Property Law, E.I.P.R. 2000, 251, 252.

30 Moran, Health: Indigenous Knowledge, Equitable Benefits, IK Notes No. 15, 1; WHO, Traditional Medicine Strategy, 1, 2.

causation such as supernatural influences by ill wishes, sorcerers, the violation of social norms or problems with ancestors and includes practices and expressions based on beliefs rather than on scientifically sound theory, such as rituals and shaman powers.[31] Consequently, while it consists mainly of plant and medical knowledge it also incorporates certain rituals and practices that stem from beliefs without scientific foundation and can thus be considered to be cultural expressions. This clearly shows the difficulties one faces when trying to find working definitions and classifications. Traditional knowledge is difficult – if not even impossible – to define as it applies to a vast variety of areas and includes numerous expressions and forms. It is to some extent incompatible with Western science-based approaches as it incorporates concepts that are uncommon to such perception and lead to the presumption that traditional medical knowledge has an obscure magical component and is thus not equally 'serious' as Western scientific knowledge.

The World Health Organization (WHO) has observed that it is not possible to assign one definition to the characteristics and elements covered by traditional medicine but notes that it is nevertheless essential to have a working definition. The WHO proposes to define traditional medicine as including diverse

> 'health practices, approaches, knowledge and beliefs incorporating plant, animal and/or mineral based medicines, spiritual therapies, manual techniques and exercises applied singularly or in combination to maintain well-being, as well as to treat, diagnose or prevent illness'.[32]

1.1.3. GENERAL CHARACTERISTICS OF TRADITIONAL MEDICAL KNOWLEDGE

It can be concluded from the mentioned attempts to describe and define the concept of traditional knowledge in general and traditional medical knowledge in particular that any attempt to find a working definition can only refer to general characteristics. These general characteristics can give some guidance when discussing the issue of traditional knowledge. For this purpose traditional medical knowledge in the context of this analysis shall include the following aspects:

---

31 Huft, Indigenous Peoples and Drug Discovery Research: A Question of Intellectual Property Rights, 89 Nw. U. L. Rev. 1678, 1695, 1696; Suchman, Invention and Ritual: Notes on the Interrelation of Magic and Intellectual Property in Preliterate Societies, 89 Colum.L.Rev. 1264, 1277, 1278.

32 WHO, Traditional Medicine Strategy, 7.

1.1.3.1. Traditional Knowledge Holders

Traditional medical knowledge refers to the knowledge held by local and indigenous groups living in close contact to nature outside mainstream civilization. Traditional knowledge holders are all persons who create, develop and practice traditional knowledge in a traditional setting and context. The lifestyles of these communities are shaped significantly by their environment.

1.1.3.2. Creation and Preservation

Traditional medical knowledge is knowledge of healing properties of plants held by local and indigenous groups. The knowledge developed over time; its creation often goes back to the prehistory of the community and it is frequently impossible to trace its origins.[33] It is often passed on orally from generation to generation and continually refined, enhanced and improved by integration of new knowledge into existing knowledge according to the changes in a society's needs.[34] Consequently the term 'traditional' does not imply that the knowledge itself is ancient or static but rather refers to the way the knowledge is acquired and used as part of the cultural traditions of a community.[35]

1.1.3.3. Ownership

Collective rights play a far greater role in indigenous cultures than they do in Western societies. Indigenous peoples submit themselves to the community and recognize group rights and collective rights.[36] However, collective ownership of the group is not the only category of rights known. Individual rights exist as well. The manner in which the knowledge is held can generally be divided into three groups: common knowledge that is widely known and may be considered to be part of the public domain; knowledge that is collectively known by a particular group but not by society as a whole; and knowledge which is known only to select members of a group.[37] In most traditional societies the knowledge is held in

---

33 Huft, Indigenous Peoples and Drug Discovery Research: A Question of Intellectual Property Rights, 89 Nw. U. L. Rev. 1678, 1700.

34 Latorre Quinn, Protection for Indigenous Knowledge: An International Law Analysis, 14 St. Thomas L. Rev. 287, 292; Mugabe, Intellectual Property Protection and Traditional Knowledge – An Exploration in International Policy Debate, 4.

35 WIPO, Intellectual Property and Traditional Knowledge, 6; Hansen/vanFleet, Traditional Knowledge and Intellectual Property, 3; Gervais, Spiritual but not Intellectual? The Protection of Sacred Intangible Traditional Knowledge, 11 Cardozo Int'l & Comp. L. 467, 472.

36 Lewinski, Indigenous Heritage and Intellectual Property, 17; Mugabe, Intellectual Property Protection and Traditional Knowledge – An Exploration in International Policy Debate, 3; Bratspies, The New Discovery Doctrine: Some Thoughts on Property Rights and Traditional Knowledge, 31 Am. Indian. L. Rev. 315, 331.

37 Correa, Traditional Knowledge and Intellectual Property: Issues and Opinions surrounding the Protection of Traditional Knowledge, 4.

different ways. Medical knowledge and practices are often exclusive knowledge of selected members of a group, e.g. healers or shamans who often use rituals as part of their healing methods which enables them to monopolize the knowledge; as opposed to this household remedies are often known by a majority of a group.[38]

Cultural or spiritual affinity to the resources leads to an increased sensitivity towards any action taken by those outside the community to exploit traditional practices and genetic resources commercially.[39]

1.2. THE ROLE OF NATURAL RESOURCES IN PHARMACEUTICAL R&D

1.2.1. OVERVIEW

Many plants possess medically useful properties. Medication originated naturally almost entirely from plants. This is to some extent still visible today. It is estimated that one fourth of modern medicines are based upon or derived from plants.[40] The 20th century witnessed a development towards the synthetic production of medicines instead of further enhancement of plant-based medication. This trend was particularly distinct in the developed world where the use of natural products was considered not to be in accordance with the science-based beliefs of the industrialized Western societies but rather to have a magical-religious significance; a perception that was naturally supported by the beliefs and rituals surrounding the use of medical plants in traditional knowledge settings.[41] However, after certain plant-derived drugs have successfully been used to treat different diseases, it has been recognized that the variety of effective remedies found in nature is far greater than the possible range of synthetically invented products and that natural products remain a crucial starting point for drug discovery.[42] Greg Vite of Bristol-Myers Squibb notes that '*the complexity and diversity of natural products can't be matched by*

38 Huft, Indigenous Peoples and Drug Discovery Research: A Question of Intellectual Property Rights, 89 Nw. U. L. Rev. 1678, 1701, 1702; Lewinski, Indigenous Heritage and Intellectual Property, 18.

39 Ong, Harnessing the Biological Bounty of Nature: Mapping the Wilderness of Legal, Socio-Cultural, Geo-Political and Enviromental Issues, in Ong, Intellectual Property and Biological Resources, 1, 4.

40 WHO, Factsheet on Traditional Medicine 2008.

41 Huft, Indigenous Peoples and Drug Discovery Research: A Question of Intellectual Property Rights, 89 Nw. U. L. Rev. 1678, 1679; Macilwain, When Rhetoric hits Reality in Debate on Bioprospecting, 392 Nature 535; Rates, Plants as Sources of Drugs, 39 Toxicon 603, 603; see also supra text accompanying note 31.

42 Asebey/Kempenaar, Biodiversity Prospecting: Fulfilling the Mandate of the Biodiveristy Convention, 28 Vand. J. Transnat'l L. 703, 706; Watal, Intellectual Property Rights in the WTO and Developing Countries, 170.

even the most innovative scientist'.[43] Furthermore, conventional medicine can be inefficient, have side effects and many forms of bacteria are meanwhile resistant to conventional medication. In consequence, many pharmaceutical companies are undertaking searches for sources of new pharmaceuticals in nature. This is a major task as it is estimated that 250.000–500.000 species can be found on the planet and that only about 10–15% of the total number of existing plants have been screened and evaluated for pharmacological activity so far, which leaves a potentially significant number of drugs remaining to be discovered.[44] The natural starting points for searches for medically effective biological resources are the tropical regions of the South which host most of the world's biological diversity.[45]

1.2.2. PHARMACEUTICAL BIOTECHNOLOGY

Medical plants are used basically in two ways. One possible therapeutic form is the direct application of a plant or parts of a plant, e.g. in the form of a tea or an ointment or the use of a mixture containing a range of constituents such as infusions, essential oils or extracts.[46] On a more advanced level plants can be subjected to successive extraction and purification procedures to isolate the active compounds.[47] The isolated compounds themselves can either be used directly or serve as a basis for the synthetic production of a drug. The goals of using plants as sources of medically effective agents are amongst others the isolation of the bioactive compounds for direct use as drugs and the production of bioactive compounds of novel or known structures as lead compounds for semi-synthesis to produce new entities of higher efficacy or lower toxicity.[48]

Biotechnology is a set of technologies that decodes cellular and molecular structures and processes in order to use biological molecules and cells to develop

---

43 In: Kalb, Pharmacy Island, Newsweek, June 10, 2005.

44 Hamburger/Hostettmann, Bioactivity in Plants. The Link Between Phytochemistry and Medicine, 30 Phyto 3864, 3864; Soejarto et. al., Ethnobotany/Ethnopharmacology and Mass Bioprospecting: Issues on Intellectual Property and Benefit-sharing, 100 J Ethnopharmacology 15, 19.

45 As noted by Huft, Indigenous Peoples and Drug Discovery Research: A Question of Intellectual Property Rights, 89 Nw. U. L. Rev. 1678, FN 2 with reference to E.O. Wilson, The Current State of Biological Diversity, 3, 8, in Biodiversity (Wilson, Ed., 1998): '*the biological richness of the tropical regions is indicated by the fact that although tropical rainforest covers only 7% of the earth land's surface, they contain more than half of the species of world's biota.*'

46 Hamburger/Hostettmann, Bioactivity in Plants. The Link Between Phytochemistry and Medicine, 30 Phyto 3864, 3864.

47 Rates, Plants as Sources of Drugs, 39 Toxicon 603, 605.

48 Fabricant/Farnsworth, The Value of Plants Used in Traditional Medicine for Drug Discovery, Environmental Health Perspectives, Environmental Health Perspectives 2001, 69, 69; Aylward, The Role of Plant Screening and Plant Supply in Biodiversity Conservation, Drug Development and Health Care, in Swanson, Intellectual Property Rights and Biodiversity Conservation, 93, 99.

products and do research.[49] It works with genetic resources using the biological base of animal, plant, microbial, and other living matter which contain the hereditary information necessary for life and are responsible for their useful properties and availability for reproduction.[50] The application of biotechnological methods allows working in many diverse fields such as pharmaceuticals, diagnostics and testing, cloning and xenotransplantation, genetic modification of seeds and foods and environmental remediation.[51]

In the pharmaceutical sector, biotechnological methods can be used to identify substances with potential pharmacologically useful properties. Application of such methods to naturally occurring substances allows the isolation and purification of the active medically useful compounds. At the end of the process stands the development of a pharmaceutical product that encompasses these compounds and has the same effects as the natural product but can be produced in a laboratory and presents itself in the form of medicine that is commonly found in pharmacies, e.g. pills, serums etc. After identification of a compound biotechnological methods can furthermore be applied in order to produce large amounts of a naturally occurring substance in cultures by transferring the gene coding for particular proteins into different organisms, e.g. by inserting the plant genes into certain microbes such as *E. coli* or *sacharomyces cerevisiae* (yeast).[52] Modern biotechnology aims at the manipulation and modification of the genetic structure of living matter in order to develop plants, animals or micro-organisms with improved characteristics. It enables the development and production of products that were not available before or at least not in such quantities or at such high quality.[53]

Although biotechnological methods are explored, used and improved since some decades R&D of pharmaceuticals from plant origin is still not a simple routine endeavor but a time-consuming and expensive process.[54] It requires multidisciplinary collaboration of scientists from different basic sciences and lengthy processes before a pharmacologically active compound is derived from a medically effective plant. The process involves collection, identification and drying of the plant material, preparation of appropriate extracts and preliminary chromatographic analysis, biological and pharmaceutical screening of crude extracts, consecutive steps of chromatographic separation, verification of the purity of isolated compounds, structure elucidation by chemical and physiochemical methods, partial or total synthesis, preparation of derivates and analogues for the investigation of

49 Sutton, Law and Biotechnology: Cases and Materials, 4.
50 Kate/Laird, The Commercial Use of Biodiversity, 1.
51 Bauer/Gaskell, Biotechnology, 1.
52 Hwang et al, Production of Plant-Specific Flavanones by Escherichia coli Containing and Artificial Gene Cluster, 69 Applied and Environmental Microbiology 2699ff.
53 Bauer/Gaskell, Biotechnology, 21.
54 Rates, Plants as Sources of Drugs, 39 Toxicon 603, 606.

structure-activity relationships and large-scale isolation for pharmacological and toxicological tests and requires the collaboration of botanists, pharmacognosists, chemists, pharmacologists and toxicologists.[55] The development of a new drug requires an investment ranging between US$ 100–360 million and a minimum of 10 years work, with only 1 out of 10.000 tested compounds being considered promising and only 1 in 4 out of these being approved as a new drug.[56] Other estimates rate the investment even at US$ 500 million in the United States and US$ 570 million in the United Kingdom and the average time for the development of a new drug to be approximately 12–15 years.[57]

1.2.3. BIOPROSPECTING RESEARCH PROJECT

Biodiversity prospecting, or bioprospecting, is the exploration of biological diversity for commercially valuable genetic resources. It encompasses the intensive search for and collection or acquisition of useful compounds from natural sources which can be developed into commercially valuable products.[58] It differs from conventional prospecting activities to the extent that the genetic resources can be reproduced and manipulated at a cellular level away from their place of extraction.[59] It needs only a small sample of a plant to start biotechnological processing. The botanical resource itself is not depleted by the extraction.

One way of drug discovery using plants is random or mass collection of plant samples which are screened for pharmacological activity. Due to the vast diversity of plants and the small chances of finding one that contains therapeutic agents, drug discovery using this method has a rather low hit rate.[60] Under a different approach the starting point for research is the chemical content of known medically active compounds and the focus of the search is on plants that

---

55 See Hamburger/Hostettmann, Bioactivity in Plants. The Link Between Phytochemistry and Medicine, 30 Phyto 3864, 3864, 3865; Rates, Plants as Sources of Drugs, 39 Toxicon 603, 604.

56 Rates, Plants as Sources of Drugs, 39 Toxicon 603, 604; Macilwain, When Rhetoric hits Reality in Debate on Bioprospecting, 392 Nature 535.

57 Kate/Laird, The Commercial Use of Biodiversity, 47.

58 Asebey/Kempenaar, Biodiversity Prospecting: Fulfilling the Mandate of the Biodiveristy Convention, 28 Vand. J. Transnat'l L. 703, 705; Ong, Harnessing the Biological Bounty of Nature: Mapping the Wilderness of Legal, Socio-Cultural, Geo-Political and Enviromental Issues, in Ong, Intellectual Property and Biological Resources, 1, 7.

59 Ong, Harnessing the Biological Bounty of Nature: Mapping the Wilderness of Legal, Socio-Cultural, Geo-Political and Enviromental Issues, in Ong, Intellectual Property and Biological Resources, 1, 7.

60 Albers-Schönberg, The Pharmaceutical Discovery Process, in Swanson, Intellectual Property Rights and Biodiversity Conservation, 67, 72.

are known to contain certain compounds or that are related to such plants. This approach is useful if the desired compound is already known.[61]

In recent years, the focus has shifted to systematic, targeted searches for new substances with medically useful properties, often conducted with the help of indigenous groups. This approach is commonly referred to as the ethnopharmacological approach. It constitutes a new form of prospecting and involves field exploration of indigenous and traditional medical knowledge and related biological diversity and the documentation and conversion of such knowledge into a commercially valuable product.[62] Although indigenous groups may not be able to identify the active ingredient in a plant, they hold vast knowledge of plants that have proven to be effective against various diseases. By concentrating the search on the plants successfully used as remedies by local or indigenous peoples, both search as well as research costs can be considerably reduced. Not only is the plant known, but also the specific part that contains the compound, the indication and method of treatment is given.[63] The long-term use of a specific plant remedy by an indigenous group implies that the respective compounds are compatible with the human body and have low human toxicity.[64] Such projects can concentrate on finding a cure against a specific disease. But traditional medical knowledge can also indicate a research path to finding new applications of a compound to cure a different disease, as in the case of the anti-aids drug Prostratin which has been developed from extracts of the tropical plant *Homalanthus nutans* used by healers in Western Samoa to treat hepatitis.[65]

In the course of a bioprospecting research project pharmaceutical companies set up teams of qualified botanists with special expertise in the field of ethnobotany who are instructed to search out and collect samples of plant surveys. During their search, shamans or other healers are interviewed about the potential uses of certain plants.[66] Alternatively these searches are conducted by intermediaries who sell their collected materials to the company.[67] The collected

61 Aylward, The Role of Plant Screening and Plant Supply in Biodiversity Conservation, Drug Development and Health Care, in Swanson, Intellectual Property Rights and Biodiversity Conservation, 93, 99; Huft, Indigenous Peoples and Drug Discovery Research: A Question of Intellectual Property Rights, 89 Nw. U. L. Rev. 1678, 1691.

62 Soejarto et. al., Ethnobotany/Ethnopharmacology and Mass Bioprospecting: Issues on Intellectual Property and Benefit-sharing, 100 J Ethnopharmacology 15, 16; Bratspies, The New Discovery Doctrine: Some Thoughts on Property Rights and Traditional Knowledge, 31 Am. Indian. L. Rev. 315, 320.

63 Yano, Protection of the Ethnobiological Knowledge of Indigenous Peoples, UCLA L. Rev. 443, 448.

64 Fabricant/Farnsworth, The Value of Plants Used in Traditional Medicine for Drug Discovery, Environmental Health Perspectives 2001, 69, 69.

65 www.aidsmeds.com/articles/hiv_prostratin_reservoirs_1667_17975.shtml (last visited on January 8, 2012); see supra Introduction.

66 Huft, Indigenous Peoples and Drug Discovery Research: A Question of Intellectual Property Rights, 89 Nw. U. L. Rev. 1678, 1703.

67 Kate/Laird, The Commercial Use of Biodiversity, 58.

materials are then screened for useful properties and the compounds responsible for the respective effect are isolated and purified. The process is complex and the final result, the drug, is expensive.[68] At the end of the project stands the development of a pharmaceutical product that possesses the medically effective properties of the plant resources but is applied in a different pharmaceutical form that is superior to the natural product. Improvements undertaken in the R&D process can take different forms and include an easier application of a drug, an increased efficiency of the active agent, better compatibility with the human body and less side effects, better production or storage availability and less use of resources by producing the active agent with biotechnological techniques. The new form also makes the drug eligible for mass production and marketing.

1.3. THE VALUE OF PHARMACEUTICAL BIOTECHNOLOGY AND TRADITIONAL MEDICAL KNOWLEDGE

1.3.1. THE VALUE OF PHARMACEUTICAL BIOTECHNOLOGICAL R&D

The work with naturally occurring products is a growing field as the demand for herbal medicines increases and the market for herbal products expands. In the developed world 50–70% of the population has used complementary or alternative medicine at least once.[69] According to the detailed study Kate and Laird undertook in 1999 on the commercial use of biodiversity and traditional knowledge, the overall annual market for products derived from genetic resources is between US$ 500 billion to US$ 800 billion. They estimate the annual global market value of pharmaceuticals to be US$ 300 billion, the contribution of natural products being between 25 to 50 per cent, hence ranging between US$ 75 to 150 billion per annum.[70] It follows from this that biodiversity conservation is also a concern for the pharmaceutical industry which depends on the availability of plant genetic resources.

Biotechnological advance in the pharmaceutical sector contributes to social welfare as it supports the development of medication and cures. Biotechnology is particularly important for drug research because it allows a targeted approach on the molecular and cellular level for the development of new pharmaceutical drugs.[71] Many beneficial achievements in the pharmaceutical sector are

68 Supra notes 54ff.
69 WHO, Factsheet on Traditional Medicine 2008.
70 Kate/Laird, The Commercial Use of Biodiversity, 246ff.
71 Gehl-Sampath, Biodiversity Prospecting Contracts for Pharmaceutical Research, 11.

contributions of biotechnological R&D; a good example is the commercial production of natural human proteins such as insulin. Many of these developments are adaptations and improvements of existing products.

Biotechnology could furthermore provide a solution to the supply problems which the growing herbal market and its commercial success cause. The demand for natural products results in over-harvesting of the raw material for herbal medicines and other natural herbal care products.[72] An example for this is Taxol, the most important natural product-derived Diterpene with anti-tumor activity found in recent years. Taxol is isolated from *Taxus (T. brevifolia* and *T. bacata).* In order to produce two and a half kilograms of Taxol 27.000 tons of *T. brevifolia* bark is required and 12.000 trees must be cut down.[73] Biotechnology can solve this problem as it works with the genetic information which can be transferred and studied, enhanced or modified without the need to use material of the primary source. This avoids depletion of the physical resource.

1.3.2. THE VALUE OF TRADITIONAL MEDICAL KNOWLEDGE

New genetic resources are an important source for the development of new drugs and R&D activities in the ethnopharmacological sector as genetic resources contain essential information for the development of herbal pharmaceuticals. The screening of biological materials has proven to be more successful than the synthetical development of chemical drugs which can by no means substitute the immense amount of medically effective combinations found in nature. Consequently, the biotechnological pharmaceutical industry depends on the availability of plant genetic resources.

Traditional knowledge of biological resources and their indication for medical treatment is another important input for pharmaceutical R&D. Its relevance is indicated by the fact that an estimated 74% of the modern pharmaceutical products derived from plants have the same or similar use by native cultures.[74] The knowledge of the effective use of a plant for disease treatment may considerably reduce the search and R&D costs and increase the success rate of a bioprospecting project. It has been stated that using traditional knowledge increases the success rate of bioprospecting project by the factor 4.[75] Similar estimates claim that the success rate of developing at least one marketable product from a thousand plant samples increases from 22% to 78%.[76] It can be

---

72 WHO, Factsheet on Traditional Medicine 2008.

73 Rates, Plants as Sources of Drugs, 39 Toxicon 603, 606.

74 Farnsworth et al, Medical Plants in Therapy, WHO Bulletin 63, 965, 967.

75 Dolder, Patente auf der Grundlage traditioneller Kenntnisse indigener Gemeinschaften, in Ann, FS König, 81.

76 Horton, Protecting Biological Diversity and Cultural Diversity under Intellectual Property Law, 10 J of Envt'l Law and Litigation 1, 5.

concluded that bioprospecting projects can be undertaken more efficiently when relying on plant-related traditional medical knowledge. Search costs as well as R&D costs are considerably reduced with the consequence that the marginal costs for developing a new drug decrease and the marginal revenues increase.

The contribution to the environment by the sustainable lifestyle of these groups is another aspect of the value of traditional knowledge. Traditional knowledge systems are more and more perceived to play an important role in the achievement of sustainable development. Biological diversity and traditional knowledge exist in a state of dependency. While an indigenous group is dependent on the biological diversity in its habitation area, the lifestyle of the group has substantial influence on the environment. To some extent traditional knowledge and practices are responsible for the conservation and enhancement of biodiversity. Their knowledge, innovations and practices contribute to the conservation, selection and improvement of biodiversity elements. Traditional knowledge groups foster a traditional lifestyle and have devised and deployed various techniques to protect and conserve the environment in general and biodiversity in particular.[77] They have learnt to adapt to their physical environment by using its biological components to sustain themselves. This close connection allows them to develop practices to manage the genetic resources in a sustainable way ensuring that they are available for future generations.[78] Indigenous people use the natural resources to enable their surviving, at the same time they contribute to the conservation of these resources.

Traditional medical knowledge clearly has an economic value. Traditional communities contribute to the discovery, development and conservation of medical plants that are used and traded on a global scale and provide inputs for R&D activities. Such R&D has a social value and generates considerable economic value. The social value in case of an improvement innovation is the difference in consumers' willingness to pay for the improved as opposed to the unimproved good.[79] Traditional knowledge is consequently relevant for plant based pharmaceutical R&D in two ways: directly as a crucial input factor for R&D and indirectly as it contributes to the conservation of biodiversity which provides the biological resources used in the R&D process.

Traditional knowledge is foremost valuable to the indigenous communities themselves as it ensures their well-being in their daily lives and enables them to

---

77 Horton, Protecting Biological Diversity and Cultural Diversity under Intellectual Property Law, 10 J of Envt'l Law and Litigation 1, 2; Hahn, Traditionelles Wissen indigener und lokaler Gemeinschaften zwischen geistigen Eigentumsrechten und der *public domain*, 47; Mugabe, Intellectual Property Protection and Traditional Knowledge – An Exploration in International Policy Debate, 4.

78 Ong, Harnessing the Biological Bounty of Nature: Mapping the Wilderness of Legal, Socio-Cultural, Geo-Political and Enviromental Issues, in Ong, Intellectual Property and Biological Resources, 1, 4.

79 Scotchmer, Standing on the Shoulders of Giants: Cumulative Research and the Patent Law, 5 JEP, 29, 31.

manage and exploit their local environment in a sustainable way.[80] The social value is embodied in the traditional knowledge asset, e.g. the products used by traditional knowledge communities. In case an initial innovation facilitates follow-on research this input in further R&D is also part of its social value.[81] The value of traditional medical knowledge thus includes also the option value of a potential application or improvement by a pharmaceutical firm.

The private value of traditional knowledge is influenced by the rights to use the knowledge and to restrict use by other. The economic value of traditional medical knowledge as an input to R&D furthermore suggests the potential to contribute to host countries' economies in the developing and underdeveloped world.

80 Dutfield, Legal and Economic Aspects of Traditional Knowledge, in Maskus/Reichman, International Public Goods and the Transfer of Technology, 495, 505.

81 Scotchmer, Standing on the Shoulders of Giants: Cumulative Research and the Patent Law, 5 JEP, 29, 31.

CHAPTER 2
THE CONVENTION ON BIOLOGICAL DIVERSITY

The Convention on Biological Diversity (CBD) is the major international agreement explicitly dealing with the protection of traditional knowledge.

The CBD was concluded on June 5, 1992 after the 1992 Rio de Janeiro United Nations Conference on Environment and Development. It is the result of increasing environmental concerns and primarily fends for the protection of biological diversity and the sustainable use thereof. It is administered by the United Nations Environment Programme (UNEP) and governed by the Conference of the Parties (COP) consisting of all governments that have signed the treaty. This includes 193 nations with the notable exception of the United States.[82] The CBD obliges the member states to implement its objectives.

2.1. BIOLOGICAL DIVERSITY

Biological diversity – commonly shortened to the term biodiversity – is generally defined to encompass the diversity of all living beings, namely

> 'the sum of all plants, animals, fungi and micro-organisms on Earth, all of their genetic variations and their phenotypic variation, and all of the communities and ecosystems that they comprise'.[83]

As an environmental concept it emerged in the early 1980s with the growing recognition of diminishing natural habitats and loss of species diversity.

2.1.1. LOSS OF BIODIVERSITY

We are currently observing a massive loss of biological diversity. Naturally, some species in the biological spectrum have always been extinct in the evolutionary

82 A list of the contracting parties is provided at www.cbd.int/convention/parties/list/ (last visited January 8, 2012).

83 Lévêque/Mounolou, Biodiversity, 5; Raven, The Epic of Evolution and the Problem of Biodiversity Loss, in McManis, Biodiversity and the Law, 27.

process. This loss is due to evolutional changes or environmental influences. However, the rate of extinction is alarmingly increasing.

The main problem in assessing the loss of biological diversity is that it is very difficult to estimate the exact number of existing species. Reliable data is only available for certain groups of species such as vertebrates, plants, butterflies and certain insects. Based on recorded extinctions in these groups over the past 300 years and fossil records, it has been estimated that the historical rate of loss of species ranged around 1–10 species per million per year while nowadays this rate has increased to hundreds or even low thousands per year which is to the greatest extent caused by a loss of habitat.[84] The rain forests, a major source of biological diversity, have been diminished by two thirds and are constantly decreasing.

2.1.2. CONSEQUENCES OF BIODIVERSITY LOSS

With the diminishing of the world's rainforests, biodiversity is severely threatened. Many species that might prove to be a valuable basis for the development of new drugs might be extinguished before they are even discovered. Surveys have been published estimating that 19 out of 20 species that are destroyed in the course of eliminating the rainforests are unknown.[85] The extinction rate also implies that genetic materials that enhance the gene pool and could be of use in plant improvement or in the biosynthesis of new compounds are no longer available.[86]

Biodiversity loss in the context of traditional medical knowledge encompasses two distinct aspects. Firstly, it implies that many potentially useful plants may be extinct before they are discovered with the consequence of depriving society at large of any beneficial applications. Secondly, indigenous communities are threatened by the extinction of biological diversity as their natural habitats decrease which ultimately causes the complete loss of their knowledge and prevents the development of new knowledge. Indigenous peoples foster a close relationship with their environment. Traditional medical knowledge is to a great degree influenced by and dependent on the natural environment of the respective local group as it encompasses the use of medically effective plants available to the holders and users. At the same time, the groups themselves depend on a sound environment for their survival. Traditional knowledge is inseparable from traditional lifestyles and traditional cultural values. The preservation of this knowledge requires sustaining the social and

84 OECD, Handbook of Biodiversity Valuation, 36; Raven, The Epic of Evolution and the Problem of Biodiversity Loss, in McManis, Biodiversity and the Law, 29, 30 with further references.

85 Raven, The Epic of Evolution and the Problem of Biodiversity Loss, in McManis, Biodiversity and the Law, 30.

86 Rates, Plants as Sources of Drugs, 39 Toxicon 603, 605.

physical environment and the cultural integrity of indigenous groups.[87] As put by McManis, the extinction of biodiversity goes hand in hand with the extinction of biocultural experience and vice versa.[88] As pointed out traditional knowledge communities contribute to the conservation of biological diversity. The groups and their knowledge are important for pharmaceutical R&D in this regard as well considering that declining biodiversity limits the potentially available resources for the development of new drugs.

The loss of biodiversity is detrimental to the general social welfare as it prevents the discovery and development of new drugs. This refers both to the resources as well as the traditional knowledge of their use as ethnopharmacology relies both on cultural and biological diversity.

2.2. MAIN OBJECTIVES OF THE CBD

The objectives of the Convention as set down in Article 1 of the CBD include the conservation of biological diversity, the sustainable use of its components and the fair and equitable sharing of the benefits arising out of the utilization of genetic resources including appropriate access to genetic resources, appropriate transfer of relevant technologies and funding.

The CBD takes a very wide view by acknowledging

> 'the intrinsic value of biological diversity and the ecological, genetic, social, economic, scientific, educational, cultural, recreational and aesthetic values of biological diversity and its components' and stating that conservation is a 'common concern of humankind'.[89]

It anticipates a broad range of environmental, economic and social benefits following from its implementation affirming that conservation and sustainable use of biological diversity is of crucial importance to deal with issues of food and health safety among other needs caused by population growth. At the same time the Convention is a statement of very broad goals. This deficit is not an uncommon phenomenon in conventions which are the result of negotiations between many parties with different interests and consequently often result in agreeing on 'the lowest common denominator'.[90] As the goals of the CBD

87 WIPO, Intellectual Property and Traditional Knowledge, 1; Hahn, Traditionelles Wissen indigener und lokaler Gemeinschaften zwischen geistigen Eigentumsrechten und der *public domain*, 9; Brush, Valuing Local Knowledge: Indigenous Peoples and Intellectual Property Rights, 4.

88 McManis, Biodiversity, Biotechnology and Traditional Knowledge Protection: Law, Science and Practise, in McManis, Biodiversity and the Law, 1, 3.

89 Preamble of the Convention on Biological Diversity.

90 Asebey/Kempenaar, Biodiversity Prospecting: Fulfilling the Mandate of the Biodiveristy Convention, 28 Vand. J. Transnat'l L. 703, 717.

become only effective once implemented in national legislation the legal initiative of the Member States will ultimately determine the success of the CBD.

2.2.1. CONSERVATION AND SUSTAINABLE USE

Conservation of biological diversity and sustainable use of its components are major objectives of the CBD. In the past decades the world has learned with increasing intensity that natural resources are not infinite. On the contrary, biological diversity has diminished vastly. As stated in the Preamble of the Convention, the CBD relies on the premise that despite requiring large investments biodiversity conservation will bring, on a long term basis, significant environmental, economic and social benefits in return.

Biological diversity is a valuable asset for current and future generations. However, this is frequently not captured by markets. Nature was for a long time considered to be an inexhaustible source of free resources but the growing scarcity of certain resources such as oil and the diminishment of many plants and animals have raised awareness of the fact that the goods and services provided in nature have economic values.[91] Significant values of biodiversity include environmental services such as oxygen production or carbon storage and the provision of food and habitats for species that provide genetic resources for the development of new products, contribute to the enhancement of the gene pool and provides for the development of new genetic resources.

Many biological products are traded on the market. The implications of the general loss of biological diversity, e.g. the environmental effects caused by the diminishing of biological diversity, however, are frequently not reflected by the market price. Market prices for products consisting of or using biological resources are not a reliable indicator of social costs as they do not capture all the effects of the use of biological resources.[92] The assessment of the economic value of biological diversity in this regard is particularly difficult because the values of these aspects of biodiversity arise out of the fact that the resources are not used. In this sense, biodiversity conservation also competes with alternative land uses.[93] This relates in particular to environmental services provided by the forest such as oxygen production and carbon storage. The costs of the non-availability of these services are not part of the price that is paid for timber or soy that stem from eroded rain forest areas. This constitutes a market failure because firms rely on the market price when deciding how much of a resource they use. A resource which has no or a low market price will be overused because the use

91 OECD, Handbook of Biodiversity Valuation, 44; Lévèque/Mounolou, Biodiversity, 208.
92 Lévèque/Mounolou, Biodiversity, 210.
93 Turner/Pearce/Bateman, Environmental Economics, 296.

incurs at no internal costs for the firm. At the same time the use creates an external cost on society.[94]

The determination of the value of biodiversity is a prerequisite to an efficient approach to resource allocation.[95] An ecological economic perspective demands the consideration of the non-priced benefits and costs in addition to those directly observed and measured in market prices. The assessment of the costs and benefits must be based on criteria other than market and utility. This can be done by determining the significance of biodiversity by valuing its contribution to human welfare and/or happiness (utilitarian or anthropocentric approach) or by according an intrinsic value to biodiversity that is independent from its contribution to human welfare and justified by the notion that each living organism has a value in its right (ecocentric approach).[96]

Economics distinguish between the direct or actual use value and indirect or non-use values. The direct use value refers to and measures the value of those assets that can be consumed directly, traded or used as an input to commercial activity.[97] Biodiversity provides food and is a significant source for drug development. Another example of a direct use value is ecotourism. These direct use values can be assessed by the market price for the respective goods. Indirect or non-use values include the long-term or option value defined as the value assigned to a natural asset because of the willingness to pay for its preservation in the anticipation of future benefits, the bequest value which is defined as the willingness to pay to preserve a natural asset with a view towards its use by future generations and the existence value which is the psychological value a person enjoys from just knowing that a species or an ecosystem exists without having any anticipated benefits in mind.[98] Obviously, it is quite difficult to determine the non-use value. In practice this can be done on the basis of the contingent valuation method whereby a fictive market is created on the basis of surveys.[99]

It can be concluded that biodiversity has great economic and non-economic values which benefit the local population and society at large. Conservation is a

---

94 Turner/Pearce/Bateman, Environmental Economics, 75; Suthersanen, Legal and Economic Considerations of Bio-Prospecting, in Blakeney, Intellectual Property Aspects of Ethnobiology, 43, 59.

95 OECD, Handbook of Biodiversity Valuation, 18.

96 Biber-Klemm/Cottier, Rights to Plant Genetic Resources and Traditional Knowledge, 7; Turner/Pearce/Bateman, Environmental Economics, 290, 291.

97 Biber-Klemm/Cottier, Rights to Plant Genetic Resources and Traditional Knowledge, 7.

98 Lévèque/Mounolou, Biodiversity, 211.

99 A contingent market defines the good itself, the institutional context in which it would be provided, and the way it would be financed. A survey assesses whether and how much respondents would be willing to pay to preserve an element of biological diversity or what they would accept as compensation for its loss. The respondents value hypothetically while it is assumed that they behave as if they were in a real market.
See: Lévèque/Mounolou, Biodiversity, 211; Turner/Pearce/Bateman, Environmental Economics, 122ff.; OECD, Handbook of Biodiversity Valuation, 107.

rational goal in global policy making but it creates opportunity costs. The markets do not ensure an economically sensible balance between the utilization of biodiversity and its conservation and maintenance. The economic failure of the market to value biodiversity adequately leads to unsustainable use of biological diversity and threatens social welfare. The costs for the use of biodiversity are too low which in itself is an incentive for over-exploitation.

2.2.2. ACCESS TO BIOLOGICAL RESOURCES AND BENEFIT SHARING

The market failure that exists in regard to biodiversity use demands for legal intervention. Biodiversity conservation can take the form of preservation by placing limits on the use of habitats, for example by the establishment of national parks or heritage sites. Another approach to conservation is by encouraging its sustainable use. The latter approach is conceptualized in the CBD and appears to be more promising as population growth and economic development make it difficult to bar large areas from human intervention but rather state a demand for access and space.[100]

The regulation of access to biological resources and inciting of benefit sharing as set out in the Preamble of the CBD and in Article 15 CBD are the proposed instruments to achieve this. Access to biological resources and benefit sharing are dealt with in the Nagoya Protocol that has been adopted at the Nagoya conference in Japan.[101] The protocol applies to genetic resources within the scope of Article 15 CBD.

Access regulation seeks to establish incentives to conserve biodiversity and sustainable use by allocating property rights to biological resources. In consequence the owners of the resource can extract benefits from their property. Protection of biodiversity may lead to a fairer distribution of the gains that recombinant genetic products provide and could give developing countries incentives to protect the rain forest and other genetically rich areas.[102] Biodiversity as the entirety of the natural environment cannot be reconciled with ownership as it is not subject to national or political boundaries and common ownership poses distinct problems. Biological resources, however, can be assigned to owners, in particular the sovereign states hosting the resources. Important concepts in regard to access are the sovereignty of nation states over the biological resources originating in their territory and the premise of treating biological resources as a common concern of mankind rather than an open source.

---

100 Turner/Pearce/Bateman, Environmental Economics, 292.

101 18th – 29th October 2010.

102 Merges/Duffy, Patent Law and Policy, 125.

2.2.2.1. *National Sovereignty*

The Convention is based on the principle of national ownership under which states have sovereign rights over their biological resources. The resources are considered to be state property subject to administration by governments. This concept is embodied in the Preamble and in Articles 3 and 15 (1) CBD. According to Article 15 paragraphs (4) and (5) access to genetic resources is furthermore contingent to prior informed consent of the respective state and mutually agreed terms. These provisions emphasize the role of the contracting nation states. On the other hand, national states are under the obligation to facilitate access to genetic resources for environmentally sound uses by other signatories, and should not impose restrictions that run counter to the objectives of the Convention.

It is an overarching principle through the entire Convention that the focus of strategies, legislative and administrative measures and policies is on the national level. The overall goal of the Convention is to develop national strategies for the conservation and sustainable use of biological diversity, recognizing the intrinsic value of biodiversity and its components and the importance of biological diversity for evolution and maintaining life sustaining systems and the diminishing of many species as a result of certain human activities.[103] Contracting parties are supposed to develop national strategies, plans or programs for the conservation and sustainable use of biological diversity and integrate the conservation and sustainable use of biological diversity into relevant plans, programs and policies.[104] National governments are to regulate access to biological resources and benefit sharing. Consequently the control over biological resources lies with the source country. National level action is also anticipated in regard to sustainable use which is the area of responsibility of the state parties. Article 10 (a) CBD requires them to integrate – as far as possible and appropriate – considerations on conservation and sustainable use of biodiversity in national decision making.

National sovereignty leads in theory to a more efficient utilization of resources as it facilitates bargaining between suppliers, in this case the national governments, and users, the transnational companies.[105] Biodiversity is the primary asset for many developing countries and it is economically beneficial if they have control over their resources because such a concept enables the source countries to negotiate bargains that allow them to extract net benefits from their resources that were unavailable before and to participate in commercial utilization.[106] National sovereignty might therefore lead to a more sustainable

---

103 Preamble of the CBD and Article 6 CBD.

104 Article 6 (a) (b) CBD.

105 Dutfield, Intellectual Property, Biogenetic Resources and Traditional Knowledge, 6.

106 Stenson/Gray, Politics of Genetic Resource Control, 122; Lerch, Intellectual Property Rights and Genetic Resources – An Economic Analysis 6.

use of genetic resources and positively influence biodiversity conservation. Thus, the principle of national sovereignty contributes to the objectives of sustainable use and might even enhance economic development.

2.2.2.2. *The Tragedy of the Commons*

The CBD recognizes that biological diversity is a common concern of mankind. This is a major change as opposed to the common heritage concept which was prevailing until the 1970s. Under this regime biological resources had been treated as being part of the public domain and thus belonging to everybody. The common heritage approach originated from unregulated distribution of biological resources in history when crops or animal and biological genetic resources were freely disseminated among farmers, diffused from their centers of domestication or introduced to other continents such as from the new to the old world after the discovery of the American continent in 1492.[107] The concept was given legal status in international conventions, e.g. the 1972 UNESCO Convention concerning the Protection of World Cultural and Natural Heritage and the 1983 Resolution of the Food and Agriculture Organization Commission which established the International Undertaking of Plant Genetic Resources. Formative of the common heritage approach is the lack of recognition of property rights, open access to genetic resources and reciprocity of access.

From an economic perspective the treatment of a physical resource as an open access source available to all poses problems as there is a tendency of over-exploitation. This problem is known as the 'tragedy of the commons' and applies to all physical goods that are rival in consumption. In this scenario the basic assumption is that the joint or public ownership of a piece of property is not efficient because each joint owner maximizes his utility by using the communal property while there is no incentive for the joint owners to take care of it and therefore overuse is the necessary result.[108] As a consequence there is a danger that conflicts arise if goods are used by an unlimited number of people. The two correctives to the open source problem are the establishment of individual property rights or the restriction of access to the common resource.[109]

Under the CBD it has been established – for the first time in international law – that the conservation of biodiversity is a common concern of mankind and an integral part of the development process.[110] The Convention incorporates property aspects by assigning ownership over biological resources to the national states. This change in perspective is influenced by two factors, the inability of the

107 Gepts, Who Owns Biodiversity, and How Should the Owners be Compensated? 34 Plant Physiology 1295, 1295.

108 Hardin, Tragedy of the Commons, 162 Science, 1243, 1244; Lerch, Intellectual Property Rights and Genetic Resources – An Economic Analysis, 2.

109 Cooter/Ulen, Law & Economics, 123.

110 Preamble of the CBD.

common heritage regime to generate incentives for sustainable use of biological resources and the growing economic importance of genetic resources.[111]

2.2.2.3. *The Role of Property Rights in Access and Benefit-Sharing Regulation*

Access regulation under the CBD has two elements: access to the biological resources in their physical form and access to the information embodied in the resource. The former is an issue of access regulation by assignment of property rights; the latter is subject to intellectual property regulation.

Property rights govern relations between individuals in regard to physical objects. Property is – from a legal viewpoint – a bundle of rights determining the extent and content of people's ownership and control over things. The essential elements of property rights are the exclusive right of individuals to use their resources as they see fit as long as they do not violate someone else's rights and the ability of individuals to transfer and exchange those rights on a voluntary basis.[112]

The need for property rights follows from the fact that physical objects are rival and thus subject to scarcity, consumption and exhaustion. Where one individual uses a thing, the use through somebody else will be affected. The use of a physical thing is thus constrained by the need and interests of others.[113] The function and justification of property rights is to prevent this conflict by allocating exclusive rights to certain individuals. Property rights are important because they internalize externalities namely the external costs and external benefits.[114] In general, the granting of property rights over a physical resource can be expected to lead to a more efficient use of the resource by preventing over-use caused by open access regimes.[115] Property rights in the biological resources within their territory would enable a source country or the landowner to harvest and market natural genetic material, e.g. with medical use, exclusively.[116]

The property rule finds its limitation when it comes to the extraction of the information embodied in the resource. This is a matter of intellectual property regulation.

Intellectual property rights deal with intangible resources, such as information, knowledge or ideas, thus ideal objects that are not bound to a physical source. Intellectual subject matter is often mentioned in the context of

111 Gehl-Sampath, Biodiversity Prospecting Contracts for Pharmaceutical Research, 18.

112 O'Driscoll/Hoskins, 482 CATO Policy Analysis 1,8; Cooter/Ulen, Law & Economics, 77, 78.

113 Cornish/Llewelyn, Intellectual Property, 1–41.

114 Demsetz, Towards a Theory of Property Rights, 57 Am. Econ. Rev. 347, 348, 349.

115 Merges/Duffy, Patent Law and Policy, 125; Demsetz, Towards a Theory of Property Rights, 57 Am. Econ. Rev. 347, 356.

116 Waldon, Preserving Biodiversity: the Role of Property Rights, in Swanson, Intellectual Property Rights and Biodiversity Conservation, 176.

public goods. Public goods have two characteristics: they are non-rival and non-excludable unless provided for by legal means.

As opposed to property in physical objects, intellectual property addresses intangible resources which are characterized by their ability to be used by many without being consumed or exhausted. The use of intellectual creations is not diminished by others using them too. Intellectual creations, information and knowledge are often also non-excludable. Once created and revealed they are available to the public. Excludability either requires secrecy as the use and distribution of intellectual creations can practically not be restricted. They can easily be copied and appropriated. Alternatively, intellectual property rights ensure exclusivity as they establish legal rules that prevent the appropriation of intellectual creations without the consent of the holder of the rights.

Genetic resources have elements of private as well as public goods depending on the method of use. A plant has different possible uses. It can be consumed directly and used as a direct source of natural compounds or it can provide information and ideas about unique ways to develop useful synthetic compounds.[117] In the first case the plant itself is used; this use is rivalrous in consumption and reduces the amount available for others. Depletion and use of a physical resource is not a question of intellectual property but of tangible property rights and environmental regulation of the source country.[118]

The application of biotechnological methods to biological resources allows the extraction of an active compound of the plant and the artificial production of this active ingredient. In this case the genetic information contained in the plant genetic resource is extracted and this extraction does not cause a significant depletion of the resource itself as only a sample of the genetic resource is needed to start the development process.[119] As a result the production of a drug derived from plants is completely independent of the original resource. In this case, the utilization is non-rival and does not affect the use of the plant by others. In this sense plant genetic resources must be allocated in the area of intellectual property as it is information that is the original producer of value and for which protection is sought.[120]

---

117 Sedjo, Property Rights, Genetic Resources, and Biotechnological Change, 35 JLE 199, 201.

118 Karjala, Biotech Patents and Indigenous Peoples, 7 Minn. J. L. Sci. & Tech. 483, 491.

119 Odek, Bio-Piracy: Creating Proprietary Rights in Plant Genetic Resources, 2 J. Intell. Prop. L. 141, 156; supra notes 48ff.

120 Sedjo, Property Rights, Genetic Resources, and Biotechnological Change, 35 JLE 199, 201; Lerch, Intellectual Property Rights and Genetic Resources – An Economic Analysis, 3ff.

2.3. ARTICLE 8 (J) CBD

The CBD specifically contains the obligation to provide for the protection and preservation of traditional knowledge in Article 8 (j) CBD. The provision holds that

> 'each contracting party shall subject to its national legislation respect, preserve and maintain knowledge, innovations and practices of indigenous and local communities embodying traditional lifestyles relevant for the conservation and sustainable use of biological diversity and promote their wider application with the approval and involvement of the holders of such knowledge, innovation and practices and encourage the equitable sharing of benefits arising from the utilization of such knowledge, innovation and practices.'

The Nagoya Protocol takes the issue of traditional knowledge protection up in Article 5*bis*.

2.3.1. THE ELEMENTS OF TRADITIONAL KNOWLEDGE PROTECTION

Article 8 (j) refers to knowledge, innovation and practices that are relevant for conservation and sustainable use of biological diversity. It recognizes the positive role of traditional groups and lifestyles in regard to conservation and sustainable use. Traditional knowledge communities exist in a state of co-dependency with their environment due to their lifestyle – in close contact to nature and frequently far off mainstream civilization – and rely on their environment for survival while at the same time enhancing a sustainable lifestyle. This positive effect on biological diversity is a prerequisite for protection. Article 8 (j) CBD refers explicitly to groups relevant for conservation and sustainable use.

By encouraging the wider application of such knowledge, the CBD accredits the value of traditional knowledge especially for follow-on research. Such application, however, shall be subject to the involvement and approval of the providers of the knowledge which is commonly understood to require some form of consent for the use of the knowledge. This element is also contained in Article 5*bis* of the Nagoya Protocol. Finally, benefit sharing is a central element of a protective regime.

2.3.2. RELATIONSHIP WITH THE OBJECTIVES

Traditional knowledge protection has interfaces with all three major CBD objectives as protection issues include conservation of biodiversity and related traditional knowledge, protection of biological and genetic heritage as well as the prevention of misappropriation and incorporate access and benefit sharing considerations.

Especially benefit sharing directly concerns the role of traditional knowledge holders in the process of protection and sustainable use of biological resources. The Convention recognizes the '*close and traditional dependence of many indigenous and local communities embodying traditional lifestyles on biological resources*' and considers equitable sharing of the benefits arising from the use of traditional knowledge, innovations and practices relevant to the conservation of biological diversity and the sustainable use of its compounds to be desirable.[121]

The CBD is based on the premise that the rainforest can generate sufficient revenues to finance conservation, e.g. from pharmaceutical R&D.[122] This notion is not undisputed. Simpson et al come to the conclusion that biodiversity is so redundant that it is virtually worthless due to the low probability of success of a bioprospecting project.[123] However, as previously stated traditional medical knowledge can be used as an initial lead in pharmaceutical bioprospecting which considerably increases the success rate of pharmaceutical bioprospecting and R&D activities. Indigenous groups contribute to sustainable use and conservation due to their lifestyle. Thus, benefit sharing can in this regard be used to channel revenues to the respective groups thereby – albeit indirectly – working towards the goal of sustainable use and conservation.

Article 8 (j) CBD corresponds with other provisions in regard to sustainable use, access and benefit sharing. Article 10 (c) CBD, for example, refers to the protection and encouragement of customary use of biological resources in accordance with traditional cultural practices that are compatible with the conservation or sustainable use requirements. Article 11 CBD encourages the adoption of economically and socially sound measures that act as incentives for the conservation and sustainable use of components of biological diversity and Article 18 (2) CBD extends technical and scientific cooperation to indigenous and traditional technologies.

---

121 Preamble of the CBD.

122 Vogel, From the 'Tragedy of the Commons' to the 'Tragedy of the Commonplace': Analysis and Synthesis through the Lens of Economic Theory, in McManis, Biodiversity and the Law, 122.

123 Simpson/Sedjo/Reid, Valuing Biodiversity for Use in Pharmaceutical Research, 104 JPE 163ff.

2.3.3. FORM OF PROTECTION

2.3.3.1. Protection by Intellectual Property Rights

The CBD stays silent in regard to the appropriate institution that should be used to put these instruments into practice. Intellectual property rights are one institution that could be used to implement the mandate. It has been held that intellectual property rights appear to be the most important tool to work towards the implementation of the CBD as they are very significant economic assets for firms and provide necessary incentives for commercially oriented R&D in the pharmaceutical sector.[124]

a. Traditional Knowledge as Intellectual Property

Traditional knowledge shares certain features with subject matter commonly considered to be an issue of intellectual property.

Firstly, the subject matter protected by intellectual property rights are abstract objects not bound to a physical source, such as ideas, information, goodwill or knowledge. Traditional knowledge is – as the term implies – information, namely knowledge. Secondly, an analogy can be found regarding the non-rivalry of knowledge and ideas. The knowledge of one person about the healing properties of a plant, for example, does not affect the use of the same plant by another person provided that the plant is available to all. Thirdly, knowledge is non-excludable. Once disclosed the use cannot be controlled or prevented without an artificially created protective system.

Thus, traditional knowledge must certainly be considered to be potential subject matter of intellectual property which can in principle be protected by conventional intellectual property laws and does not lose its intellectual property significance as to its being referred to as 'traditional'.[125] As pointed out above, the knowledge must not be understood in the sense of being ancient or static.[126]

b. Biotechnological Inventions as Intellectual Property

The result of the wider application of traditional knowledge of the medical use of the plants is a biotechnological enhanced pharmaceutical drug. These biotechnological enhancements derived from biological resources also have interfaces with intellectual property. Biotechnological inventions are clearly potential subject matter of intellectual property, namely patents. They incorporate ideas as to how to apply information embodied in genetic resources.

---

124 Dutfield, Intellectual Property, Biogenetic Resources and Traditional Knowledge, 12.

125 Lewinski, Indigenous Heritage and Intellectual Property, 92.

126 Supra note 35.

Patent law requires a reduction to practice for an invention; but it is the abstract object that is appropriated by intellectual property rights.[127]

Consequently, traditional knowledge, biotechnological innovation and biological diversity are interrelated and closely linked. This is particularly true in regard to medical knowledge, pharmaceuticals and medically effective plants.

2.3.3.2. Positive and Negative Approaches to Protection

Positive protection aims at the allocation of rights to the holders of the knowledge. Primarily discussed are enhancements and modifications of existing intellectual property regimes or the introduction of new *sui generis* regimes. Negative protection regimes seek to address the misappropriation claimed to exist under the current legal framework. Possible approaches encompass the introduction of prior informed consent and disclosure requirements in varying intensity into the existing patent laws or the establishment of databases containing traditional knowledge to improve the success rate of searches for invalidating prior art.[128] The focus has so far been on defensive approaches but positive protection is becoming more relevant as several developing countries are making use of their traditional knowledge as a basis for R&D. This can be seen on the example of patent filings in relation to the *Neem* tree where an increasing proportion of indigenous innovation can be observed.[129] Benefit sharing can be the result of a positive right that can be licensed or a legal rule establishing an obligation to compensate for the use. In part 3, the different proposals will be dealt with in detail.

127 Funder, Biology, Information and Property, 24.

128 India is a particularly strong proponent of traditional knowledge databases and has set up the Traditional Knowledge Digital Library (TKDL). The TKDL contains information about traditional knowledge and aims at improving the efficiency of prior art searches conducted by the patent offices.

129 Lewinski, Indigenous Heritage and Intellectual Property, 94.

CHAPTER 3

TRADE-RELATED INTELLECTUAL PROPERTY RIGHTS AND TRADITIONAL MEDICAL KNOWLEDGE

The implementation of the objectives of the CBD and the regulation of traditional medical knowledge use in biotechnological pharmaceutical R&D projects by intellectual property rights affect global relations. The functioning of intellectual property rights in the global market and the justification of legal invention are economic concerns. The Agreement on Trade-Related Intellectual Property Rights (TRIPS Agreement) provides the legal framework in regard to intellectual creations on an international level. Given that traditional medical knowledge and biological resources are mainly found in the developing countries, it is important to examine the impact of intellectual property regimes on these countries as well. A discussion of the appropriate applicable rights and the interfaces between the TRIPS Agreement and the CBD concludes this part.

3.1. THE TRIPS AGREEMENT

The economic importance of rights in intangible goods has vastly increased. Technology innovation has become a major factor in national wealth and international competition. The laws governing intellectual property were designed when the production and dissemination of knowledge were comparatively small scale activities. Trade in goods embodying intellectual property rights has substantially increased in the last decades and no longer takes place within national borders but on an international scale. Due to these changes intellectual property is now the basis for growth and competitiveness on a worldwide level.[130]

---

130 Guellec/van de Potterie, The Economics of the European Patent System, 2.

3.1.1. INTRODUCTION

3.1.1.1. The International Legal Developments

Intellectual property rights are territorial rights granted by a sovereign government and valid only within the territory of the granting authority. The principles of territory and independence of intellectual property rights have the effect that a right can be granted in one country but have no protective effect in another country. All intellectual property systems have an element of domestic regulation. National intellectual property systems focused long time on the optimal regulation of the national market leading to strong regimes in countries with much innovative and creative activity and weaker systems in countries with only few potential creators and innovators.[131] The emphasis on domestic concerns, however, is especially problematic because the emergence of global markets demands for global regulation.

Globalization of the international economy and the growing importance of international trade and international markets led to a situation that demanded having the same or similar protection in foreign markets as in the national markets. Intellectual property rights harm the free market flow as they allow control over the activities of others as they give the owner the exclusive right to use, sell and market his work and to exclude others from using, selling and marketing it. Due to this effect intellectual property rights constitute limited monopolies as exceptions to the principle of free competition. A consequence of the principle of territoriality is that nationals see themselves exposed to unfair competition by unprotected foreign works or inventions.[132] Lack of intellectual property protection in foreign countries or differing standards can thus both amount to a new type of non-tariff barriers to trade because they result in unfair advantages that allow cheap copying of technologies and reduce the competitive advantage of the exporting firms.[133]

There have been several attempts to have multilateral cooperation in the field with the objective to harmonize intellectual property protection on an international level.

The 1883 Paris Convention for the Protection of Industrial Property and the 1886 Berne Convention were the first important international treaties aiming at the establishment of global regimes in the area of intellectual property. They

131 Falvey/Martinez/Reed, Trade and the Globalisation of Patent Rights, GEP Research Paper No 02/12, 1.

132 Trebilcock/Howse, The Regulation of International Trade, 397; Gervais, The Internationalization of Intellectual Property: New Challenges From the Very Old and the Very New, 12 Fordham Intell. Prop. Media & Ent. L.J. 929, 930.

133 Abbott/Cottier/Gurry, The International Intellectual Property System, 2; Hoekman/Kostecki, The Political Economy of the WTO, 372; Falvey/Martinez/Reed, Trade and the Globalisation of Patent Rights, GEP Research Paper No 02/12, 2, 3.

govern patents, trademarks and copyright, and have ultimately led to the establishment of the World Intellectual Property Organization (WIPO) in 1967. The main flaws of these agreements are the absence of detailed rules on the enforcement of rights and the absence of a binding and effective dispute settlement mechanism.[134]

The most important international agreement governing intellectual property rights in a global context today is the TRIPS Agreement which was negotiated as part of the Uruguay round in 1994 and became effective on January 1, 1995. All members of the World Trade Organization need to comply with the provisions set out in TRIPS. The TRIPS agreement establishes minimum universal standards on patents, copyrights, trade marks, industrial design, geographical indications, integrated circuits and undisclosed information. It aims at the harmonization of the substantive and some procedural rules on intellectual property rights and provides for a dispute settlement body.

3.1.1.2. The Economic Rationale of Intellectual Property Protection

Some things in nature are economically scarce and in regard to these things the exclusion of others is necessary and justified. Consequently, property rights are only applicable to scarce resources. Intellectual property, on the other hand, is basically information and as such not scarce. Access and use through one person does not lead to limited access through somebody else.[135] Information is rather characterized by its ability to be possessed and used non-exclusively. It is not a restricted resource in the sense physical property is.[136] The tragedy of the commons is not imaginable when talking about information. The nature of abstract objects permits the unlimited use by many at the same time without the consequence of exhaustion or overuse. While property rights in tangible objects are a necessary consequence of scarcity, intellectual property rights rather create artificial scarcity.

Intellectual property laws give creators enforceable rights that put them in a position where they can protect their ideas from appropriation. Classical theories saw the justification of intellectual property rights based on the Lockean labor theory in the right to earn the fruits of one's labor or followed the Hegelian philosophy which assumed a right in the expression of one's personality in creative endeavors. Economic theory, on the other hands, evaluates market failures and considers the maximization of social welfare. In the light of economic theory the establishment of an intellectual property system serves to create a market for intangibles that would otherwise be non-tradable common goods. The two economic objectives underlying the protection of intellectual

134 Gervais, The TRIPS Agreement: Interpretation and Implementation, E.I.P.R. 1999, 156.

135 Posner, Intellectual Property: The Law and Economics Approach, 19 JEP 57, 64.

136 Cornish/Llewelyn, Intellectual Property, 1–41.

property are the promotion of investment in knowledge creation and business innovation by establishing exclusive rights to use and market newly developed products and the encouragement of widespread dissemination of new knowledge in the market by encouraging and requiring inventors to reveal their inventions.[137]

Intellectual creations are beneficial and contribute to social welfare. The exclusion of consumers from the use of an intellectual creation appears to be undesirable when considering that due to their non-rivalry intellectual creations can be used by an unlimited number of consumers without additional costs.[138] Efficient utilization in terms of static efficiency would hence require not putting a price on the knowledge and letting everyone enjoy the benefits. However, economic theory dictates that at zero price only knowledge that can be produced at zero cost will be produced.[139] The costs of creating intellectual property, on the other hand, are often very high.

Another aspect is that the creation of a market for creative or innovative work is only possible if the value of an idea can be assessed in advance. This, however, means revealing the idea to a potential buyer who will then have already acquired the idea at zero costs and can reproduce it.[140] This is problematic because the marginal costs of reproducing an intellectual creation tend to be low or even near zero which leads to the phenomenon of free-riding – the use of the creative or innovative work of somebody else with little costs – and poses the danger of appropriation by third parties without adequately compensating the original inventor. Intellectual creations are especially susceptible to exploitation and misappropriation. Obviously, an innovation has little value for the creator once reproduction occurs at zero costs. This implies that a market for intellectual creations cannot exist or will be at least inefficient.[141] Incentives for the generation of ideas will be low or even non-existent. The result is an undersupply in innovative output and knowledge creations and a loss in social welfare in terms of dynamic efficiency.[142]

Undersupply in knowledge creations constitutes a market failure and implies the need for protection that sets incentives for the investments in new and useful

137 Maskus, Intellectual Property Rights and Economic Development, 32 Case W. Res. J. Int'l L., 471, 473; Cooter/Ulen, Law & Economics, 124f.

138 Lévêque/Ménière, Economics of Patents and Copyright, 5; Stiglitz, Knowledge as a Public Good, in Kaul/Grunberg/Stern, Global Public Goods, 309; Hoekman/Kostecki, The Political Economy of the WTO, 371.

139 Stiglitz, Knowledge as a Public Good, in Kaul/Grunberg/Stern, Global Public Goods, 309.

140 Arrow, Economic Welfare and the Allocation of Resources for Invention, 609, 615.

141 Fisher, M., Fundamentals of Patent Law, 65; Kampermann Sanders, Intellectual Property Treaties and Development, in Gervais, Intellectual Property, Trade and Development, 157, 163; Suchman, Invention and Ritual: Notes on the Interrelation of Magic and Intellectual Property in Preliterate Societies, 89 Colum.L.Rev. 1264, 1269.

142 Dutfield/Suthersanen, Global Intellectual Property Rights, 50; Lévêque/Ménière, Economics of Patents and Copyright, 5.

creations and the publication of the creative and innovative output. Intellectual property rights provide a solution as they allow the proprietor to exclude others from using his creative work and enable him to charge a price above marginal cost (monopoly price). This in turn excludes all those consumers from enjoying the product that are not willing to pay that price.

The optimal diffusion of existing products at lowest possible cost is best reached when a competitive environment leads to allocative efficiency and the price of a product equals the marginal cost of producing it.[143] In the area of intellectual creations, however, free and unrestricted competition can deter investments in innovation and decrease the dynamic efficiency of markets ultimately leading to market failure. Under a protective system, artificial scarcity is created which allows producers to charge prices above marginal cost in order to recoup their investment in the creation of the intellectual work. This leads to a decrease in static efficiency by inflicting social costs as some individuals are excluded from the use because they are not willing to pay the monopoly price. These social costs, also referred to as the dead-weight loss, are traded-off against expected future dynamic gains by the creations of incentives to invest in intellectual creation and to disclose them to the public. The public at large can enjoy the benefits of the intellectual work and build upon it after the monopoly has expired.

To sum up, the enforcement of intellectual property rights serves the investment in innovation as well as the prevention of market failure by establishing the same barriers to entry for all competitors.[144] New intellectual creations provide dynamic efficiency gains but come at the costs of a welfare loss in terms of static efficiency. Intellectual property regulation has to find the optimal trade-off between the welfare loss and the welfare gains.

3.1.2. OBJECTIVES OF THE TRIPS AGREEMENT

The TRIPS Agreement translates these economic principles into the most significant international legal framework. It consists of four main elements. Firstly, it establishes minimum standards for intellectual property protection aiming at some harmonization of the intellectual property systems on an international level. These standards apply to availability, scope and use of intellectual property rights. Secondly, the agreement incorporates provisions on the enforcement of intellectual property rights. Thirdly, a dispute settlement

143 Correa, Managing the Provision of Knowledge: The Design of Intellectual Property Laws, in Kaul et al, Managing Global Public Goods, 411.

144 Kampermann Sanders, Intellectual Property Treaties and Development, in Gervais, Intellectual Property, Trade and Development, 157, 163.

mechanism is employed. And finally, TRIPS encompasses general rules and principles that preside over the obligations under the Agreement.

The objectives of the TRIPS Agreement are set out in the Preamble and in Article 7 TRIPS.

3.1.2.1. Promotion of Free Trade

The first paragraph of the Preamble states that the goal of the TRIPS Agreement is the reduction of distortions and impediments to international trade and recognizes the need to promote intellectual property rights protection. The Agreement does not aim at the protection of intellectual property but at the promotion of free trade through adequate protection of intellectual property. It clearly indicates that protection has to be adequate and must not itself become a barrier to trade.[145]

In regard to measures and enforcement procedures, the TRIPS Agreement is based on the notion that overly excessive protection could have a similar restrictive effect as a lack of protection and may lead to distortions. This assumption does not extend to the substantive standards of protection.[146] Consequently, under TRIPS the Member States are free to the extent that they can determine how the specified minimum standards are implemented, Article 1 (1) TRIPS. This provision applies to the implementation of substantive standards only. In relation to enforcement rules, the obligations are mostly phrased in a mandatory way. Thus, Members may implement more extensive protection in regard to substantive standards, but not in regard to procedural rules.

The concept that inadequate protection of intellectual property can act as a barrier to trade is a fundamental change as compared to the rules of the General Agreement on Tariffs and Trade (GATT). As opposed to TRIPS, under GATT the protection of intellectual property was conceptualized as an exemption to free trade.[147] The approach taken in the TRIPS Agreement is unique in the WTO context. The agreements administered by the WTO have so far only concerned the issue of freeing trade by providing for the exclusion or penalization of the use of certain policies that are presumed to negatively affect trade (so-called negative integration). The TRIPS Agreement, on the other hand, imposes obligations on national governments to adopt a set of substantial rules in a field that is commonly considered to be the subject of domestic regulation

---

145 The Preamble of the TRIPS Agreement reads:
'[...] Desiring to reduce distortions and impediments to international trade, and taking into account the need to promote effective and adequate protection of intellectual property rights, and to ensure that measures and procedures to enforce intellectual property rights do not themselves become barriers to legitimate trade; [...].'

146 Carvalho, The TRIPS Regime on Patents, 36.

147 Article XX (d) GATT.

having a direct effect of national regulatory and legal regimes (positive integration).[148]

Free competition is believed to be the best way to evaluate competing economic interests and to satisfy supply and demand and maximize wealth in society as a whole. Interference in the market should be as little as possible and if interference occurs it should result in a social benefit.[149] Imperfect knowledge disturbs the functioning of a market. Perfect knowledge, on the other hand, will induce a situation where the spontaneous interaction between knowledge possessors will lead to a state of equilibrium and the optimum distribution of resources in society.[150] Hence, legal intervention should aim at providing an environment where perfect knowledge induces perfect competition. Modern economic theory is concerned with the establishment of a workable competitive market which demands efficient allocation of resources. Any social institution must be aimed at the maximization of social net welfare by providing for a competitive environment and inducing an optimal and efficient allocation of resources in a market economy which responds to peoples' needs and generates the highest possible level of social wealth.[151]

3.1.2.2. Promotion of Economic Development

It is a major concern to enhance economic growth in the world economy. Innovation and transfer of technology are key factors to growth and productivity in the economy. Availability and enforcement of intellectual property protection can influence both innovation and transfer of technology.

Innovation occurs largely in advanced economies where commitments to R&D are strong, the political and economic environments are stable, barriers to starting new business are low, and intellectual property rights are respected.[152] The relationship between innovation and growth is well-established in modern economics. It appears to be quite obvious that innovators will be reluctant to invest in innovation if they cannot expect large returns in the future. Companies, the main investors in innovation, act out of profit-maximizing motivation. Economic incentives need to take this motivation into account. In consequence of the nature of ideas future profits from innovation are not secure in the absence of a protective system.[153]

---

148 Hoekman/Kostecki, The Political Economy of the WTO, 370; Petersmann, From Negative to Positive Integration in the WTO: The TRIPS Agrement and the WTO Constitution, in Cottier/Mavroidis, Intellectual Property: Trade, Competition, and Sustainable Development, 23.

149 Kampermann Sanders, Intellectual Property Treaties and Development, in Gervais, Intellectual Property, Trade and Development, 157, 158.

150 Cooter/Ulen, Law & Economics, 32ff.

151 Dutfield/Suthersanen, Global Intellectual Property Rights, 49.

152 Shapiro/Hassett, The Economic Value of Intellectual Property, 7.

153 Supra Part 1:2.1.1.2.

Technology transfer occurs mainly through three different channels, namely international trade in goods and services, foreign direct investment and licensing of technologies. Trade in intellectual property creations goes hand in hand with the transfer of the embodied technology as technological advance can be accomplished by reverse engineering. Licensing also plays a central role in technology transfer because it enables the licensee to acquire expertise without undertaking own research endeavors.[154] A major stimulator for economic growth is furthermore the ability to attract Foreign Direct Investment. Foreign Direct Investment (FDI) is the act of establishing or acquiring a foreign subsidiary over which the investing firm has substantial management control.[155] It constitutes an important channel of technology diffusion by backward and forward linkages, demonstration effects, competition effects, learning-by-doing which strengthens human capital and knowledge spill-overs.[156]

Local protection of intellectual property rights has some influence on technology transfer through each of these channels. Differences in intellectual property regimes across countries can act as non-tariff barriers to trade and weak or lack of intellectual property regimes in a particular market can effectively discourage rights holders to make their innovation available there, be it through trade, direct investment or licensing.[157]

The promotion of economic development is a fundamental objective of the TRIPS Agreement embodied in paragraph 5 of the Preamble and correspondingly in Article 7 TRIPS. According to Article 7 TRIPS, the objective of intellectual property protection and enforcement contributes to the promotion of technological innovation but also to the transfer and dissemination of technology. Intellectual property rights are expected to foster investment in R&D and knowledge creations. With regard to patents and copyright this refers to innovation; in the area of trademarks investment in a reputation is the basis for protection. In effect, only those intellectual property rights which refer to subject matter with a technical nature such as patents can actually contribute to

154 Lippoldt, Can stronger Intellectual Property Rights boost Trade, Foreign Direct Investment and Licensing in Developing Countries?, in Perez Putach, The Intellectual Property Debate, 44, 54.

155 Maskus, The Role of Intellectual Property Rights in Encouraging Foreign Direct Investment and Technology Transfer, 9 Duke J. Comp. & Int'l L. 109, 119.

156 Lippoldt, Can stronger Intellectual Property Rights boost Trade, Foreign Direct Investment and Licensing in Developing Countries?, in Perez Putach, The Intellectual Property Debate, 44, 48; WTO, A Taxonomy on Country Experiences on International Technology Transfers, 3; Primo Braga/Fink/Sepulveda, World Bank Discussion Paper No. 412, 32.

157 Maskus, Intellectual Property Rights and Economic Development, 32 Case W. Res. J. Int'l L., 471, 481; Falvey/Foster/Greenaway, Intellectual Property Rights and Economic Growth, Research Paper 2004/12, 3ff.; Lippoldt, Can stronger Intellectual Property Rights boost Trade, Foreign Direct Investment and Licensing in Developing Countries?, in Perez Putach, The Intellectual Property Debate, 44, 45.

promotion of technological innovation and dissemination of technology while trademarks and geographical indications cannot.[158]

3.1.2.3. *Intellectual Property Rights and Developing Countries*

In the aftermath of the founding and successful extension of the WTO and the integration of many countries all over the globe into the WTO, globalization progresses and intellectual property protection is becoming more and more internationalized and harmonized. Traditional medical knowledge has a strong international component as a transfer of knowledge and resources takes place between South and North.

Intellectual property protection in general and traditional medical knowledge use in particular are fundamental North-South issues viewed differently in the biodiversity-rich countries of the South and the technology-rich countries in the North. Article 7 TRIPS tries to strike a balance between opposing interests of developed and developing countries taken into the negotiations during the Uruguay round. While the developed countries' interest was primarily to secure the rights of intellectual property owners and allow them to exploit those rights in all countries of the WTO, developing countries feared that strong intellectual property protection would weaken their economies and limit access to and transfer of technology.[159] Countries with a comparative advantage on imitation rather than innovation naturally have an interest in less stringent intellectual property protection.

The effect of intellectual property protection on developing countries' economies is not undisputed. The TRIPS Agreement recognizes the need for some flexibility in implementing the TRIPS obligations in regard to the least developed countries; this has found entry in Article 66 TRIPS.

a. General Observations

The concept of positive integration deserves a different economic evaluation than negative integration. While the mutually beneficial economic effects of reciprocal trade liberalization are generally accepted by economists, there is some support for the argument that the positive affirmation obligations under TRIPS are potentially harmful for developing countries.

Up to date, the economies of developing and underdeveloped countries are primarily dependent upon agricultural production.[160] In the area of innovation developing countries rely mainly on incremental innovation by adaptation or

158 Carvalho, The TRIPS Regime on Patents, 122.
159 Correa, Trade Related Aspects of Intellectual Property Rights, 91.
160 Homere, Intellectual Property Protection, Trade and Development: A View from the United States, in Gervais, Intellectual Property, Trade and Development, 333, 343.

even imitation of existing technologies rather than by original innovation.[161] In general, developing countries are working towards the establishment of a sound agricultural and industrial base which includes the stimulation of commercial activity and economic growth.

National regimes of intellectual property protection depend to a large extent on the level of economic development. While governments tend to strengthen their intellectual property systems as their economies become wealthier it is debatable whether stronger intellectual property systems promote technological change and development.[162] It can be observed that the trade-off between promotion of innovation and its dissemination causes major trade tensions in the contemporary world. The developed countries create far more innovations that are eligible for intellectual property protection than developing countries. Consequently, there is a case for strong intellectual protection in the developed world, while the developing countries are rather importers of innovative technologies and expertise and benefit from diffusion of technology at low cost.[163]

The introduction of stronger intellectual property systems causes both costs as well as benefits for the engaged countries. The assumed costs of required changes can be quite significant and include additional administration and enforcement costs, increase in payments for foreign proprietary knowledge, price increases as a result of greater market power of knowledge producers, the costs of displacement of pirate activities, and the opportunity costs of additional R&D.[164] These costs constitute a net welfare loss in the short run as they might result in diminished access to technological information and cause harm to economic development by raising costs of imitation and permitting monopolistic behavior by owners of intellectual property rights. The potential benefits include the promotion of innovation, product development and technical change fostered by higher levels of R&D on a domestic and international level, technology transfers and greater FDI flows.[165] Unemployment as a consequence of displacement of pirates does not necessarily occur as these activities may be replaced by legal ones operating under licensing agreements, resources employed

161 Correa, Managing the Provision of Knowledge: The Design of Intellectual Property Laws, in Kaul et al, Managing Global Public Goods, 413; Maskus, Intellectual Property Rights and Economic Development, 32 Case W. Res. J. Int'l L., 471, 478, 489.

162 Maskus, Intellectual Property Rights and Economic Development, 32 Case W. Res. J. Int'l L., 471, 476.

163 Cooter/Ulen, Law & Economics, 125, 126; Shapiro/Hassett, The Economic Value of Intellectual Property, 10.

164 Primo Braga/Fink, The Economic Justifications for the Grant of Intellectual Property Rights, in Abbott/Gerber, Public Policy and Technological Integration, 106.

165 Primo Braga/Fink, The Economic Justifications for the Grant of Intellectual Property Rights, in Abbott/Gerber, Public Policy and Technological Integration, 106; Maskus, Intellectual Property Rights and Economic Development, 32 Case W. Res. J. Int'l L., 471, 479.

in imitation might be devoted to R&D and new business opportunities will arise.[166]

b. Empirical Surveys

Numerous studies have been undertaken to evaluate the effects of intellectual property protection on the economies in the developing countries. Only a fraction can be presented here.

Intellectual property protection in developing countries was long viewed skeptically. Opponents of the extension of traditional intellectual property rights to developing nations claim that protecting innovation does not benefit the people in developing countries but rather the innovators who are frequently situated in the developed world. Many economists are reluctant to the introduction of strong intellectual property systems in developing countries. This view is based on the assumption that non-industrialized developing or underdeveloped countries gain little from granting patents to foreign inventors as long as the country itself does no patenting abroad. The historic development of the patent systems supports this argument. Patent laws have generally been imposed only after a country has reached a certain industrial standard. An empirical study by Ginarte and Park who constructed an index of patents rights for 110 countries for the period 1960–1990 points in the same direction.[167] Their empirical data suggests that more developed countries tend to provide stronger intellectual property protection and that a country requires a certain critical size of an innovation sector before it has an incentive to engage in the establishment of a patent system.

On the other hand it has been stated that the adverse effects on developing countries are outweighed by the contributions of innovation to growth and productivity in the developing countries markets to which transfers of innovation take place as well as the countries that are engaged in innovative activity themselves.[168] There are quite a few studies supporting the latter point of view.

Mansfield surveyed 100 firms from twelve different industries in the United States and found that patent protection is judged to be essential for the development or introduction of 30 percent or more of the inventions in only two industries, namely chemicals and pharmaceuticals.[169] In a subsequent study he showed that a firm's decision to engage in FDI depends on the type of investment in question and that increased FDI is positively correlated with higher levels of

---

166 Carvalho, The TRIPS Regime on Patents, 55; Primo Braga/Fink, The Economic Justifications for the Grant of Intellectual Property Rights, in Abbott/Gerber, Public Policy and Technological Integration, 119.

167 Ginarte/Park, Determinants of Patent Rights: A Cross-national Study, 26 Res. Pol'y 283ff.

168 Shapiro/Hassett, The Economic Value of Intellectual Property, 12.

169 Mansfield, Patents and Innovation: An Empirical Study, 32 Management Science 173, 174ff.

intellectual property as far as protecting production and R&D facilities is concerned but not in regard to protecting sales and distribution outlets.[170] Again it proved that the chemical and pharmaceuticals sectors relied most on intellectual property protection which can be attributed to the fact that R&D is costly in these sectors while copying is cheap. As opposed to this, producers of products and technologies that are difficult to imitate will not be as concerned about intellectual property protection.[171]

Gould and Gruben find a positive impact of intellectual property protection on growth. In their study they examine data on patent protection from 95 countries over a period of 28 years (1960–1988) and conclude that intellectual property rights had a significant effect on growth in open economies with liberal markets which was largest in high income countries where innovations were developed and in low income countries in which strong patent protection encouraged imports and inward FDI flows of innovations.[172]

In a more recent study Falvey, Foster and Greenaway observe significant effects of increased intellectual property protection in high as well as low income countries, but not in middle income countries.[173] They attribute these findings to encouraged imports and inward FDI flows from advanced countries. In case of middle income countries, the positive impact on growth is likely to be offset by negative impacts slowing down the diffusion and dissemination of knowledge thereby discouraging imitation which is especially relevant for middle income countries with little innovative activity but rather a focus on adaptation and imitation activities. It is worth noting that the authors do not find any negative effects of increased intellectual property protection on growth.[174]

Maskus concludes that stronger intellectual property rights as part of a pro-competitive market environment have potentially significant and positive impacts on the transfer of technology in developing countries through trade, FDI and licensing especially for complex but easily copied technologies.[175]

---

170 Mansfield, Intellectual Property Protection, Foreign Direct Investment and Technology Transfer, World Bank Discussion Paper No. 19, 1ff.

171 Mansfield, Intellectual Property Protection, Foreign Direct Investment and Technology Transfer, World Bank Discussion Paper No. 19, 1, 11f.

172 Gould/Gruben, The Role of Intellectual Property Rights in Economic Growth, 48 J. Dev. Econ., 323, 334ff.

173 Falvey/Foster/Greenaway, Intellectual Property Rights and Economic Growth, Research Paper 2004/12, 1, 5ff.

174 Falvey/Foster/Greenaway, Intellectual Property Rights and Economic Growth, Research Paper 2004/12, 1, 17.

175 Maskus, Intellectual Property Rights and Economic Development, 32 Case W. Res. J. Int'l L., 471, 483ff.; Maskus, The Role of Intellectual Property Rights in Ecouraging Foreign Direct Investment and Technology Transfer, 9 Duke J. Comp. & Int'l L. 109, 119ff.; Maskus, Saggi, Puttitanum, Patent Rights and International Technology Transfer through Direct Investment and Licensing, in Maskus/Reichman, International Public Goods and the Transfer of Technology, 265ff.

A study by Smarzynska supports the introduction of strong intellectual property systems in developing countries and shows that strong regimes attract foreign investment in the form of a transfer of production technologies and manufacturing while weak regimes tend to attract foreign direct investment with focus on developing distribution channels for their products.[176]

Overall, the findings suggest that the impact of intellectual property protection on growth depends on the level of development of the respective countries. Developed nations generally benefit from strong intellectual property protection as innovative activity primarily originates from such nations. For developing countries the benefits of intellectual property rights are likely to exceed the costs of implementation but the positive effects of strengthened intellectual property systems in developing countries, especially in those with low per capita incomes by encouraging technology transfers from more advanced countries through direct imports and foreign direct investment will rather show in the long run.[177] Patent protection does not ensure that new products will be supplied in the short term but rather prevents the provision of products in markets that would supply the goods if imitation was possible. They do, however, play a positive role in attracting FDI and enhancement of technology transfers.

c. Conclusion

The mere implementation of an intellectual property regime will not enhance technological innovation and dissemination of technology. Rather, intellectual property rights can enhance such effects if integrated in a legal system of protection of private property that promotes free competition.[178] They play a positive role in encouraging new business development, rationalization of inefficient industries and inducing technology acquisition and creation.[179]

Overall, it appears that countries with advanced economies profit from strong intellectual property protection on an international level. Generally, the level of development has an influence on the impact of intellectual property protection on economic growth. However, on the long term increased protection – thereby fulfilling obligations under TRIPS as members of the WTO – could accrue benefits for developing countries. Intellectual property rights are not the

---

176 Smarzynska, The Composition of Foreign Direct Investment and Protection of Intellectual Property Rights. Evidence from Transition Economies, 48 Europ. Econ. Rev. 39, 45ff.

177 Homere, Intellectual Property Protection, Trade and Development: A View from the United States, in Gervais, Intellectual Property, Trade and Development, 333, 343; Shapiro/Hassett, The Economic Value of Intellectual Property, 1, 12f.; Lippoldt, Can stronger Intellectual Property Rights boost Trade, Foreign Direct Investment and Licensing in Developing Countries?, in Perez Putach, The Intellectual Property Debate, 49ff.

178 Carvalho, The TRIPS Regime on Patents, 126.

179 Maskus, Intellectual Property Rights and Economic Development, 32 Case W. Res. J. Int'l L., 471, 472.

sole determinant to growth but must be part of a pro-competitive environment. Harmonization of intellectual property regimes is necessary in order for developing countries to bridge the gap and achieve a level on which they can be competitive with developed countries. This result is important because a discussion of intellectual property protection for traditional medical knowledge would make little sense if the countries providing such knowledge had no incentives to support the establishment of sound intellectual property systems.

3.1.3. GENERAL PRINCIPLES OF NON-DISCRIMINATION

General principles of the General Agreement of Tariffs in Trade (GATT) such as the rules in regard to non-discrimination were incorporated into the TRIPS Agreement. The most important principles in regard to non-discrimination are the most-favoured-nation clause (Article 4) and national treatment (Article 3).

3.1.3.1. National Treatment

The national treatment principle embodied in Article 3 TRIPS is not a new one. It was incorporated in the Paris Convention and several other intellectual property conventions. Under GATT national treatment applies to goods, under TRIPS the application of the principle is extended to persons. It essentially prevents discrimination between foreigners and nationals. A Member country must not accord to nationals of other signatories less favorable treatment than it accords to its own nationals. The rationale of this rule is that domestic producers who do not face competition will charge higher prices from consumers and while becoming at the same time uncompetitive in international markets.[180] It follows from this that there is no reason to prohibit a more favorable treatment of foreigners than nationals. The national treatment principle is not one of reciprocal treatment. Thus, if a country denies rights to its national as well as foreigners another Member cannot accord reciprocal treatment as retaliation towards the nationals of the Member country.[181]

3.1.3.2. Most-Favoured-Nation Clause

The most-favoured-nation principle also stems from GATT. It is a new element in the international property framework as it has no equivalent in other agreements relating to intellectual property rights protection. In essence it

---

180 Abbott/Cottier/Gurry, International Intellectual Property in an Integrated World Economy, 45.

181 Carvalho, The TRIPS Regime on Patents, 86; Abbott/Cottier/Gurry, International Intellectual Property in an Integrated World Economy, 49.

determines that any advantage, favor, privilege or immunity a Member States grants to the nationals of any other country must be accorded unconditionally and immediately to the nationals of all Member countries ensuring uniformity of the multilateral trade environment.[182] There are some exemptions to the most-favoured-nation principle, e.g. the exclusion of judicial assistance and law enforcement agreements. In regard to patent protection the most-favoured-nation principle does not apply to favors, privileges or immunities deriving from international agreements related to the protection of intellectual property provided that these agreements are notified to the TRIPS council and do not constitute an arbitrary or unjustifiable discrimination against nationals of other Member States.[183]

3.2. THE INTERNATIONAL LEGAL AND ECONOMIC FRAMEWORK OF PATENTS

The choice of the appropriate intellectual property right depends on the kind of knowledge in question. Patents are granted for inventions that fulfill the requirements of usefulness, novelty, non-obviousness or inventive step. Copyright is a right given against the copying of defined types of cultural, informational and entertainment productions.[184] Copyrights protect the form of expression but not the underlying idea. Trademarks as expressions of goodwill are attached to a market symbol. They indicate origin and are thus a valuable help to consumers to distinguish between different products. Trademarks prevent a competitor from using the protected mark in order to facilitate his market entry.

Traditional knowledge can be found in variety of area. Geographical indications might be adequate to provide protection for products from a specific area as for example *Basmati* rice. Folklore is often associated with copyright. Traditional medical knowledge and pharmaceutical products are most closely related to patents because they incorporate inventions in a technical field. Genetic resources and the related knowledge about their use are valuable sources of information. The information contained in the genetic structure of a plant resource combined with the knowledge of the disease for which the active compounds of the plant provide a cure can serve as a source for new pharmaceutical products. The use of knowledge provided by the traditional knowledge community in the course of a bioprospecting research project and the subsequent use of the knowledge therefore poses questions of intellectual property rights as R&D efforts might lead to the development of new patentable products.

182 Gervais, The TRIPS Agreement, 188.
183 Article 4 (d) TRIPS.
184 Cornish/Llewelyn, Intellectual Property, 1-06.

3.2.1. HISTORICAL DEVELOPMENT OF TODAY'S PATENT LAWS

The exact origin of modern patent law is unknown and may date as far back as ancient Greece. Historically, patents were granted as monopolies by a sovereign authority. The first known system of intellectual property protection is the Statute of Venice promulgated in 1474 which codified a system of granting patents on inventions in the useful arts in a general patent statute. Under the Venetian system an inventor was granted the exclusive right to practice his arts for a specific period between 10 and 15 years. The Statute influenced the conception of patents in various European countries. The English Crown followed the Venetian model and granted patents with the primary intention to control industries that were considered to be of political importance. In 1623 the Statute of Monopolies codified this system and laid the foundations for an independent system of patents and innovations. Other European states followed. In 1791 the French enacted similar legislation as did Austria, Russia, Belgium, the Netherlands and several German states between 1810 and 1843.[185]

The patent system in its current form goes back to the 19th century. Today we speak of intellectual property rather than intellectual monopoly. Our patent regimes, although changed slightly and named differently are strongly shaped by 19th century culture and beliefs.

Intellectual property protection nowadays faces new challenges. Knowledge expands rapidly, technologies become more advanced and discovery in many areas becomes easier. The economic role of patents in the knowledge economy, for example, is immense. In 2006 the European Patent Office received more than 200.000 patent applications, an increase of 150% since 1995.[186] The upwards trend is continuing. In 2010, the European Patent Office has received 235.000 patent filings.[187] This trend implies that innovators have less time to offer their innovations without competition from substitutes. Consequently firms tend to recoup their expenses more quickly by expanding their worldwide market.[188]

3.2.2. OVERVIEW ON TRIPS RULES ON PATENTS

With the TRIPS Agreement minimum standards for patent protection in regard to substantive standards and enforcement procedures were enacted. Particularly relevant in this context is Article 27 TRIPS which provides rules for the scope,

185 Fisher, M., Fundamentals of Patent Law, 23ff.

186 Guellec/van de Potterie, The Economics of the European Patent System, 1.

187 European Patent Office, Press conference on patent statistics 2010, 13 April 2011, available at http://documents.epo.org/projects/babylon/eponot.nsf/0/6be088f728f3e2dcc125787000384641/$FILE/20110413_press_folder_en.pdf (last visited 16 January, 2012).

188 Shapiro/Hassett, The Economic Value of Intellectual Property, 10.

use and effect of patents. This section was a particularly difficult part of the negotiations as it involves a number of North-South issues.[189] The conclusion of norms that define the scope of patents in an international agreement rather than relying on domestic laws was a major step forward. Under TRIPS, Members are obliged to provide certain minimum standards for patent protection. Article 27 (1) TRIPS holds any inventions, whether products or processes, which '*are new, involve an inventive step and are capable of industrial application*' patentable. With regard to the patentability requirements Member States are free to adopt different standards as to each of the requirements.[190]

3.2.2.1. Patentable Subject Matter

Article 27 (1) of the TRIPS Agreement stipulates that '*patents shall be available for any inventions, whether products or processes, in all fields of technology*'. The inclusion of this provision in the Agreement puts an end to the debate on standards for patentability. While countries in the developed world have a long tradition on protecting inventions by patents, patent protection was long not an issue in the developing countries and viewed skeptically there. With the adoption of the TRIPS Agreement a general principle of eligibility for patent protection has been established. Any exclusion from patentability is now an exception to the general rule.

Article 27 (1) TRIPS incorporates a very broad definition of patentable subject matter, namely any invention in all fields of technology. It provides for the availability of patents for inventions that are new, involve an inventive step and are capable of industrial application. The requirement of inventive step may be deemed to be synonymous with non-obviousness; capable of industrial application may be interpreted in the same way as useful.[191] Some Member States have made use of this provision. The differences between the respective concepts will be discussed later.[192]

As with most patent laws in the world, there is no reference as to matters that do not constitute an invention which leaves room for national legislation. But it can be concluded that a broad approach to the concept of invention is intended because TRIPS requires compliance with the Paris Convention which states in Article 1 (3) that a broad approach to the definition of industrial property of which patent law is a part is required.[193]

---

189 Gervais, The TRIPS Agreement, 220.

190 Carvalho, The TRIPS Regime on Patents, 191; see supra Part 1:3.2.2.1.

191 Article 27 (1) n.5 TRIPS.

192 See infra Part 2:1.2.3. and Part 2:1.2.4.

193 Article 1 (3) of the Paris Convention states that industrial property is to be understood 'in the broadest sense'. The Paris Conventions is deemed applicable by Article 2 (1) TRIPS. See also Van den Bossche, The Law and Policy of the World Trade Organization, 52.

3.2.2.2. *Rules on Biotechnological Inventions and Biological Resources*

It has been observed that intellectual property has always adapted to important technological changes without major problems.[194] One of the core challenges to modern patent law is the biotechnological advance and the modification of natural products. The TRIPS Agreement contains some rules in this regard.

Firstly, the general patentability of altered biological material is established. The language of Article 27 TRIPS is held quite broadly and thus allows the interpretation that altered biological matter is generally covered.[195] A restriction to the rule of general eligibility is contained in Article 27 (2) TRIPS which allows for the exclusion of inventions from patentability in case their commercial exploitation would contravene *ordre public* or morality within the concerned Member state.

Article 27 (3) (b) TRIPS provides for another exception to the principal patentability which refers in particular to biotechnological inventions and may become relevant in regard to the protection of pharmaceutical patents based on plant genetic resources and associated traditional medical knowledge. According to this provision, members may exclude from patentability

> 'plants and animals other than micro-organisms, and essentially biological processes for the production of plants or animals other than non-biological and microbiological processes.'

The provision refers to plants and animals and not a certain classification thereof. It follows from this that the exception is to be interpreted in broad terms including animals and plants as such. The exclusion of microbiological processes specifically excludes traditional breeding methods from patentability while the possibility to obtain protection, for instance, on developments based on cell manipulation or, with the advances in biotechnology, the transfer of genes, remains. There is some flexibility as to the form of protection which can be undertaken by patents, effective *sui generis* systems or a combination thereof. It has with good reason been criticized that an instrument that aims at the harmonization of law and the establishment of universal standards, has not settled the issue of the form of protection in this particular case in a more straightforward way.[196]

---

194 Gervais, The Internationalization of Intellectual Property: New Challenges From the Very Old and the Very New, 12 Fordham Intell. Prop. Media & Ent. L.J. 929, 949 with further references.

195 Latorre Quinn, Protection for Indigenous Knowledge: An International Law Analysis, 14 St. Thomas L. Rev. 287, 300.

196 Correa, The GATT Agreement on trade-related Aspects of Intellectual Property Rights: New Standards for Patent Protection, 16 E.I.P.R. 327, 329; Carvalho, The TRIPS Regime on Patents, 216, 217; Gervais notes that there is still considerable uncertainty and debate surrounding

3.2.2.3. *Disclosure*

In exchange for the exclusive right to use the invention during the patent term, the innovator must disclose how the invention works so that the public at large can enjoy and use it fully once the patent term has expired. Enabling disclosure as a formal and mandatory requirement is set out in Article 29 TRIPS. It obliges to disclose an invention in a manner that makes it comprehensible by others. The scope of the enabling disclosure requirement is defined by two elements: reasonableness and purpose.[197] Disclosure must be sufficient for a person skilled in the art to understand and carry out the invention. It must not contain irrelevant information.

3.2.3. THE ECONOMIC UNDERLYINGS OF PATENTING

As with intellectual property in general, an invention that has been reduced to practice should from a welfare point of view be available free of charge to ensure optimal utilization.[198] The marginal cost of sharing something existing is low; the social value of an invention is not lessened by its use through many. It can even be argued that the attendant benefit of use increases the value of an invention since society can enjoy the invention more fully and that it seems rather more wasteful to restrict use.[199] However, the reduction of an idea to practical use usually requires the input of financial resources and there would be no incentive for investment in R&D without a prospect to recoup expenses. Many inventions can be copied at low cost. Without a protective system the market would be inefficient.[200] Consequently, economic argument calls for some sort of protection that produces scarcity of the goods and creates incentives to invest in the creation of innovation.

3.2.3.1. *The Incentive-to-Invent Theory*

Economy theory suggests different approaches to patenting; the most popular economic theory claims that patents generate incentives to invent. The incentive to invent theory is based upon the assumptions that growth and industrial progress is socially desirable; innovation is necessary for such progress; the level of invention will be sub-optimal without incentives and finally, that patents are

Article 27 (3) (b) of the TRIPS Agreement, Gervais, The TRIPS Agreement, 351 with further references.

197 Carvalho, The TRIPS Regime on Patents, 255.

198 Arrow, Economic Welfare and the Allocation of Resources for Invention, 609, 616, 617.

199 Fisher, M., Fundamentals of Patent Law, 64.

200 Supra note 141.

the most efficient way to promote incentives.[201] It goes back to Arrow's basic work in which he presents a basic model for invention, R&D, innovation and imitation.[202] He concludes that there is a tendency in the industry to underinvest in R&D from society's point of view which is due to the difficulties that firms face in appropriating the economic benefits of their R&D activities caused by imitation. According to Arrow, patent protection is one way of solving this problem since it delays the entry of imitation in the market. The price society has to pay in exchange for stimulating investment is that of a higher price, the monopoly price, during the patent period.

This is the classic patent trade-off. Patents create limited monopolies as exceptions to free competition thereby allowing the patent holder to charge prices above marginal costs for a certain time. From a consumer welfare point of view pricing at marginal cost is optimal to maximize static efficiency and achieve a maximum diffusion of existing products.[203] In the knowledge sector this may lead to a sub-optimal rate of investment in innovation. The monopoly price allows the proprietor to recoup his investment in the process of developing the new product by obtaining higher rents. The other side of the coin is a reduction of the output below the socially optimal level as a result of monopoly pricing thereby creating a current static loss to consumers. Additional costs imposed by patent systems include also the costs created by giving exclusive rights for inventions that would also have been produced in the absence of a patent system, opportunity costs incurred on duplication research undertakings and attempts to invent around a patented invention, the cost of allocating resources to research areas that are potentially capable of patent protection to the detriment of research in areas that are not, and finally the administrative costs of running a patent system.[204] This welfare loss (dead-weight loss) is traded-off against anticipated future dynamic gains by increased incentives to innovate and invest in the production of technology and the disclosure thereof.[205]

Patents incite the creation of knowledge and innovation. They also facilitate the dissemination of knowledge and innovation by making them available to the public. Furthermore, innovation adds to the public stock of knowledge thereby lowering the costs of future innovation.[206] This, however, requires that the invention is fully accessible to future innovators including their understanding

---

201 Fisher, M., Fundamentals of Patent Law, 75.

202 Arrow, Economic Welfare and the Allocation of Resources for Invention, 609ff.

203 Primo Braga/Fink/Sepulveda, World Bank Discussion Paper No. 412, 27; Correa, Managing the Provision of Knowledge: The Design of Intellectual Property Laws, in Kaul et al, Managing Global Public Goods, 411.

204 Homere, Intellectual Property Protection, Trade and Development: A View from the United States, in Gervais, Intellectual Property, Trade and Development, 333, 341, 342 (citing Turner, 44 New York LR 450, 454 – 455).

205 Supra Part 1:3.1.1.2.

206 Falvey/Foster/Greenaway, Intellectual Property Rights and Economic Growth, Research Paper 2004/12, 2.

of how it works. A patentee, on the other hand, will be reluctant to disclose his invention because by doing so he enables other actors to reproduce. The disclosure requirements in patent laws are the embodiment of this reasoning and counter the tendency to keep disclosure to an absolute minimum.[207] By requiring disclosure of the technical information of an invention, patent law stimulates the acquisition and dissemination of knowledge.[208]

The publicity of an innovation can be beneficial to other researchers who use the knowledge as inputs for further research. Cumulative innovation describes scenarios in which one innovation inspires other researchers to an innovation that is linked to the first innovation. This link can be of different intensity. Firstly, it is possible that the second innovation would not have occurred without the first. Secondly, the first innovation can reduce the costs of the second innovation or accelerate the development of the second invention.[209] Both scenarios can occur in ethnopharmacological bioprospecting projects. Traditional medical knowledge can reduce the costs of follow-on R&D in a pharmaceutical product. It is also possible that the second invention would not have occurred without the traditional knowledge input or that the knowledge leads the researcher towards a new research path.

Patents are justified when the consumer surplus from new and better products, albeit limited by the implications of monopoly pricing, is greater than the consumer surplus from current products in the absence of exclusive rights.[210]

3.2.3.2. Patent Scope

The Coase theorem applied to patents holds that the best manner to incite economic actors to extract the highest aggregate output from conflicting economic interests is to establish effective property rights.[211] Strong patent regimes and enforcement mechanisms contribute to the reduction of transaction costs and increase efficiency in allocation of resources to R&D activities.[212]

The patent leads to monopoly pricing and it takes information out of the public domain which could otherwise be used in further research. Consequently, the coverage of a patent affects both static and dynamic efficiency.[213] An overly

207 Seville, EU Intellectual Property Law and Policy, 72.

208 Maskus, Intellectual Property Rights and Economic Development, 32 Case W. Res. J. Int'l L., 471, 481.

209 Scotchmer, Standing on the Shoulders of Giants: Cumulative Research and the Patent Law, 5 JEP, 29, 31.

210 Correa, Managing the Provision of Knowledge: The Design of Intellectual Property Laws, in Kaul et al, Managing Global Public Goods, 413.

211 Carvalho, From the Shaman's Hut to the Patent Office: A Road Under Construction, in McManis, Biodiversity and the Law, 241, 246.

212 Carvalho, The TRIPS Regime on Patents, 52, 53.

213 Correa, Managing the Provision of Knowledge: The Design of Intellectual Property Laws, in Kaul et al, Managing Global Public Goods, 414.

protective intellectual property system facilitating broad claims could limit the social benefit from an invention by reducing incentives to disseminate its fruits and might restrict follow-on innovation as researchers can hardly further develop a technology without infringing the original patent; a weak system could reduce innovation by failing to provide adequate compensation for investment in R&D and creates negative externalities.[214] A careful policy balance has to be found that considers market conditions and encourages growth.

Patent law has two mechanisms that influence the value of a patent by allowing for control of the effects, namely patent breadth and patent length.

a. Patent Breadth

Patent breadth is interpreted by the patent officers and courts. The breadth of a patent is determined by the claims which have to be in accordance with the description of the innovation and the patent criteria of novelty and non-obviousness.[215] It is in the patentee's interest to draft wide claims in order to enjoy wide protection and cover as broad a range of substitutes as possible. From society's point of view, on the other hand, broad claims take much knowledge out of the public domain. Although patent breadth is subject to legal rules, overall it is an economic principle subject to economic concerns rather than a legal one.[216]

b. Patent Duration

Patent duration is the second main policy lever that affects the value of patents. A long duration allows the patent holders to obtain high profits at the cost of suboptimal use during the patent term and consequently leads to reduced static efficiency.[217] Longer patent terms might increase the incentives to invest in costly innovation which might not be developed if patent life is short. But innovators can not reliably anticipate future profits because non-infringing substitutes may be developed. Economic theory supports the notion that the prospect to recoup investment in the far future has less incentive effects and – albeit inciting costly R&D – longer durations of patents unjustified subsidize less costly innovation.[218]

The duration of a patent is set by law and is currently 20 years although there are exceptions for certain products that are subject to regulatory approval and

214 Maskus, Intellectual Property Rights and Economic Development, 32 Case W. Res. J. Int'l L., 471, 474; Primo Braga/Fink/Sepulveda, World Bank Discussion Paper No. 412, 28.

215 Merges/Nelson, On the Complex Economics of Patent Scope, 90 Colum. L. Rev. 839, 840; Lévêque/Ménière, Economics of Patents and Copyright, 30.

216 See infra Part 3:1.2.2.1.

217 Correa, Managing the Provision of Knowledge: The Design of Intellectual Property Laws, in Kaul et al, Managing Global Public Goods, 417, 418.

218 Lévêque/Ménière, Economics of Patents and Copyright, 27.

suffer as a result a delay in marketing, such as pharmaceuticals, providing effectively for a longer term of protection.[219]

3.3. THE INTERACTION BETWEEN TRADITIONAL MEDICAL KNOWLEDGE, THE TRIPS AGREEMENT AND THE CBD

3.3.1. TRADITIONAL KNOWLEDGE IN THE TRIPS CONTEXT

Despite being a major issue in developing countries hosting biological resources and traditional knowledge communities, traditional knowledge is not explicitly mentioned in the TRIPS Agreement. This does not imply that traditional knowledge is not a TRIPS issue because the TRIPS Agreement is a framework agreement. Rather, the WTO Ministerial Conference included the interaction between the TRIPS Agreement and the CBD, the commercial use of traditional knowledge and genetic materials by other parties besides the traditional knowledge groups and the source countries as well as the relationship of TRIPS with conservation and sustainable use issues in the list of topics to be discussed in the course of the review of Article 27(3) (b) thereby admitting that a linkage may exist between the TRIPS Agreement and the CBD.[220] The emphasis on Article 27 (3) TRIPS in respect to traditional knowledge is also a political issue which relates to the fact that the strengthening of patent protection for biotechnological inventions is frequently considered to be interrelated with rights in genetic resources and traditional knowledge.[221]

The knowledge of traditional communities can be innovative to the extent that it adapts to a changing environment and provides a solution to needs of a group. In the absence of a protective system traditional knowledge providers cannot exclude others from using their knowledge. Consequently, they are not in a position to negotiate about the use of their knowledge. The intellectual property rationale hence applies to traditional communities as well. Traditional healers, for example, have employed time and efforts to find new materials that provide cures. They are at disadvantage if they have to compete with foreign imitators who use their medication.[222]

---

219 Article 33 TRIPS stipulates a minimum of 20 years protection from the date of filing. Protection for pharmaceuticals can be extended under EC legislation, see Tritton, Intellectual Property in Europe, 2–013. In the United States extension is regulated by the Hatch-Waxman Act.

220 WTO, The Relationship Between the TRIPS Agreement and the CBD, 4, 9; Carvalho, The TRIPS Regime on Patents, 227.

221 Lewinski, Indigenous Heritage and Intellectual Property, 38.

222 Carvalho, The TRIPS Regime on Patents, 233.

3.3.2. INTELLECTUAL PROPERTY RIGHTS AND THE CBD

Intellectual property rights may have an impact on several provisions of the CBD, be it directly or indirectly. Intellectual property rights are explicitly considered as a possible way to promote the objectives of the CBD and ensure conservation of biological diversity and achieve fair and equitable benefit sharing.[223] Looking at the issues the CBD addresses it becomes clear that they are related to areas commonly regulated by intellectual property rights. The CBD focuses in large parts on the value of biological diversity as a source for genetic resources which in turn constitute valuable sources of information for beneficial developments, e.g. inputs for research and development of new products in different fields. The CBD furthermore deals with the transfer and exchange of technologies, both biotechnologies as well as indigenous innovations.

An intersection between the CBD and TRIPS Agreement is especially given in the area of traditional knowledge protection (Article 8 (j) of the CBD), access to genetic resources and benefit sharing (Article 15 of the CBD and Articles 27 and 28 of the TRIPS Agreement), access to and transfer of technology and technical and scientific cooperation (Articles 16 and 18 of the CBD and Articles 7, 8, 27, 28, 30 and 31 of the TRIPS Agreement).

3.3.2.1. *Article 8 (j) CBD – Preservation of and Respect for the Knowledge, Innovations and Practices of Traditional Communities*

The Conference of the Parties has discussed issues relating to intellectual property rights since 1996[224] focusing on the implementation of Article 8 (j) of the Convention. The knowledge and practices of indigenous and local communities embodying traditional lifestyles is important in achieving the CBD objectives of sustainable use and conservation of biological diversity as the knowledge and practices provide insights into biological resources and ecosystems. Furthermore, their knowledge provides an important source for the development of new, socially beneficial, products.

Intellectual property rights can possibly encourage investment by local and indigenous peoples in maintaining their traditional lifestyles practices and thus contribute to preservation of and respect for their knowledge, innovation and practices. Innovations refer directly to intellectual property, particularly patents. Intellectual property rights can possibly set incentives for the preservation of traditional practices. The efficiency of intellectual property rules could require that means to prevent misappropriation are incorporated.[225]

---

223 Article 16 (5)CBD.

224 E.g.: 3rd Session November 1996; 4th Session May 1998; Inter-Sessional Working Group on Article 8 (j), COP Decision IV/9.

225 Mashelkar, Intellectual Property Rights and the Third World, 81 Current Science 955, 957.

3.3.2.2. *Conservation and Sustainable Use of Biodiversity*

Conservation of biodiversity and sustainable use of its components is the major objective of the CBD and directly linked to many of the provisions of the CBD. An interaction with intellectual property rights – although presumably indirect – appears to be given as well as the genetic resources comprising biological diversity can serve as sources for the development of new products such as pharmaceuticals. As intellectual property rights create incentives for investment in innovation and R&D they could indirectly provide economic incentives for conservation and promote the conservation and sustainable use of the resources required for the development of such inventions.

3.3.2.3. *Article 15 CBD – Access to Genetic Resources and Fair and Equitable Benefit Sharing*

Access to genetic resources is firstly a matter of property rights in tangible objects. The use of the information contained in the resources, on the other hand, is an issue for intellectual property rights.

If genetic resources are employed in inventions the creators may receive intellectual property protection. The scope of such intellectual property rights defines who can exploit the information contained in genetic resources, and consequently influences the distribution of the benefits flowing from the utilization of the resource.[226] Access and benefit sharing could possibly be incorporated into an intellectual property regime fit to govern use and protection of traditional knowledge.

3.3.2.4. *Article 16 CBD – Access to and Transfer of Technology*

The transfer of technology on a quid pro quo basis for access to genetic resources is another field where intellectual property rights will affect the CBD. New technologies are often subject to intellectual property protection, particularly patents, and thus the exchange provision has a close connection with intellectual property rights. This is particularly true for biotechnologies. Although the language of the provision which uses the term 'may' in Article 16 (5) CBD implies that the negotiators were not sure whether intellectual property rights would have positive or adverse effects on the implementation of the objectives, they are nevertheless considered to be one possible tool to achieve the objectives.

---

226 CIEL, Biodiversity and Intellectual Property Rights, 3.

3.4. SUMMARY OF THE MAIN RESULTS OF PART 1

Ethnopharmacology is one field of research in which cultural and biological diversity are interlinked and used to produce products that are of great value in economic terms. It has been established that a close relationship exists between biological diversity, traditional medical knowledge and biotechnological pharmaceutical R&D.

The biotechnological sector works with and depends to a considerable extent on the availability of plant genetic resources which can provide pharmacologically active compounds for the development of pharmaceuticals. Traditional and local indigenous communities who live in close contact with and are dependent on the biological resources in their environment have developed practices to manage genetic resources in a sustainable way and can provide valuable information to other users of genetic resources. This refers inter alia to the knowledge of the medical use of plants which is vast in traditional knowledge settings and can be beneficial in pharmaceutical R&D. Plant related traditional medical knowledge can considerably reduce costs and increase the success rate and efficiency of pharmaceutical R&D projects.

Bioprospecting activity carries a considerable risk of failure and requires the input of large financial resources. It involves issues of ownership and control over biological resources. In order to maximize social welfare the valuable information embodied in plant genetic resources and the traditional knowledge of their use must be available to pharmaceutical firms that invest in R&D and produce end products for commercial sale. The availability of genetic resources, however, depends on the willingness of source countries and traditional knowledge holders to provide access to these resources and the knowledge of their use.

The Convention on Biological Diversity is the first international agreement dealing with the protection of traditional knowledge, innovation and practices. Its focus is on setting incentives for conservation and sustainable use of biological diversity. This is supposed to address the economic failures that stem from the current incentive structure which facilitates over-exploitation of biological resources and contributes to the diminishing of the habitats and loss of biodiversity. This is mainly due to the fact that the value of biodiversity is not reflected adequately in the price. For many of the outputs a market does not exist.

In order to change the situation different principles are proposed including the common concern approach and the concept of national sovereignty. Access and benefit sharing regulation are considered to be fundamental premises to achieve the objectives. Traditional knowledge protection can be expected to have positive impacts on the conservation and sustainable use of biodiversity because of the sustainable lifestyle of the respective groups. Traditional knowledge is recognized to be a valuable resource – not only in terms of contribution to conservation and sustainable use of biological diversity but also in economic terms. This assumption finds proof in theory and practice. The sharing of benefits arising from the utilization of genetic resources and associated traditional medical knowledge is therefore a major concern.

The intellectual property rights framework is one institution that may be used to regulate the use of biological resources and related traditional knowledge and to address benefit-sharing issues. The grant of patents for the biotechnologically altered end products links traditional medical knowledge, biological resources and pharmaceutical R&D. Access to and use of plant genetic resources and the treatment of contributions of local and indigenous peoples to an end product based on genetic resources are governed by the Convention on Biological Diversity. The objectives of the CBD are closely linked to intellectual property rights. This potential role of intellectual property for implementation is explicitly stated in the text of the Convention. Intellectual property rights have an impact on several provisions of the CBD. While property rights lead to a more efficient utilization of physical resources, intellectual property rights have a distinctly different economic effect as knowledge and ideas cannot be exhausted by use. Intellectual property rights monopolize knowledge which on the one hand sets incentives to invest in the creation of knowledge; at the same time a deadweight loss is caused due to monopoly pricing and restricted access to the new knowledge. It has to be evaluated whether these incentive structures are applicable to traditional medical knowledge use.

The international component must be considered as well. The CBD recognizes the relevance of global trade issues which is crucial for any agreement that aims at successful implementation on an international level. The implementation must be reconciled with the TRIPS Agreement which is the most important international agreement governing intellectual property rights. TRIPS establishes minimum standards for intellectual property protection. In regard to patents it provides rules as to the scope, use and effect of patents and settles the debate surrounding the patentability of biotechnological products and processes. As traditional medical knowledge and biological resources are mainly found in the developing countries, the effects of intellectual property regimes on the economies of these countries have been discussed. There is support for the assumption that intellectual property protection in combination with a competitive environment is on the long term beneficial for development.

The protection of traditional knowledge raises a number of policy issues such as the modalities and extent of protection and the implications for global trade and economic development. The issues are complex as to the uncertainties of the subject matter in question, the rationale for protection and the instruments that should be used to achieve protection.

PART 2

THE STATUS QUO – PROTECTION OF TRADITIONAL MEDICAL KNOWLEDGE AND BIOTECHNOLOGICAL INVENTIONS UNDER CURRENT PATENT LAW

Intellectual property rights have been discovered to be one possible tool to regulate some of the issues dealt with in the CBD, namely access to and trade with genetic resources and protection of traditional knowledge. Patents are the intellectual property right used to protect biotechnological inventions in the pharmaceutical field. They may be applicable to traditional medical knowledge as well. Considerable movement has taken place in the area of patent regulation in recent years. The negotiations on and implementation of the TRIPS Agreement emphasize the growing importance of intellectual property rights and the international recognition thereof, especially in regard to patents and their interfaces with biotechnology. Similar developments can be noted on the national level. The US has enhanced the protection of its industry by extending patent protection to living organisms. Europe has taken steps in the same direction with the enactment of the Biotechnology Directive.

In case a bioprospecting research project has come to a successful end a pharmaceutical company will have developed a new remedy. At the beginning of the R&D process stands an indigenous group that holds and shares specific knowledge of the healing properties of a plant resource and provides a method to apply the plant to cure a certain disease, often in a rather simple form such as a tea or an ointment. A team of bioprospectors uses this knowledge to identify plants with medically active agents in the habitat of the indigenous group. In a highly equipped laboratory plant genetic resources are processed. This includes analyzing the genetic structure of the plant, isolating the effective compounds and undertaking a long process of purification, testing etc. At the end stands the final medical product which differs in appearance as well as in effectiveness to some degree from the plant remedy used by the indigenous group. While they may have made a tea or an infusion the medical product later is a pill or a serum. This final product bears improvements over the natural product such as an increased efficacy, targeted application and better absorption rate or longer storage stability.

Property rights on the improved end product can be discussed in regard to the original traditional medical knowledge and its reduction to practice by an indigenous group as well as for the altered end product. The owners of the right can be the traditional knowledge group or the biotechnological company. The mere existence of traditional medical knowledge may already influence the claims on the final product. A product that merely copies an existing product is obviously not patentable as patents reward innovations. In case the new product differs considerably from something existing, it will be patentable. Problems arise where the new product is only slightly different or if the same result is achieved by different means. Here, the scope of a conferred patent monopoly needs to be carefully determined.

The first chapter of this part gives an overview of general patent requirements in US and European law with emphasis on the concepts that affect biotechnological patenting and traditional knowledge. In the second chapter the concepts are applied to biotechnological enhanced pharmaceutical products. Chapter 3 evaluates the degree of protection that is awarded to traditional medical knowledge and the distribution of rights under the contemporary regimes.

CHAPTER 1
PATENTABILITY CRITERIA IN THE US AND THE EU

The developing countries that host biological resources and traditional medical knowledge are generally in favor of protection. Many countries have already taken legislative steps towards the implementation of the CBD.[227] However, in a globalized world only uniform rules that overcome the territoriality of patents will accomplish the mandate. Thus, the developed world's approach will severely influence the successful implementation of the issues addressed in the treaty. The US and European law have been chosen as examples for approaches to patenting in national patent laws in the developed world. They are currently among the most active players in the biotechnology sector and consequently generate the highest profits. Their patent laws can be used as a good indicator on whether the protection of traditional knowledge and biodiversity is adequate.

The patent regimes of the EU and the US also show the opposing effects of the first-to-file versus the first-to-invent approach.[228] Finally, it is interesting to note that the US is not a signatory to the CBD while most European countries are.

---

227 The Costa Rican Biodiversity Act provides that intellectual property rights using biological resources can only be granted if a certificate of origin and a statement on prior informed consent is provided to the organs instituted under the Act (Biodiversity Act 1998). The amended Indian Patents Act includes a requirement concerning the disclosure of the geographical source of the biological materials used in an invention (Patent Amendment Act 2002). The South African Patent Act contains a similar requirement (Patents Amendment Bill 2005). The South African law even takes it a step further by requiring the disclosure of traditional knowledge and traditional uses. The Philippines have implemented legislation that requires the prior informed consent from the communities (Indigenous Peoples Rights Act of 1997).

228 The US is the only jurisdiction with a patent law that follows the first-to-invent approach. Under this approach the person who first invented an asset is entitled to the patent. As opposed to this, under the first-to-file approach the patent is assigned to the person who first applies for it. The different approaches influence the determination of the priority date. However, the change to the first-to-file approach has now been decided by the Smith-Leahy America Invents Act, infra Part 2:1.1.1.2.

1.1. LEGAL FOUNDATIONS FOR (BIOTECHNOLOGICAL) PATENTS IN THE US AND THE EU

Invention, novelty, inventive step or non-obviousness and utility or capability of industrial application are prerequisites to patentability found in literally all patent laws. But it shows that there is room for interpretation as to how to apply the standards. Biotechnology industries are mainly found in the developed countries, especially in the US and Europe. The patent laws of these countries provide examples of strong patent systems.

1.1.1. SOURCES OF US PATENT LAW

1.1.1.1. The Constitution

The statutory foundation for US patent law is embodied in Article I, section 8 of the United States Constitution which confers congressional power

> 'to promote the Progress of Science and useful Arts, by securing for limited Times to Authors and Inventors the exclusive Right to their respective Writings and Discoveries.'[229]

This so called intellectual property clause covers patents as well as copyright. At the time the constitution was ratified in 1787 the term 'Science' referred to knowledge and learning in general; 'Arts' covered technologies and industries thereby including patentable subject matter.[230]

The Supreme Court has interpreted the clause to not only grant power to congress but also to limit this power. It held that patents may not be obtained for technologies in the public domain and for obvious variations of such technologies.[231]

1.1.1.2. Federal Statutes and Regulations

The first Patent Act was enacted in 1793 under Thomas Jefferson and provided in quite broad terms for the patentability of

229 U.S. Const. Article 1, §8, cl 8.

230 Mueller, An Introduction to Patent Law, 30; Walterscheid, The Nature of the Intellectual Property Clause: A Study in Historical Perspective (Part I), 83 Pat. & Trademark Off. Soc'y 763, 781.

231 *Graham v John Deere Co.*, 383 U.S. 1 (1966). The case is discussed in greater detail below, see infra Part 2:1.2.3.1.a.

> '[...] any new and useful art, machine, manufacture, or composition of matter, or any new or useful improvement [thereof] not known or used before the application [...].'[232]

This broad definition of patentable subject matter remained in subsequent patent statutes of 1836, 1870 and 1874 and is also the underlying concept of current statutory US patent law as embodied in the Patent Act[233] which goes back to the Patent Act of 1952 with several amendments. It states in Section 101 that

> 'whoever invents or discovers any new and useful process, machine, manufacture, or composition of matter, or any new and useful improvement thereof, may obtain a patent, subject to the conditions and requirements of this title.'

The Patent Act of 1952 also introduced the statutory requirement of non-obviousness to US patent law in Section 103. The Patent Act of 1952 is subject to some amendments by the Leahy-Smith America Invents Act which has been signed on September 16th, 2011 and will become effective 18 months after enactment, i.e. in March 2013 for most applications. The major changes concern the abandonment of the first-to-invent principle and a new definition in regard to the content of the prior art.[234]

The statutory provisions of the Patent Act are implemented through the United States Patent and Trademark Office's regulations which are found in Title 37 of the Code of Federal Regulation.

1.1.1.3. Case Law

Since 1982 the U.S. Court of Appeals for the Federal Circuit is the major decisional authority in interpreting the patent statute and regulations. It generally decides appeals in patents cases through panels of three Circuit judges. Decisions of the Federal Circuit panels are binding precedent on later panels and only the *en banc* court which consists of all active status judges of the Federal Circuit can overrule existing decisions.[235] The Federal Circuit has adopted the decisions of its predecessors, the Court of Customs and Patent Appeals and the appellate decisions of the Court of Claims as binding precedent. The decisions of the Federal Circuit are subject to review by the U.S. Supreme Court whose decisions bind the Federal Circuit.

---

232 Section 1, Patent Act of 1793, Ch. 11 1 Stat., 318–323.

233 Title 35 of the US States Codes (U.S.C.); all references to the US Patent Act refer in the following to Title 35 U.S.C. unless otherwise indicated.

234 Infra Part 2:1.2.2.1.

235 See Fed. Cir. R. 35(a); Mueller, An Introduction to Patent Law, 32.

1.1.2. EUROPEAN PATENT LAW

European patent law has first evolved within the domestic jurisdictions of the European States. In the process of harmonizing the law, the European Patent Convention (EPC) has been concluded in 1973 governing the patent laws of all participating states. Directives and national patent laws and court decision give some guidance as to the interpretation of the EPC. In regard to biotechnological patents the Directive on the Legal Protection of Biotechnological Inventions is an important legal instrument.

1.1.2.1. The European Patent Convention

The European Patent Convention (EPC) in its amended form EPC 2000[236] forms the legal framework for European patents providing the law that regulates the application for, granting of and opposition to European patents.

The European patent system exists in parallel to national patents. A patent in a Contracting State can be obtained either by application for a European patent to the European Patent Office (EPO) or by application for a national patent to the national patent office. These procedures are mutually exclusive as to one invention. A European patent is a bundle of national patents valid in those EPC Member States that have been designated by the applicant and granted through the EPO.[237] Once granted the patent is enforced by the national courts.

The EPC obliges the Member states to harmonize their substantive patent law as it establishes that European patents have the same effect and are subject to the same conditions as national patents[238]; confer on the proprietor the same rights as would be conferred to by a national patent[239]; are given the same or more protection upon publication of the application as that of a published national patent application[240]; can only be revoked on the grounds specified in the Treaty[241]; and must have the same prior right effect as a national patent application and a national patent.[242] As to the harmonization of the national laws, the EPC 2000 is in particular relevant in regard to the requirements for patentability and the interpretation of patent claims.

According to Article 52 (1) of the European Patent Convention,

> 'European patents shall be granted for any inventions which are susceptible of industrial application, which are new and which involve an inventive step.'

---

236 All reference to the EPC refer in the following to the EPC 2000 unless otherwise indicated.
237 Article 67 (1) EPC; Hacon/Pagenberg, Concise European Patent Law, 1.
238 Article 2 EPC.
239 Article 64 EPC.
240 Article 67 EPC.
241 Article 138 EPC.
242 Article 139 (1) EPC.

The EPC 2000 is supplemented by the Implementing Regulations to the European Patent Convention 2000 as adopted by decision of the Administrative Council of December 7, 2000.

1.1.2.2. The Biotechnology Directive

A 1996 EU study found that the US issued 65% of the world's patents for biotechnological research and had 1.300 biotechnological firms as opposed to the EU which issued only 15% of the world's patents and had 485 firms.[243] A reason for this development was seen in the great differences in national laws in relation to the protection of biotechnological inventions. While some countries granted patents on biotechnological inventions quite early[244] the general perception was that uncertainty in regard to biotechnological patenting dominated and caused the European countries to fall seriously behind the US in attracting biotechnological R&D industries.[245] Biotechnology was generally viewed skeptically in Europe. In addition legal uncertainties caused, for example, by the morality exception in Article 53 (a) EPC led to European patent law being less predictable than for example US patent law.

In response to these disadvantages for the biotechnology sector in Europe the Directive on the Legal Protection of Biotechnological Inventions[246] was finally implemented after long and controversial discussion. This demonstrates that the importance of biotechnological patenting, its adequate protection and the need to ensure harmonized standards in all Member States were finally recognized.

The Biotechnology Directive intends the promotion of effective and harmonized patent protection throughout the Member States, encouragement of investment in the biotechnology sector, enhancement of progress and growth as well as competition.[247] The Directive also seeks to clarify the legal protection of biotechnological inventions, acknowledging that clarification and harmonization of the law is required to eliminate barriers to trade and enable proper functioning of the internal market.[248] According to Article 249 of the EC Treaty a Directive is binding on the results it intends to achieve but needs to be implemented by the Member States leaving the national authorities the choice of forum and method. Only in case a Directive is not properly implemented within the implementation period it becomes directly effective. National courts are

243 Opinion of the Economic and Social Committee on the 'Proposal for a European Parliament and Council Directive on the Legal Protection of Biotechnological Inventions' 1996 O.J. (C 295) 11 at §§1.2.2.-1.3.2 cited in Chow/Lee, International Intellectual Property, 349.

244 E.g. BGH X ZB 15/67 – *Rote Taube.*

245 Bauer/Gaskell, Biotechnology, 59, 60; Chow/Lee, International Intellectual Property, 348.

246 Directive 98/44/EC enacted on July 1998; referred to as 'Biotechnology Directive' in the following.

247 Recitals 1–3 of the Directive.

248 Recitals 4–6 of the Directive.

under the obligation to interpret national law in accordance with the intention of the Directive.[249]

1.1.2.3. National Laws and Court Decisions

The European Patent Convention contains autonomous law which is separate and independent from the patent systems of the Member states as far as the application and grant of a European patent is concerned.[250] After the European patent has been granted national laws are to a greater degree applicable.[251] The Member States have implemented the rules of the EPC into their national laws. Although the EPC and national laws are independent and the Member States are not bound by the EPO's decisions and vice versa, harmonization endeavors require that interpretation of legal norms is undertaken uniformly and the national courts and patent offices interpret their patents laws in conformity with the Convention.[252] As far as the Convention law applies, findings and decisions by the national courts and scientific discussions can only be used to interpret the terms in accordance with the Convention.[253]

1.2. SUBSTANTIVE PATENT REQUIREMENTS

1.2.1. PRODUCTS OF NATURE

Patents are granted for inventions and innovations. Under TRIPS patents shall be available for inventions in all fields of technology. Certain categories of subject matter may be excluded from patentability and most countries have decided to make use of this authorization. This applies for example to diagnostic, therapeutic and surgical methods for the treatment of humans or animals and to plants and animals other than micro-organisms and essentially biological processes for the production of plants and animals other than non-biological and microbiological processes. Certain exclusions are based on morality and public policy considerations; others are justified on the grounds that they refer to wide concepts. The grant of a temporary monopoly in these cases causes a great deadweight loss and may hinder further research and development by taking too much information out of the public domain.

249 Case C-14/83 *Von Colson and Kamann v Land Nord-Rhein-Westfalen*; Tritton, Intellectual Property in Europe, 1–027.

250 Article 1 EPC.

251 E.g. Article 2 (2) EPC, Article 64 EPC; Singer/Stauder, Europäisches Patentübereinkommen, Article 1 note 2, Article 2 notes 7, 8.

252 E.g. BGHZ 98, 12, 18 – *Formstein*; House of Lords GRUR Int. 1993, 325, 328f – *Tumornekrosefaktor*; Tribunale di Milano GRUR Int. 1993, 249, 251 – *Epilady XI*.

253 Singer/Stauder, Europäisches Patentübereinkommen, Artikel 60 note 5 (in regard to the term inventor).

The first threshold for a patent claim is that the subject matter in question indeed qualifies as an invention. The distinction between discovery and invention is especially relevant in the area of patenting plants, genetic resources or plant-derived biotechnological pharmaceutical drugs.

The ordinary meaning of the term 'invention' implies the output of an intellectual activity in the form of new knowledge of a technical nature and suggests a distinction between creation and mere discovery.[254] A discovery is understood to be the unearthing of causes, properties or phenomena already existing in nature whereas invention is the application of such knowledge to the satisfaction of social needs.[255] Put differently, a discovery lies in finding something existing which was unknown before while an invention requires the creation of something that does in this state not occur in nature. A discovery may include the identification of unknown properties and utilities.[256] The distinction between invention and discovery becomes blurred when patenting products of nature is at issue. This is an especially relevant concern in the area of biotechnology as this technology predominantly works with originally naturally occurring products and processes and a crucial point in the discussion of patenting of traditional medical knowledge and plant-based biotechnological inventions.

1.2.1.1. US Patent Law

Under Section 101 of the US Patent Act one finds the following phrasing: '*[...] whoever **invents or discovers** any new or useful [...]* (emphasis added)'; Section 100 (a) defines the term 'invention' to mean *invention or discovery.*

Although discoveries are thus literally patentable subject matter under US patent law, it is recognized that the laws of nature, physical phenomena and abstract ideas are not patentable and courts have established exemptions to patentability on a case law basis. US patent related case law has a long tradition of denying patents for products of nature.

The first major case setting forth the rule that natural products are unpatentable is *Funk Brothers Seed Co v Kalo Inoculant Co.*[257] An inventor claimed a patent for a mixture of bacteria that fixed nitrogen in soil. By infecting the roots of plants with this mixture, the plants themselves could absorb nitrogen more easily. The Supreme Court held in its decision that this mixture of bacteria as a product could not be subject to a patent since each of the bacteria existed in nature and their combination was merely a discovery on which a

254 Correa, Trade Related Aspects of Intellectual Property Rights, 272.
255 Cornish/Llewelyn, Intellectual Property, 5–56.
256 Sena, Directive on Biotechnological Inventions: Patentabiliy of Discoveries, IIC 1999, 731, 733.
257 76 U.S.P.Q. 280 (1948).

monopoly could not be claimed. Mixing the strains did not change the natural function of the bacteria.

An exception to the general rule that renders natural products unpatentable has been recognized in *Merck & Co Inc. v Olin Mathieson Chemical Corp.*[258] The ruling in this case held that a natural product that was purified or modified by men could be patented. The court considered the purified product (vitamin B 12) to be sufficiently different from the substance found in nature and therefore a new and useful composition that was entitled to patent protection. Furthermore, it held that the new product must differ *'not only in degree but in kind'* as well as have *'unexpected properties'*.[259] In *Merck* the purified matter was medically useful. Earlier cases had already emphasized that purification of natural products must lead to a superior quality, substantial advantage or unexpected results.[260]

The reduction of a natural substance to its pure form has also been discussed in *Cochrane v Badische Anilin & Soda Fabrik.*[261] In this case the court considered a patent for a synthetic form of dye, alizarine, to be invalid because alizarine occurred naturally in its pure state as the extraction of the madder root and consequently the synthetic product was not a new development.[262] In *Ex parte Latimer* the patent commissioner argued similarly and found that a fiber of a tree was unpatentable because such a patent would exclude all other men from the use of a natural product.[263] A patent on an isolated and purified hormone adrenaline was granted and upheld in *Parke-Davis & Co v H.K. Mulford & Co.*[264] The difference in this case is that adrenaline does in its pure form not exist in nature. Prior to the invention, dried and powdered superadrenal glands had been used to treat patients suffering from low blood pressure. In its decision the Court emphasized the greater value of the new form for the justification of the patent claim. Beside being more cost-effective, the new substance also had greater utility for disease treatment.

A line of argument has developed that requires two criteria to be fulfilled in order to overcome the products of nature doctrine. Firstly, the pure form of a product must not occur in nature. Secondly, the pure form must have greater value than the natural occurring substance.

Advances in biotechnology research finally enabled scientists to alter naturally occurring organisms. Consequently, courts were forced to define their position in regard to granting patents on living matter. The reasoning in regard to patents on products of nature found its summit in the decision in *Diamond v*

---

258 253 F.2d 156 (1958).

259 Id at 162.

260 E.g. *Kuehmsted v Farbenfabrikanten of Elberfeld Co.*, 179 F. 701, 705 (1910).

261 111 U.S. 293 (1884).

262 Id at 297.

263 1889 Dec. Comm'r Pat. 123, 126 (1889).

264 196 F.2d 641 (1929).

Chakrabarty.[265] The respondent Chakrabarty filed a patent application for a human-made, genetically engineered bacterium that is capable of breaking down multiple components of crude oil. *Diamond v Chakrabarty* was the first case stating that an end product micro-organism itself was patentable. Prior to *Diamond* the courts had denied patent protection to living organisms. This decision determines the limits of the natural products doctrine. It clearly states that living organisms are patentable subject matter and covered by patent law despite the fact that two statutes have been enacted providing special forms of patent protection for certain living organism.[266]

The goal of US patent law is the promotion of advances in its technology sector. This is already codified in the Constitution and was subsequently manifested by amendments of the statute and judicial interpretation. The biotechnological sector is large in the US and this can to a fair extent be attributed to its patent law and policy. The broad concept of patentable subject matter ultimately led to the acceptance of 'patents on life' which provides the foundation for the growth of the biotechnological industry. Critics claim that this decision has opened the floodgates for patenting any man-made living organisms which ultimately results in the legitimization of biopiracy.[267]

However, the decision is from a legal perspective by no means inconsistent with the underlying distinction between discovery and invention. The bacteria claimed in *Funk* were merely identified. They still had the same composition and performed the same function as they did in their natural state. As opposed to this the respondent's claim in *Diamond v Chakrabarty* referred to a non-naturally occurring manufacture or composition of matter. He did not simply combine two naturally occurring bacteria which still performed in their natural way and thus discovered a hitherto unknown natural phenomenon but produced a new modified organism that did not previously exist in nature but is the result of human intervention. Similarly, the alleged patents in *Cochrane* and *Latimer* claimed naturally occurring substances. *Parke Davis*, on the other hand, differs as to the degree of human intervention which led to the production of a new product that did in this form not exist in nature.

1.2.1.2. European Patent Law

The EPC does not give a statutory definition of the concept of an invention. A non-exhaustive list of unpatentable subject matter is provided for in Article 52 (2) (a) – (d) EPC which takes items that are abstract in nature and lack technical

265 447 U.S. 303, 100 S. Ct. 2202, 65 L.Ed.2d 144 (1980).

266 1930 Plant Patent Act; 1970 Plant Variety Protection Act.

267 Stenton, Biopiracy within in the Pharmaceutical Industry: A Stark Illustration of how Abusive, Manipulative and Perverse the Patenting Process can be Towards Countries of the South, E.I.P.R. 2004, 17, 19; Shiva, Global Trade and Intellectual Property: Threats to Indigenous Resources, in Krimsky/Shorett, Rights and Liberties in the Biotech Age, 98.

characteristics out of the definition scope of what is considered to be an invention. This includes specifically discoveries, scientific theories, and mathematical formula as stated in Article 52 (2) (a) EPC.

The Biotechnology Directive contains the general obligation to protect biotechnological inventions in Article 1. On the other hand, Article 52 (2) (a) EPC deems discoveries unpatentable. A definition of a biological invention is not contained in the Convention. The explicit exclusion of discoveries 'as such' as opposed to the inclusion of biological materials in the scope of the Directive exemplifies the difficulties at the borderline between biotechnological inventions and discoveries.

Sena, for examples, argues that biotechnological inventions are truly discoveries and the exclusion of discoveries 'as such' refers to scientific theories and mathematical formulas but not to material objects with previously unknown properties.[268] It appears more practicable, however, to distinguish a discovery from an invention. A discovery as such is abstract in nature and has no technical character in itself and is thus excluded from patentability but it can form the basis for an invention if it is practically applied in some form.[269] This can be derived from Article 52 (3) EPC which limits the restrictions as to exclusions from patentability to the extent to which the claim relates to that subject matter as such. While a claim that covers an item specified in Article 52 (2) EPC is not patentable, this limitation does not extend to claims that encompass both technical and non-technical subject matter. The exclusion of discoveries 'as such' is commonly understood to refer to the mere recognition of what already exists but human intervention or interaction of a technical nature with something that has been merely discovered can thus constitute a distinction between 'discovery as such' and 'invention' and render a claim patentable.[270] Furthermore, the alleged invention is considered as a whole and features that are excluded from patentability may nevertheless contribute to novelty and inventive step.[271]

Paragraph 1 of rule 26 of the Implementing Regulations states that the EPC shall be applied and interpreted in accordance with Directive 98/44 which is to be used as a supplementary means of interpretation. Rule 26 of the Implementing Regulations provides some general definitions which are further specified in rules 27 – 29. Biotechnological inventions are defined as '*inventions which concern a product consisting of or containing biological material or a process by means of which biological material is produced, processed or used*'[272] and

268 Sena, Directive on Biotechnological Inventions: Patentabiliy of Discoveries, IIC 1999, 731, 734.

269 Hacon/Pagenberg, Concise European Patent Law, EPC 2000, Article 52 EPC note 4; Guidelines for Examination in the European Patent Office, Part C, Chapter IV, 2.3.1.

270 Paterson, The European Patent System, 7–18.

271 Hacon/Pagenberg, Concise European Patent Law, EPC 2000, Article 52 EPC, note 10.

272 Rule 26 Paragraph 2 of the Implementing Regulations.

biological material as '*any material containing genetic information and capable of reproducing itself or being reproduced in a biological system*'.[273]

Patent protection under the Biotechnology Directive extends to products consisting of or containing biological material and to processes by which biological materials are produced, processed or used.[274] Article 8 (2) makes it clear that patent protection does not refer to the process by which biological material is altered or produced but extends to the material itself. Article 3 (2) of the Biotechnology Directive states that '*biological material which is isolated from its natural environment or produced by means of a technical process may be subject of an invention even if it previously occurred in nature*'. This definition is also contained in rule 27 (a) of the Implementing Regulation to the EPC. It does not affect the distinction between discovery and invention. Biological discoveries remain unpatentable but a patent on biological material can be obtained either for biological material that previously occurred in nature but has been identified and isolated or biological material that has been altered or produced by means of a technical process.[275] As in the US, microbiological inventions are also patentable under European law. This includes the patentability of micro-organisms *per se* if they are capable of producing novel compounds or known compounds more efficiently and of the microbiological process, in addition to patentability of the novel product.[276]

Article 53 (b) EPC excludes subject matter that concerns plant and animal varieties and essentially biological processes for the production of plants and animals from patentability. It does, however, not extend this exemption to microbiological processes. Essentially biological processes are those that consist entirely of natural phenomena such as crossing and selection.[277] The rationale behind this limitation is presumably to avoid double protection by both plant variety rights and patents and to prevent restrictions on long-standing practices of animal breeding.[278] The Biotechnology Directive provides for exemptions for plants and animals and essentially biological processes in Article 4. The interpretation of the non-patentability of animal and plant varieties and of essentially biological processes is narrowly construed under European law today.[279] Illustrative in regard to animal patents is the acceptance by the

273 Rule 26 Paragraph 3 of the Implementing Regulations.

274 Article 3 (1) Biotechnology Directive.

275 Articles 3 (1), 3 (2) and 8 (2) Biotechnology Directive; Tritton, Intellectual Property in Europe, 2–017; Benkard-*Melullis*, Europäisches Patentübereinkommen, Article 52 note 68.

276 T 356/93 – *Plant Genetic Systems*, [1995] O.J. EPO 545; Grubb/Thomson, Patents for Chemicals, Pharmaceuticals and Biotechnology, 229.

277 Rule 26 Paragraph 5 of the Implementing Regulations.

278 Hacon/Pagenberg, Concise European Patent Law, EPC 2000, Article 53 EPC, note 1.

279 Tritton, Intellectual Property in Europe, 2–110ff; Correa, The GATT Agreement on trade-related Aspects of Intellectual Property Rights: New Standards for Patent Protection, 16 E.I.P.R. 327, 328.

European Patent Office of a patent on the '*Harvard Mouse*'[280], and the decision in the *Lubrizol* case[281] in connection with the concept of essentially biological processes for the production of plants and animals.

To sum up, in Europe the problem of excluding discoveries from patent protection while at the same time providing for biotechnological patents has been solved by granting patents on substances found in nature only if those substances are isolated from their natural environment and are new in the sense that they were not available to the public previously.

1.2.2. NOVELTY

Once it has been established that the alleged subject matter indeed qualifies as an invention and is not merely a discovery, it has to be determined whether it is novel. An invention that already exists and has fallen in the public domain cannot be patented since there is no need to award a monopoly in this case. Patents on known products would only take information that has been available before out of the public domain and cause social loss as well as hinder further developments and would have quite the opposite effect of the original intention of patent law.

In technical terms an invention is only considered to be novel if it does not form part of the state of the art. The state of the art consists of the knowledge available to the public. The extent of the relevant prior art, however, differs considerably in the US and EU jurisdiction.

1.2.2.1. The State of the Art in US Patent Law

The novelty requirement is embodied in Section 101 ('new') and in Section 102 ('novelty'). Despite the different terminology in the provisions 'new' and 'novel' are treated as one criterion. Section 102 defines the relevant prior art that anticipates an invention and deems it not to be novel.[282]

---

280 T 19/90 – *Harvard/Onco-mouse* [1990] E.P.O.R. 501.

281 T 320/87 – *Lubrizol/Hybrid plants* [1990] O.J. EPO 3.

282 According to Section 102, novelty is denied if '*(a) the invention was known or used by others in this country, or patented or described in a printed publication in this or a foreign country, before the invention thereof by the applicant for patent, or (b) the invention was patented or described in a printed publication in this or a foreign country or in public use or on sale in this country, more than one year prior to the date of the application for patent in the United States [...].*'
Note: Section 102 (a), (e) and (g) constitute novelty requirements. An invention that passes those requirements could be patented. As opposed to this Section 102 (b) – (d) are statutory bars that may cause the loss of the right to patent, see Merges/Duffy, Patent Law and Policy, 359.

The state of the art encompasses prior use and knowledge as well as patents and publications. US patent law does not work with an 'absolute novelty' definition but makes a distinction between printed published knowledge and unpublished knowledge or use; the latter is only relevant if it occurred within the US.

Printed publication encompasses all publications regardless of the place of origin. With regard to what qualifies as a publication of an invention the statute stays silent. The Supreme Court relies on the '*Seymour* standard' holding that a prior publication must contain and exhibit a substantial representation of the patented improvement in clear and full terms enabling a person skilled in the art to make and work the invention.[283] Crude and imperfect experimentation is hence not sufficient. This implies that a detailed description clearly qualifies as relevant prior art while a mere mention in passing of an invention will not suffice. It can be concluded that any published disclosure that allows one to make an invention without any additional inventive contribution such as conceptual advance in the prior art, for example, suffices.[284]

Foreign prior art is only included in the state of the art if it is embodied in written form, such as a publication or a patent. Unpublished knowledge from abroad, on the other hand, is disregarded in the course of the novelty assessment. Publication is the only activity outside the US that can destroy novelty.

The Leahy Smith – America Invents Act incorporates changes in regard to the scope of the prior art which shall include offers for sale, public uses, patents and printed publications and items otherwise available to the public including uses anywhere in the world.[285] The changes will become effective starting in March 2013. However, the existing prior art definition will continue to apply for the patents now in force, the applications that are currently been examined and the patents that issue on them, the applications that are currently pending at the PTO and the patents that issue on them and the applications that will be filed before the effective date of March 16, 2013 and the patents issuing on them which will likely reach into the decade of the 2030s.[286]

US patent law uses the first-to-invent principle under which the relevant date of invention which determines whether prior art anticipates an invention is the date when the inventor has reduced his invention into practice.[287]

283 *Seymour v Osborne*, 78 U.S. 516, 517 (1870).

284 Huft, Indigenous Peoples and Drug Discovery Research: A Question of Intellectual Property Rights, 89 Nw. U. L. Rev. 1678, 1721.

285 Leahy-Smith America Invent Act, §3, enacting new 35 U.S.C. §102.

286 Janicke, A Commentary on the New Patent Law of the United States, GRURInt. 2011, 887, 893.

287 Merges/Duffy, Patent Law and Policy, 359; Halpern/Nard/Port, Fundamentals of United States Intellectual Property Law, 211; *Mahukar v C.R. Bard, Inc.*, 79 F.3d 1572, 1577, 1578 (1996). Actual reduction to practice occurs when the invention is shown to be suitable for its intended purpose. Constructive reduction to practice occurs when the patent application is filed regardless of whether anything has been built, see Halpern/Nard/Port, Fundamentals of

1.2.2.2. The European Approach to Novelty

European patent law follows a distinctly different prior art definition. According to Article 54 (2) EPC

> 'everything made available to the public by means of written or oral description, by use, or in any other way, before the filing date of the European patent application'

is part of the state of the art.

Article 54 EPC specifies three types of disclosure, namely written description, oral description and use. By recognizing 'any other way' as disclosure any information made available to the public is included in the state of the art. Thus, information available to the public refers to all information regardless of the source or means of transmission, such as written and oral descriptions and other means of information.[288] The relevant public refers to the general public at large in the sense that an unlimited number of individuals have the possibility of accessing the knowledge. This excludes knowledge from the state of the art that is only available to a limited number of people provided that it is impossible for the information to leak out.[289] Finally, availability requires the objective possibility of access. The mere existence of prior art is consequently not sufficient but it is also not required that the public actually learns about the knowledge as long as it could learn the teaching. In case of oral disclosure it has been held that 'public' means skilled person.[290] This makes sense because disclosed knowledge is theoretically available for the person skilled in the art regardless of the place of the disclosure whereas oral disclosure requires the attendance of a person skilled in the art at the time of disclosure. Oral disclosure before people that do not understand the information and are thus unable to reproduce it, cannot anticipate an invention.[291] All types of disclosure must provide the skilled person 'direct and unambiguous' access; the invention must be derivable from the prior art which does not require identity of the words in the prior art source and the patent claim but must enable the skilled person to carry out the invention without undue burden.[292] In regard to chemical patents, courts have established the rule that the disclosure of a general structural formula does not disclose every individual compound that falls under that formula; there has to be some

United States Intellectual Property Law, 211; the abandonment of the first-to-invent approach is also part of the Smith-Leahy America Invents Act, supra Part 2:1.1.1.2.

288 Schulte, Patentgesetz, §3 notes 19–25.

289 Seville, EU Intellectual Property Law and Policy, 105; Schulte, Patentgesetz, §3 notes 26 – 34.

290 T 877/90 *Hoopert/T-Cell Growth Factor* [1993] E.P.O.R. 6.

291 Tritton, Intellectual Property in Europe, 2–055.

292 G1/92 – *Availability to the public* [1993] E.P.O.R. 241; Hacon/Pagenberg, Concise European Patent Law, EPC 2000, Article 54 note 9 and 15.

kind of indivualization that enables the person skilled in the art to perform the invention in order to destroy novelty.[293]

The relevant date is the date of filing which is considered to be the priority date for the purposes of Article 54 (2) and (3) EPC, Article 89 EPC. The state of the art encompasses all those inventions which have been filed but not published, Article 54 (3) EPC.

The different concepts in regard to determining the state of the art are quite influential in the area of anticipation of an invention based on traditional medical knowledge. Under a domestic prior art limitation traditional knowledge will often not qualify as invalidating prior art. Under European law, however, prior art is judged on an absolute, global scale and includes printed publications as well as unpublished information from abroad thereby rendering knowledge from everywhere around the world to be the state of the art.

1.2.3. INVENTIVE STEP AND NON-OBVIOUSNESS

The patent laws further require an inventive step or non-obviousness of the alleged invention. European patent law speaks of *inventive step*; US patent law uses the term *non-obviousness*. There are some differences between the concepts. While inventive step implies that an intellectual process has taken place to develop a new product or process, non-obviousness could be predicated with regard to subject matter in cases of discovery as well as invention.[294] This is in line with the broader concept of invention in the US Patent Act which literally encompasses discoveries.

This requirement is the most important standard in patent law and also the most difficult to asses. Its rationale is to keep trivial advancements in the public domain and to ensure that those improvements that constitute only the next logical step in a development and could occur to anyone skilled in particular field of expertise are not protected exclusively for a period of 20 years. In many situations valuable innovations are obvious responses to changes in economic, social or technological circumstances. Where those changes are not within the sphere and responsibility of the person applying for a patent, it is not economically sensible to confer an exclusive right. Secondly, granting patents to obvious inventions may diminish the incentives that the patent system provides to develop non-obvious inventions. And finally, the non-obviousness requirement prevents the proliferation of economically insignificant patents that are expensive to search and license.[295]

---

293 BGH X ZR 89/07 – *Olanzapin*; BGHZ 103, 150 – *Fluoran*.

294 Correa, Trade Related Aspects of Intellectual Property Rights, 276.

295 Merges/Duffy, Patent Law and Policy, 614, 615.

Even if an invention is novel it can still be obvious if it is not significantly different from the prior art. Generally speaking, the requirement is fulfilled when a person skilled in the art under consideration of the prior art does not regard the invention to be obvious. The assessment appears to be necessarily subjective.

1.2.3.1. US Patent Law – Non-Obviousness

Prior to the 1952 Patent Act the assessment of non-obviousness was not codified in the statute. Patent officers and courts evaluated non-obviousness as part of the examination of whether the claimed act constituted an invention. The first important case in this regard was *Hotchkiss v Greenwood* where the Supreme Court held that patentability requires something more than novelty and defined invention in the sense that it had to show more ingenuity and skill than possessed by an ordinary mechanic.[296] US courts subsequently applied a rather rigid standard rewarding only substantive departures from the prior art. As put in *Atlantic Works v Brady*[297] patent law was not designed to

> 'grant a monopoly for every trifling device, every shadow of a shade, of an idea, which could naturally and spontaneously occur to any skilled mechanic or operator in the ordinary progress of manufacturing'.

Later courts even demanded that an invention *'must reveal the flash of creative genius'*.[298] From *re Kepler*[299] and other contemporaneous cases the rationale was drawn that a claimed invention could be invalidated by showing that the departure from the prior art as undertaken by the patentee would have been 'obvious to try' which provided viable ground for denying patentability as to a lack of inventiveness.[300] As this level proved to be too vague and ambiguous and resulted in inconveniently high bars to patentability, the Patent Act 1952 introduced the requirement of non-obviousness in Section 103 to replace the assessment within the concept of invention.

---

296 *Hotchkiss v Greenwood*, 52 U.S. 248 (1850), 11 How. 248, 13 L. Ed. 683; Lange/LaFrance/Myers, Intellectual Property, Cases and Materials, 474.

297 107 US 192; 2 S.Ct. 225, 27 L.Ed. 438 (1883).

298 *Cuno Engineering Corp.*, 314 US 84, 51 U.S.P.Q. 1 (1941).

299 132 F.2d 130 (1942).

300 Trask, 'Obvious to Try': A Proper Patentability Standard in the Pharmaceutical Arts? 76 Fordham Law Rev., 2625, 2638, 2639.

a. The Graham Factors

The standard test for non-obviousness was subsequently established in a set of cases commonly referred to as *Graham v John Deere Co.*[301] The rationale from the cases is that the ultimate determination of non-obviousness is a question of law based on several factual inquiries. Firstly, the content and scope of the prior art must be considered. In a second step, the differences between the prior art and the alleged invention have to be determined. Finally, the level of skill in the prior art is assessed in order to resolve whether one skilled in the art could have reasonably thought of or readily produced the changes.[302] The relevance of secondary considerations is acknowledged. Considerations to be taken into account in the course of the assessment include commercial success, the fulfillment of a historical need for the invention, failure of others and the unexpectedness of the results. Obviousness may furthermore be implied where several persons independently develop similar solutions at the same time.[303]

The properties of chemical compounds which are mainly intended for use in highly complex systems such as living systems are generally unpredictable. Small alterations in the chemical structure can result in great differences in the therapeutical effectiveness.[304] This reasoning must also apply in cases in which the preparation of a product involves a complex system as in biotechnology. Here the process of obtaining the compound is equally unpredictable.[305] In regard to biotechnological patent cases the impropriety of an obvious-to-try standard had presumably been settled in *re O'Farrell*[306] and *In re Deuel.*[307] It was held that in the area of biotechnology a general incentive or the existence of a technique does not render a result obvious.[308]

b. Combining References: TSM

Unlike the relevant prior art disclosure in Section 102 which needs to encompass every element of what the patentee claims as his invention in order to anticipate the invention, a reference does not need to disclose the entire invention to bar a

---

301 *Graham v John Deere Company Kansas City, Calmar, Inc., v Cool Chemical Company, Colgate-Palmolive Company v Cool Chemical* Company, 383 U.S.1, 86 S.Ct. 684, 15 L.Ed. 2d 545, 148 U.S.P.Q. 459 (1966).

302 Id at 17; Davis, The Patenting of Products of Nature, 21 Rutgers Computer & Tech. L. J. 293, 304.

303 Lange/LaFrance/Myers, Intellectual Property, Cases and Materials, 480.

304 Wegner, Chemical and Biotechnology Obviousness in a State of Flux, 26 Biotechnolgy L. Rev. 437, 440.

305 Ducor, Patenting the Recombinant Products of Biotechnology and Other Molecules, 22.

306 853 F.2d 894 (1988).

307 52 F.3d 1552 (1995).

308 Id at 1559; Burk/Lemley, Is Patent Law Technology-Specific? 17 Berkeley Tech. L.J. 1155, 1179. See also infra Part 2:2.1.3.1.

patent under Section 103.[309] Frequently, obviousness is claimed arguing that disclosure of two or more prior art references rendered the alleged invention obvious.

In regard to this issue the Federal Circuit introduced the 'teaching, suggestion, or motivation' test. This concept attributes to the fact that '*the genius of invention is often a combination of known elements which in hindsight seem preordained*'. In order to prevent hindsight invalidation it is not sufficient to show that every element of an invention was independently known in the prior art. Rather a patent is only proven obvious if '*some motivation or suggestion to combine the prior art teachings*' can be found in the prior art, the nature of the problem, or the knowledge of a person having ordinary skill in the art.[310]

This approach, however, has become increasingly formalistic as to the conception of teaching, suggestion or motivation. As stated in *McGingley v Franklin Sports, Inc.* '*the tests of whether to combine references need to be applied rigorously*'.[311] This led to patents on inventions that combined prior art sources that did not explicitly contain a suggestion or motivation to combine but were nevertheless predictable. In the recent case *KSR International Co. v Teleflex Inc.*,[312] the application of the TSM test was finally challenged.

c. The Implications of *KSR v Teleflex*

This case concerned a mechanical patent for a position-adjustable vehicle pedal which combined elements from two prior art sources. The patent was deemed to be obvious due to the combination of prior art sources. The court held that the combination of known elements yielded predictable results.

The Supreme Court applied an obvious-to-try standard under which not only the immediate problem the patentee was trying to solve but any problem in the field as well as all uses of prior art disclosure beyond their primary purpose were considered. Despite the fact that the prior art sources addressed different problems than those the patentee tried to solve, the combination of the elements was nevertheless considered to be obvious to a person skilled in the art. The court furthermore held that a patent can be proven to be obvious merely by showing that a combination was obvious to try provided that there is a design need or market demand to solve a problem and there are a finite number of predictable solutions.[313]

---

309 *Re Vaeck*, 947 F.2d 488 (1991); Merges/Menell/Lemley, Intellectual Property in the New Technological Age, 226.

310 *McGingley v Franklin Sports, Inc.*, 262 F.3d 1339, 1351 (2001); *Al-Site Corp. v. VSI Int'l, Inc.*, 174 F.3d 1308, 1323–1324 (1999).

311 Id at 1351.

312 127 S.Ct. 1727 (2007).

313 Id at 1732.

The Supreme Court thereby rejected the rigid application of the TSM test by the Court of Appeals and stated that in regard to the question of obviousness, Supreme Court case law set forth an expansive and flexible approach under which secondary considerations can be taken into account while rigid rules limit the obviousness inquiry in a way that contradicts the diversity of inventive pursuit and of modern technologies.[314] Overall, this establishes a higher threshold in regard to non-obviousness as opposed to the approach under the TSM test.

It remains to be seen how this decision affects biotechnological patent cases. If the principle was extended, the existence of a technique and a general incentive to apply a certain method could, contrary to the current interpretation, indeed render the result obvious.[315]

1.2.3.2. European Patent Law – Inventive Step

The EPC refers to inventiveness in Article 56 EPC stating that

> 'an invention shall be considered as involving an inventive step if, having regard to the state of the art, it is not obvious to a person skilled in the art'.

a. Problem-and-Solution Approach

The test used in order to assess inventiveness is an objective one, the so-called 'problem-and-solution approach'. The problem-and-solution approach comprises three major stages: (1) determining the closest prior art, (2) establishing the objective technical problem to be solved, and (3) considering whether or not the claimed invention, starting from the closest prior art and the objective technical problem, would have been obvious to the skilled person.[316]

In determining the closest prior art it is assumed that the inventor relied on the document that comes closest to the alleged invention which addresses the same technical issue and constitutes the most promising starting point towards the development of the claimed invention.[317] The technical problem posed by the prior art is then identified through the eyes of the skilled person at the priority date. Obviousness will be given if the skilled person starting with the closest prior art and being confronted with the technical problem would have solved the

314 Id at 1731.

315 Infra Part 2:2.1.3.1.

316 T 1/80 – *Bayer/Carbonless copying paper*, [1979–85] E.P.O.R. B250; T 24/81 – *BASF/Metal refining*, [1979–85] E.P.O.R. B354; Guidelines for Examination in the European Patent Office Part C, Chapter IV, 11.5.

317 Brinkmann/Tilmann, EPÜ-Handbuch, 167; Benkard-*Jestaedt*, Europäisches Patentübereinkommen, Article 56 note 32; Hacon/Pagenberg, Concise European Patent Law, EPC 2000, Article 56, note 10.

problem by means of the invention claimed in the patent application.[318] The decisive view is the view of a person skilled in the art which will be presumed to be an ordinary practitioner with specific knowledge in the relevant field of expertise, common general knowledge in the art and knowledge he would gain from routine work and experimentation but not possessing any inventive capability.[319]

The 'could-would test' holds that in order to deny an inventive step it is not sufficient that the skilled person *could* have made the invention but rather whether he *would* have done so thereby requiring some kind of motivation or reasonable expectation of success.[320] Unexpected or surprising effects are consequently an indication of inventiveness. The assessment is supposed to avoid an *ex post facto* analysis.[321] The 'could-would test' is similar to the 'obvious-to-try' inquiry undertaken in US law. If a particular solution is obvious to try with a reasonable expectation of success an inventive step will be denied.

b. Subsidiary Criteria

It is frequently difficult to answer the question whether the skilled person would have solved the technical problem in the same way the inventor did. The EPO has developed several subsidiary criteria that may give guidance.

Combining references from different prior art sources may render an invention obvious. This, however, will only be the case if the content of the different sources makes it likely that the person skilled in the art would have taken them into consideration. The more sources are to be combined the greater the likelihood that the combination was not obvious.[322]

Other secondary indications in determining an inventive step are similar to those found in US law and include the departure from a beaten track, the satisfaction of a long felt need, commercial success, the overcoming of a technical prejudice or an achievement that experts have long tried.[323]

Especially in biotechnology, a research path may have been indicated by the prior art, but it was expected that the research would be difficult or require long and complex techniques or take a long time. In such cases the person skilled in

---

318 Hacon/Pagenberg, Concise European Patent Law, EPC 2000, Article 56, note 12, Guidelines for Examination in the European Patent Office Part C, Chapter IV, 11.5.3.

319 T 39/93 – *Allied Colloids*, [1997] O.J. EPO 134; Tritton, Intellectual Property in Europe, 2–074; Hacon/Pagenberg, Concise European Patent Law, EPC 2000, Article 56, note 3; Schulte, Patentgesetz, §4 notes 42–47.

320 T 2/83 – *Rider*, [1984] O.J. EPO 265; Benkard-*Jestaedt*, Europäisches Patentübereinkommen, Article 56 notes 60, 61; Schulte, Patentgesetz, §4 note 61 with further references.

321 T 465/93 ABl 96, 32; Tritton, Intellectual Property in Europe, 2–076.

322 Hacon/Pagenberg, Concise European Patent Law, EPC 2000, Article 56 note 14.

323 Benkard-*Jestaedt*, Europäisches Patentübereinkommen, Article 56 notes 67ff. Hacon/Pagenberg, Concise European Patent Law, EPC 2000, Article 56 notes 20–23; Tritton, Intellectual Property in Europe, 2–078ff.

the art might be unlikely to try as there is no real expectation of success.[324] Such circumstances can hint at inventiveness.

1.2.4. UTILITY AND INDUSTRIAL APPLICATION

US patent law requires an invention to be useful while European patent law speaks of a capability for industrial application. It should be noted that useful is a much broader term than industrial application and encompasses some more assets. Until recently it seemed that this patentability requirement did not constitute a strong threshold in the application process and could usually be easily complied with.[325] It mainly excluded inoperable inventions from patentability. In relation to biological or pharmaceutical patents, however, some critical issues arose that should be mentioned.

1.2.4.1. US – Utility

The utility requirement is included in Section 101 which requires an invention to be 'useful' as well as in Section 112 which requires an applicant to disclose 'the manner and process of making and using the invention.' The provisions imply that an alleged invention has some beneficial use for society. Cases that discuss a lack of utility are rare.[326] It is indeed hard to imagine that someone would bother to apply for a patent for a useless and thus probably invaluable invention. However, it is quite possible that an invention has no current but rather an evolving or future use. Also, the opinions on whether an invention is useful may differ. Utility rules are supposed to limit strategic patenting by ensuring that patents on basic research are not granted, delaying the point in the development of a new product in which a patent can be obtained and reducing the costs of searches by screening out useless inventions.[327] Utility poses a greater concern for biological inventions. Often those inventions have an evolving utility. Inventors might identify a compound without a known current use relying on knowledge on the behavior of related compounds and assuming to develop some application in the future.[328] It may be a process until a biotechnological compound can be effectively used. Furthermore, biotechnological inventions are often controversial and the beneficial use is questioned

324 T 223/92 – *Genentech/HIF-Gamma* [2003] E.P.O.R. 10; Tritton, Intellectual Property in Europe, 2–085; Schertenleib, The Patentability and Protection of DNA Based Inventions in the EPO and the European Union, E.I.P.R. 2003, 125, 129.

325 Abbott/Cottier/Gurry, The International Intellectual Property System, 26.

326 Halpern/Nard/Port, Fundamentals of United States Intellectual Property Law, 232.

327 Landes/Posner, The Economic Structure of Intellectual Property Law, 302.

328 Thomas, Pharmaceutical Patent Law, 60.

Within the question of utility three issues can be distinguished: operational or general utility[329], beneficial utility[330] and practical or specific utility.[331] Generally speaking, some minimal current use suffices.

Practical or specific utility can become relevant in chemical or biotechnological cases. Frequently inventions of chemical or biological compounds are made that do not have a value at that time but become valuable when research and understanding continue and expand. Allowing patents on such inventions could easily impede further research and development.

In US law this conflict has been solved by requiring more than the production of something that may be an object of scientific research. The applicant needs to show some specific benefit of his invention in its current available form. The first case highlighting this issue was *Brenner v Manson*.[332] A researcher invented a novel process for making a known steroid. At that time, however, while a research interest clearly existed, an application or utility of the steroid was not known. The court decided that a mere interest for research or further investigation was not sufficient to approve the utility of chemical compounds but that a specific or substantial utility was required. The court emphasized that encouraging disclosure and inhibiting secrecy are only one side of the coin and argued that a patent on a process in a chemical field which has not yet been developed to the point of practical utility creates a monopoly on knowledge which may cover a vast area without clearly determined boundaries and may confer the power to block off whole areas of scientific development without compensating any benefit to the public.[333] The rational of this approach is clearly to avoid blocking of further research by requiring that a certain degree of practicable applicability must be reached which determines the boundaries of the claim. At the same time, however, the requirement of proving a practical or specific utility as stated in *Brenner v Manson* has an adverse effect on disclosure and further going research. Obviously, a researcher who invents a new compound has an incentive to keep it secret until the use is discovered.[334]

Another issue is what the applicant must prove regarding the practical utility of his invention. In *re Brana*[335] and *Fujikawa v Wattansin*[336] this was discussed

---

329 Operational utility is given if an invention can actually accomplish the utility alleged by the inventor. This excludes any fantastic or impossible inventions, e.g. a perpetual motion machine as claimed in *Newman v Quigg*, 877 F.2d 1575 (1989).

330 Beneficial utility ascertains whether an invention is socially beneficial or rather socially harmful or has a deleterious purpose. Here morality considerations can become important and may have an effect, e.g. on biotechnological inventions, Merges/Duffy, Patent Law and Policy, 208.

331 Merges/Duffy, Patent Law and Policy, 208.

332 383 U.S. 519, 148 U.S.P.Q. (BNA) 689 (1966), 86 S.Ct. 1033, 16 L.Ed.2d 69.

333 Id at 533; Lange/LaFrance/Myers, Intellectual Property, Cases and Materials, 426.

334 Merges/Duffy, Patent Law and Policy, 228.

335 51 F. 3d 1560, 34 U.S.P.Q. 2d 1436 (1995).

336 93 F.3d 1559 (1996).

with regard to pharmaceutical inventions. It was found that an applicant needs to establish some pharmacological activity. Tests on animals suffice to claim a practical utility as Food and Drug Administration (FDA) approval is no prerequisite for utility in the context of patent law. The burden of proof only shifts to the applicant once the United States Patent and Trademark Office (USPTO) challenged a presumptively correct assertion of the utility of a device and provides evidence that someone with ordinary skill in the art would reasonably doubt the asserted utility.

1.2.4.2. EU – Industrial Application

Industrial application as required under European Patent law is broadly defined, and includes making and using the invention in any kind of industry, including agriculture, Article 57 EPC. Especially the Biotechnology Directive puts emphasis on the capability of industrial application.

The rationale for this requirement is to limit patent protection to technical inventions which belong to the practical and useful arts and to prevent protection of such inventions that are merely aesthetic creations.[337] Consequently, industry is understood in the broadest sense and defined to mean activities carried out continuously, independently and for financial gain.[338] The possibility of commercial application and success suffices. Industrial applicability excludes private and personal use but it will be sufficient if a product that serves only private or personal use can be produced industrially or if the industrial application is one possible use among others.[339] While disclosure of a practical application is required it is sufficient to show the possibility of applicability besides other uses.[340] Inoperative inventions do not satisfy the requirement.[341]

Morality considerations that are discussed in the context of utility under US patent law are subject to a separate provision under European patent law, Article 53 EPC. Article 53 (2) EPC exempts methods for the treatment of the human or animal body by surgery or therapy and diagnostic methods as unpatentable. These provisions were formerly placed within Article 54 (2) EPC 1973 and excluded from patentability on the grounds of lack of industrial applicability. The placement within Article 53 EPC 2000 reflects the fact that the exemption is based on public policy considerations. Products such as substances

---

337 Guidelines for Examination in the European Patent Office, Part C, Chapter, IV, 5.1; this concept correlates with the explicit exemption of aesthetic creations in Article 52 (2) (b) EPC.

338 T-144/83 – *Du Pont/Appetite suppressant* [1987] E.P.O.R. 6.

339 Benkard-*Jestaedt*, Europäisches Patentübereinkommen, Article 57 note 3; Hacon/Pagenberg, Concise European Patent Law, EPC 2000. Article 57 note 2.

340 Tritton, Intellectual Property in Europe, 2–088; Schulte, Patentgesetz, §5 note 8.

341 Court of Appeals, GRUR Int. 1998, 419 – *Hepatitis-C-Virus II*; Benkard-*Melullis*, Europäisches Patentübereinkommen, Article 52 note 4; Hacon/Pagenberg, Concise European Patent Law, EPC 2000, Article 57, note 3.

and compositions for use of treatment, however, are not exempted from patentability.[342] Morality considerations are introduced in Article 6 (1) of the Biotechnology Directive. Inventions that are contrary to the *ordre public* or morality are unpatentable.[343]

1.3. SPECIFICATION

The main formal requirement contained in the patent laws is the specification of the invention. Specification consists of the written description and the patent claims. The description provides for disclosure. As the patent is only rewarded in exchange for the publicity of the invention the inventor must disclose the invention in a manner sufficient to enable a person skilled in the art to carry out the invention (enabling disclosure). The specification furthermore consists of the patent claim which determines the scope of the patent right.

1.3.1. DISCLOSURE OF THE INVENTION

Formally, the patent applicant has to specify his claims including the full disclosure of his invention by a written description. The provisions on disclosure enact the underlying rationale of patenting, namely that the patent is only granted in exchange for publicity of the invention. US and European patent law both have established similar principles as to the necessary disclosure of the invention. The patent claim must be proportionate to the effective disclosure and enablement of the subject matter of protection.[344]

Due to the complexity of living systems the sufficient and reproducible disclosure by a written description alone can be difficult or even impossible in case of biotechnological inventions.[345] In order to overcome this hurdle most patent laws provide for a deposit requirement. This concept has been introduced into international law with the Budapest Treaty which entered into force in 1980.

1.3.1.1. US Patent Law

Section 112 sets out the requirements for specification.[346] According to Sec. 112 the patent applicant needs to disclose his invention fully by providing a written description enabling any person skilled in the art to make and use the invention.

342 Article 57 (2) (1) EPC.
343 Case C-34/10 – *Oliver Brüstle/Greenpeace e.V.*
344 Funder, Biology, Information and Property, 188.
345 Grubb/Thomson, Patents for Chemicals, Pharmaceuticals and Biotechnology, 226; Mgbeoji, Patents and Traditional Knowledge of the Use of Plants: Is a Communal Patent Regime Part of the Solution to the Scourge of Bio Piracy? 9 Ind. J. Global Legal Stud. 163, 184.
346 Section 112 reads: '*The specification shall contain a written description of the invention, and of the manner and process of making and using it, in such full, clear, concise and exact terms as to*

a. Written Description and Deposit Requirement

The patent applicant must provide a written description of the alleged invention. In order to comply with this requirement the applicant must prove with reasonable clarity to persons skilled in the art that he was 'in possession' of the subject matter subsequently claimed as the invention.[347] This does not necessarily require that the applicant describes the invention in words. It is also permissible to provide drawings.[348]

Providing a written description can be problematic in cases claiming patents on biological materials. In these cases the written description requires a precise definition as to the structure, formula, chemical name or physical properties of the claimed substance because only by providing this information, the applicant proves that he is in possession of the complete and operative invention.[349] The revised US guidelines 2001 stated that completeness of the invention can be shown by a sufficiently detailed disclosure identifying relevant characteristics, i.e. including complete or partial structure, other physical and/or chemical properties, functional characteristics when coupled with a known or disclosed correlation between function and structure, or some combination of such characteristics.[350] The applicant must provide a deposit of the biological material in addition to the written disclosure but the courts even allow the deposit to satisfy the written description requirement.[351] The deposit requirement is subject to some critique. While disclosure serves the purpose of allowing easy access of the public to the information (e.g. for use in follow-on research), deposited biological material is not easily accessible or reproducible by the public.[352]

b. Enablement

Enablement is given when the disclosure in the patent application is sufficient to allow a person skilled in the art to both make and use the claimed invention. Its rationale is to ensure that the public is 'in possession' of the subject matter of the claimed invention and can reproduce it after the patent has expired.[353] The

---

enable any skilled person in the art to which it pertains, or with which it is most nearly connected, to make and use the same [...].'

347 E.g. *Vas-Cath v Mahurkar*, 935 F.2d 1555, 1561 (1991).

348 Id at 1565.

349 *Regents of the University of California v Eli Lilly & Co.*, 119 F.3d 1559, 1566 (1997); Burk/Lemley, Is Patent Law Technology-Specific? 17 Berkeley Tech. L.J. 1155, 1176.

350 Guidelines for Patent Applications under the 35 U.S.C. §112, 'Written Description' Requirement, 66 Fed. Reg. 1099, 1106.

351 *Enzo Biochem, Inc. v Gen-Probe Inc.*, 323 F.3d 956 (2002).

352 Mgbeoji, Patents and Traditional Knowledge of the Use of Plants: Is a Communal Patent Regime Part of the Solution to the Scourge of Bio Piracy? 9 Ind. J. Global Legal Stud. 163,.

353 *Christianson v Colt Industries Operating Corp.*, 820 F.2d 1992 cert. denied, 493 U.S. 822, 110 S.Ct. 81, 107 L.Ed.2d 47 (1989).

application of the enablement requirement by the Courts results in the invalidation of patent claims which are too broad and require 'undue experimentation' in the course of reproducing them. Undue experimentation is determined by the *Wands* factors which take into account the quantity of experimentation required, the amount of guidance provided, the presence or absence of working examples, the nature of the invention, the state of the prior art, the relative skill of those in the art, the predictability or unpredictability of the art and the breadth of the claims.[354]

Predictability is frequently given in mechanical and electrical arts while chemical and biotechnological arts are at least in parts unpredictable as minor changes in the physical property of a molecule or compound can result in major changes in its properties or functions. This puts the burden on the applicant to provide a greater degree of information on how to make and use the invention in patent applications in these areas.[355]

c. Best Mode Requirement

US patent law furthermore encompasses the best mode requirement which considers a disclosure to be sufficient only if it contains the best way known by the inventor of carrying out the invention.[356] This requirement obliges the patent applicant to disclose any specific instrumentalities or techniques he may have developed if these constitute the best way to carry out the invention.[357]

1.3.1.2. Europe

Article 83 EPC requires that the invention must be disclosed sufficiently clear and complete for it to be carried out by a person skilled in the art. A lack of disclosure is a ground for opposition, Article 100 (b) EPC, as well as a ground for revocation, Article 138 (b) EPC.

a. Description and Enablement

Disclosure must be clear and complete. As opposed to US patent law this does not require the disclosure of the best mode to carry out the invention. The application must disclose at least one way of carrying out the invention in detail as to enable the person skilled in the art to put the invention into practice.[358]

---

354 *Re Wands*, 858 F.2d 731 (198); *Enzo Biochem, Inc. v Calgene, Inc.*, 188 F.3d 1362 (1999).

355 *Amgen, Inc. v Chugai Pharm. Co.*, 927 F.2d 1200, 1214, cert. denied, 502 U.S. 856 (1991); Mueller, An Introduction to Patent Law, 91.

356 *Christianson v Colt Industries Operating Corp.*, id at note 353.

357 *Spectra-Physics, Inc. v Coherent, Inc.*, 827 F.2d 1524, 1532 (1987).

358 T 292/85 – *Gentech* [1989] O.J. EPO 275; Hacon/Pagenberg, Concise European Patent Law, EPC 2000, Article 83 note 3.

Sufficiency of disclosure is assessed on the basis of the application including the description, the drawings and the claims.

As the patent application is addressed to a person skilled in the art, the point of view to determine sufficient disclosure is that of such a person who is assumed to have read the application carefully and may rely on common knowledge as well as other documents referred to in the specification.[359]

The EPO has established the general principle that the patent application must enable the invention to be performed to the full extent of the legal monopoly claimed, i.e. disclosure 'across the breadth of the claim' enabling the skilled person to reproduce substantially all embodiments of the claimed subject matter.[360] In general, a broad claim requires a more detailed disclosure of technical information and alternative embodiments.[361] As in US patent law, the invention must be reproducible without undue burden but a reasonable amount of trial and error will not render the disclosure insufficient.[362] Especially in the area of biotechnological patenting it may be difficult to reproduce an invention exactly. This does not hinder the application provided that the skilled person is able to put the invention into practice without undue burden.[363]

Rule 31(1) of the Implementing Regulations provides for the deposit of biological materials in case an invention that involves the use of such material cannot be described in manner as to enable the invention to be carried out. The Biotechnology Directive contains the details of description and deposit of biological material in Article 13.

b. Disclosure of the Source

Recital 27 of the Biotechnology Directive incorporates a voluntary disclosure requirement that obliges the applicant to disclose the origin of biological material used. It applies only if the applicant knows the origin of the source of the material and non-compliance and has no effect on the validity of his rights.

---

359 T 611/89 *Hüls Troisdorf AG* (not reported); T 267/91 *Plus-Staufer AG* (not reported); Hacon/Pagenberg, Concise European Patent Law, 99 (citing the cases); Benkard-*Schäfers*, Europäisches Patentübereinkommen, Article 83 note 11.

360 T 409/91 – *Exxon/Fuel oils* [1994] O.J. EPO 653.

361 Guidelines for Examination in the European Patent Office, Part C,Chapter II, 4.9.

362 T 014/83 – *Sumitono/Vinyl chloride resins* [1979–85] E.P.O.R. C737; Hacon/Pagenberg, Concise European Patent Law, EPC 2000, Article 83 note 5.

363 T 301/87 – *Biogen* [1990] O.J. EPO 195; T 281/86 – *Unilever* [1989] O.J. EPO 202.

1.3.2. PATENT CLAIMS

1.3.2.1. Claim Categories

Patent law supports different categories of claims. Product claims are claims to produce substances and confer protection over all uses regardless of how a substance was derived.[364] Process claims, on the other hand, protect activities such as methods, uses or processes. Protection extends to the products directly obtained by the process and third parties are not allowed to sell market or use the product.[365] A subset of process claims are the use claims which allow for patenting of a particular indication such as a second medical use (Swiss claim).[366] Since the disclosure of a previously unknown indication of a known substance can well constitute a valuable contribution to the state of the art, patent protection for these claims is recognized.[367] Finally, product-by-process applications claim a patent for a product produced by a particular method. The USPTO and the EPO both recognize such claims – primarily used in chemical and biotechnological inventions but not limited to these – where the product is too complex and cannot be defined in reference to its composition or structure.[368] A product-by-process claim extends the patent right to the product and is not limited to the process steps recited in the claim.[369]

1.3.2.2. Claim Drafting

The patent claim determines the scope of the right to exclude. It is to be distinguished from the written description which provides for disclosure and enablement.

a. US

The claim consists of a single-sentenced definition of the scope of the patent right. Section 112 (2) of the Patent Act requires that each patent concludes with one or more claims that

---

364 G2/88 – *Mobil/Friction reducing additive* [1990] O.J. EPO 93; Seville, EU Intellectual Property Law and Policy, 97.

365 Article 64 (2) EPC; Benkard-*Schäfers*, Europäisches Patentübereinkommen, Article 84 note 30.

366 Article 54 (5) EPC; G05/83 – *Eisai* [1985] O.J. EPO 64; Benkard-*Schäfers*, Europäisches Patentübereinkommen, Article 84 note 31; Hacon/Pagenberg, Concise European Patent Law, EPC 2000, Article 53 EPC, note 9.

367 Benkard-*Schäfers*, Europäisches Patentübereinkommen, Article 84 note 31.

368 T 150/82, *IFF/Claim Categories* [1984] O.J. EPO 309, 310–11; *Re Bridgeford*, 537 F.2d 679, 682 (1966); Benkard-*Schäfers*, Europäisches Patentübereinkommen, Article 84 note 33; Seville, EU Intellectual Property Law and Policy, 97.

369 Mueller, An Introduction to Patent Law, 77.

> 'particularly point out and distinctively claim the subject matter that the applicant regards as his invention.'

This requirement is commonly referred to as the definitiveness requirement. In the course of defining novel and possibly unknown technologies the patent applicant may create new words and be 'his own lexicographer'.[370] Sufficient particularity and distinctiveness are determined from the point of view of the person skilled in the art which might be distinguished even from the inventor's perspective.[371]

Claim drafting in US patent law is based on the principle of peripheral definition. As opposed to central claiming which was used earlier and where the scope of the patent is determined by the description in the specification that recites the preferred embodiment of the invention but encompasses all equivalents and lead to very broad claims, peripheral claiming marks the outer boundary, or periphery, of protection.[372] Hence, the extent of protection is determined by the scope of the claims which has the advantage of clearly notifying the public of the extent of the patentee's monopoly.[373]

b. Europe

Article 84 EPC has settled the different traditions prevailing in Europe as to claims drafting. Germany, for example, applied central claiming[374] while the UK considered the patent claims to define the peripheral boundaries of the claim.[375] This dispute has been settled by requiring the applicant to define the alleged subject matter clearly and definitely in a manner that allows outsiders to predict the scope of the patent. According to Article 84 EPC the claims shall be clear, concise and supported by a description. The claim must encompass all essential features of the invention that are necessary for solving the technical problem. The patent claim must relate to one invention or to a group of inventions which form a single inventive concept, according to Article 82 EPC.

370 Mueller, An Introduction to Patent Law, 56.

371 E.g. *Solomon v Kimberley-Clark Corp.*, 216 F.3d 1372 (2000).

372 Mueller, An Introduction to Patent Law, 54; Fisher, M., Fundamentals of Patent Law, 178, 180.

373 Fisher, M., Fundamentals of Patent Law, 181.

374 BGHZ 98, 12, 18ff – *Formstein*; BGH GRUR 1995, 330, 331ff – *Elektrische Steckverbindung*; VFG GRUR 1998, 1003ff – *Leuchtstoff*; Benkard-*Schäfers*, Europäisches Patentübereinkommen, Article 84 note 5.

375 RiLi/PatOffUK No. 14.112 with reference to *Electrical and Musical Industries Ltd v Lissen Ltd*, 56 RPC 23: '*The function of the claims is to define clearly and with precision the monopoly claimed so that others may know the exact boundaries of the area within which they will be trespassers. Their primary object is to limit and not to extend the monopoly.*'; see also Benkard-*Schäfers*, Europäisches Patentübereinkommen, Article 84 note 6.

1.4. CONCLUDING REMARKS

Both US and EU patent law provide in general for patentability of inventions in all technical fields. Exclusion from patentability are the exception to the general rule that deems any new invention that involves sufficient progress from the prior art patentable provided that it is susceptible of industrial application or has some utility, respectively. Natural occurring materials are in both jurisdictions potential patentable subject matter if they are removed from their natural environment, processed and improved.

Major differences between US and EU patent law can be found in regard to the different prior art definitions. Under US patent law oral prior art can only invalidate a patent if it originates within the territory of the United States. Foreign activities are only relevant if they are manifested in printed form. The prior art definition in European patent law, on the other hand, is global in scope and encompasses all sources regardless of their form and place of origin. The European Union applies the first-to-file approach whereas US patent law relies on the first-to-invent principle. This influences the determination of the priority date. However, US patent law is subject to some changes in regard to the determination of the priority date and the first-to-invent principle by the Smith-Leahy America Invents Act. Differences can furthermore be found in the assessment of non-obviousness as opposed to inventive step requirement.

Morality considerations which are discussed within the context of utility in US law and are rather limited in application have greater weight in European Law. Especially in regard to biotechnological progress and patenting of live forms the Members of the European Union have undergone lengthy discussions before they came to terms with the adoption of the Biotechnology Directive.

Overall, the substantive patent requirements in the US tend to set a lower standard whereas European patent law contains more potential limitations. The formal requirements, on the other hand, are less stringent in the EU where for example only one way to carry out an invention needs to be indicated.

CHAPTER 2

BIOTECHNOLOGICAL PATENTS ON PHARMACEUTICAL DRUGS DEVELOPED IN BIOPROSPECTING RESEARCH PROJECTS

At the end of a bioprospecting research project stands the development of a pharmaceutical drug. This drug can be an improvement of an existing traditional remedy with basically the same function or a new drug with different properties and application. Patents for plant-derived products can cover the structure of the compound (product patent), the process of isolation (process patent) or the specific use of a drug (use patent). Patents for biotechnological inventions can be claimed for a biotechnological process or a product that is the result of the application of such a process. Product patents in particular can be the result of a bioprospecting research project. In case of ethnopharmacological bioprospecting these patents incorporate traditional medical knowledge.

2.1. THE PATENTABILITY OF BIOTECHNOLOGICAL INVENTIONS USING TRADITIONAL MEDICAL KNOWLEDGE

Biotechnological patents have to be discussed in regard to the products of nature exclusion as they stem from biological resources. The novelty and non-obviousness requirements must be carefully examined as well. The traditional medical knowledge contributions may have influence on the assessment of these requirements.

2.1.1. NATURAL PRODUCTS DOCTRINE

Biotechnological products consist of biological material that has been isolated from its natural environment, altered and purified by using biotechnological techniques such as genetic engineering. The first threshold is the question whether these enhancements must be excluded from patentability under consideration of the products of nature doctrine or on the grounds that they are really discoveries, respectively.

Under US patent law, exceptions have been established in regard to altered products that have an increased therapeutic or commercial value as opposed to the natural substance. There is a large amount of case law and the issue is largely settled. Pharmaceutical drugs that consist of active ingredients that do not exist in their pure form in nature are patentable. The extraction of pharmacologically active compounds from plant genetic resources, their purification or production with the use of biotechnology frequently results in the manufacture of a substance that does in this form not exist in nature. The processing often leads to improvements that can be considered to have greater value as the natural products be it in terms of increased efficiency, fewer side effects or longer durability.

Products consisting of or containing biological material are not *per se* barred from patentability under European patent law. The same applies to processes by means of which biological material is produced, processed or used and extends to the materials resulting from such processes. The Biotechnology Directive requires isolation of biological material or production by a technical process. Products that are derived from biological resources are thus patentable subject matter if biological material that previously occurred in nature has been identified and isolated, altered or produced by means of a technical process. Pharmaceutical drugs isolated from biological sources or produced with biotechnological methods meet these requirements.

The natural products doctrine and the exclusion of discoveries generally do not constitute bars to patentability of biotechnologically enhanced pharmaceuticals that are derived from natural products.

2.1.2. TRADITIONAL MEDICAL KNOWLEDGE AS INVALIDATING PRIOR ART

Biotechnological products are derived from naturally occurring substances and it is questionable whether the existence of the natural product or the prior disclosure of a possible use anticipates a claim for the final product. Given that the results of biotechnological work are generally unpredictable, the mere existence of the natural product will not render the invention unpatentable. The existence of traditional uses, however, is not as obviously irrelevant in the patent proceedings. In case the biotechnological invention consists of the isolated and purified active ingredient of a plant resource that has been used by a traditional knowledge community for the same purpose before the biotechnological invention was filed for a patent, an anticipation of the claim by the prior art must certainly be discussed. In order to anticipate a claim on grounds of lack of novelty, the alleged invention must form part of the state of the art at the priority date.

The different approaches as to what the state of the art encompasses become relevant here. This is also nicely exemplified by the *Neem* patent cases.[376]

2.1.2.1. The Neem Patents

Neem has been the object of many patent proceedings. Literally all parts of the *Neem* tree contain valuable components. Quite instructive is the controversy around the patents held by the US based company W.R. Grace. Grace obtained more than 40 patents in the US and at least 150 worldwide which are related to the *Neem* tree.

Neem tree oil can for example be used as an insecticide. Indian farmers have long extracted *Neem* oil by soaking the crushed seeds in water or alcohol. The disadvantage of this extraction method is that gained oil becomes ineffective after 24 hours. Grace discovered that water degraded the composition of the active ingredient and made it ineffective. Grace subsequently claimed a patent in the US for a new formulation of a *Neem* based insecticide which can be stored for up to two years.[377] The company also applied for a European patent at the EPO claiming a novel pesticide composition for controlling insects and fungi on plants by the aid of hydrophobic extracted *Neem* oil.[378] In the patent application the use of the *Neem* tree in tropical countries as a source of insecticides was explicitly acknowledged. The patent was nevertheless granted after the patent specification and the claims had been redrafted and limited to the fungicidal effect of *Neem* tree oil. An in-depth prior art search was not conducted. The Indian Government challenged the patents, both in the US and in the EU, on the basis that the *Neem* oil has been used since centuries as an insecticide and fungicide in India and argued that the prior use either anticipated the claim or rendered the use of a different solvent at least obvious.

While Grace maintains valid patent claims in the US for lack of evidence of publications at the time of the complaint, the EPO has revoked the *Neemfungicide* patent in 2005.[379] This decision is so important because it is the first case in which the EPO has revoked a patent with subject matter based essentially on traditional knowledge and stated explicitly that traditional knowledge may constitute invalidating prior art and consequently challenge novelty and inventiveness of a patent application. Although the case concerns an agricultural product the findings can well be applied to the pharmaceutical field.

---

376 Although the EPO's ruling is based on lack of inventiveness the case also demonstrates the extent of traditional knowledge consideration in the prior art assessment.

377 Supra Introduction.

378 Application number 90250319.2; Dolder, Traditional Knowledge and Patenting: The Experience of the Neemfungicide and the Hoodia Cases, 26 Biotechnology L. Rep. 583.

379 T 0416/01.

2.1.2.2. *Analysis of the Prior Art Assessment in the Neem Proceedings*

The prior art definition as found in US patent law recognizes existing knowledge and use from abroad only if it is published in written form or contained in a patent application. Unpublished foreign knowledge does not form part of the state of the art. The prior use by a traditional knowledge group thus has generally no influence on the patent as this use or knowledge is frequently not documented in written form.

In the *Neem* case prior traditional use occurred in India and hence outside the US. In the proceedings before the USPTO India finally withdrew its opposition to the patent because it was unable to present published evidence of prior use.[380] European patent law, on the other hand, does not limit the relevant prior art to knowledge that has been used within national borders. Rather, unpublished prior knowledge from outside serves as invalidating prior art. The EPO consequently allowed oral evidence in the proceedings. The *Neem* decision nevertheless shows the difficulties unpublished knowledge faces in patent proceedings.

Firstly, there are obvious practical problems. Traditional knowledge is often not available in a manner that makes it accessible to prior art search. And even if evidence of prior traditional knowledge exists it shows that in practice traditional knowledge is at disadvantage if not documented in printed form. The *Neemfungicide* case supports this assumption. It demonstrates that proper prior art searches are rarely conducted even if there is evidence hinting at prior use.

Secondly, it can be observed that there is a tendency of the EPO to rely on evidence published in printed form in scientific journals rather than unpublished evidence such as affidavits or oral statements. The Appeal Board allowed oral evidence in the form of affidavits and a testimony but was nevertheless reluctant to decide the case on the oral evidence alone. It rather consulted a printed documentation.[381] It has been held that the presented affidavits and oral evidence were far more technical in detail and should have been considered to constitute the closest prior art.[382] On the other hand, one must take into account that oral evidence such as affidavits and testimonies are indeed less reliable, especially when some time has passed since the actions and the proceedings and it is only natural that the EPO demands precise information as to the content and circumstances of prior disclosure to the public. The case highlights that the EPO applies a high standard for proof of prior traditional knowledge use in the absence of supporting printed evidence. However, this standard is justified due

380 Moyer-Henry, Patenting Neem and Hoodia: Conflicting Decisions Issued by the Opposition Board of the European Patent Office, 27 Biotechnology L. Rep. 1, 5.

381 T 0416/02, 4.2.

382 Dolder, Traditional Knowledge and Patenting: The Experience of the Neemfungicide and the Hoodia Cases, 26 Biotechnology L. Rep. 583, 587.

to the limited evidentiary value of oral knowledge as opposed to written knowledge. On the other hand, if oral knowledge is persuasively presented, it must be taken into account and may anticipate a claim.

2.1.2.3. The Standard of Disclosure

Much has been written on the perceived misconception of the exclusion of certain prior art sources under the US approach to determine novelty. Critics claim that the lack of documentation and the domestic prior art definition in US patent law creates loopholes and favors the unfair exploitation of traditional knowledge.[383] This is one of the core arguments of the 'biopiracy' position. The US approach to novelty is claimed to facilitate the misappropriation of traditional knowledge. Under a domestic prior art definition as in the US, an invention is not anticipated as long as the prior art in question exists only in oral form in a country other than the US. Traditional knowledge that exists only in oral form is treated as though it was never disclosed.[384] This conception is harshly criticized as being detrimental to traditional knowledge holders and enabling biopiracy. It is also claimed that the distinction between oral and printed documentation constitutes an anachronism that has lost its justification nowadays.[385] The 'absolute' prior art definition, on the other hand, in theory avoids neglecting unpublished traditional knowledge. Practical problems such as the detection of such knowledge in the course of a prior art search or the impact of rules of evidence, however, remain. The existence of traditional knowledge or evidence thereof is not necessarily discovered in a prior art search. The *Neemfungicide* case[386] is only one example in which a proper search was not undertaken even though there was evidence of prior traditional knowledge use.

The establishment of traditional knowledge databases is supposed to solve this problem by making traditional knowledge and prior use available. It appears, however, that publication alone does not solve the problems of biopiracy. Traditional knowledge databases may improve the efficiency of the prior art search and in theory address the problem of disregarding oral knowledge from abroad and the disadvantages oral knowledge faces even under

---

383 Conforto, Traditional and Modern-Day Biopiracy: Redefining the Biopiracy Debate, 19 J. Envtl. L. & Litig. 357, 364; Garcia, Fighting Biopiracy: The Legislative Protection of Traditional Knowledge, 18 Berkeley La Raza L.J. 5, 12; Kadidal, Subject-Matter Imperialism? Biodiversity, Foreign Prior Art and the Neem Patent Controversy, 37 IDEA 371, 375, 376.

384 Moyer-Henry, Patenting Neem and Hoodia: Conflicting Decisions Issued by the Opposition Board of the European Patent Office, 27 Biotechnology L. Rep. 1, 5.

385 Mgbeoji, Patents and Traditional Knowledge of the Use of Plants: Is a Communal Patent Regime Part of the Solution to the Scourge of Bio Piracy? 9 Ind. J. Global Legal Stud. 163, 176; Kadidal, Subject-Matter Imperialism? Biodiversity, Foreign Prior Art and the Neem Patent Controversy, 37 IDEA 371, 385ff.

386 Supra Part 2:2.1.2.1.

a global prior art criterion.[387] However, the problems lie also in the highly technical nature of patent specifications. Even if the qualities of a new biotechnologically produced pharmaceutical product have been known previously by a traditional knowledge group and databases prove the existence of prior knowledge, the novelty is often still given. The scope of the relevant knowledge is in many cases not sufficient to anticipate the claim. The traditional knowledge community may know the application but it does not know the active ingredient, its chemical structure or a method for isolating it.[388] Anticipation, however, occurs only if the active ingredients in an isolated or purified form are already taught by the prior art which in regard to biotechnological and chemical inventions refers to the chemical structure of the product.[389] Publication of indigenous medical practices does not disclose the structure of the essential compound or a method for isolating it. It is not sufficient merely to know the formula, let alone the application. The patent claim encompasses the chemical structure of the product and not the product itself. Consequently the knowledge of the traditional community can often not anticipate the patent claim for the biotechnological invention. The prior art does not only need to describe the chemical structure or provide a formula but has to contain information that enables a person skilled in the art to make the compound without undue burden.[390]

2.1.3. NON-OBVIOUSNESS IN BIOPROSPECTING RESEARCH PROJECTS

The most critical point in biotechnological patenting is the question of non-obviousness or inventiveness. Research is often cumulative and builds upon prior inventions. Much research activities aim at making improvements or finding new applications of previous discoveries.[391] This is also true for biotechnology R&D which works with the application of methods and

387 Traditional knowledge databases are supposed to destroy novelty. At the same time they are detrimental to some extent as they do not contribute to social welfare. They even put more knowledge in the public domain.

388 Huft, Indigenous Peoples and Drug Discovery Research: A Question of Intellectual Property Rights, 89 Nw. U. L. Rev. 1678, 1726.

389 Tritton, Intellectual Property in Europe, 2–056; Grubb/Thomson, Patents for Chemicals, Pharmaceuticals and Biotechnology, 214.

390 Benkard-*Mellulis*, Europäisches Patentübereinkommen, Article 54, note 164; Hacon/Pagenberg, Concise European Patent Law, EPC 2000, Article 54, note 15 (c); Dutfield, Legal and Economic Aspects of Traditional Knowledge, in Maskus/Reichman, International Public Goods and the Transfer of Technology, 495, 509ff.

391 Gallini/Scotchmer, Intellectual Property: What is the Best Incentive System? Innovation Policy and the Economy, 2 Innovation Pol'y and the Economy 51, 65.

techniques to biological materials in order to make improvements. Especially in pharmaceutical and biotechnological research radical innovation is rare.[392]

The reliance on traditional knowledge can influence the outcome of the assessment of the inventive step. Novelty and non-obviousness have partially overlapping contents which sometimes leads to errors. This is presumably why it has for example been stated that the non-obviousness requirement is not a bar to patenting traditional knowledge because the indigenous groups often cannot identify the exact active ingredient.[393] As explained previously this lack of knowledge is relevant within the assessment of novelty. Non-obviousness, on the other hand, concerns the question whether the contribution of the patentee was obvious-to-try for a person skilled in the art thereby constituting merely the next logical step which cannot justify the award of the advantages associated with the patent grant. Here, a possible objection is that the step from the traditional knowledge use to the final drug is only a minor improvement. In particular the application of a known method in order to process the biological resources and isolate the active compound could render the result obvious. A pharmaceutical drug which has been developed based on traditional medical knowledge of the healing properties of a plant by isolation and purification of said plant could furthermore be obvious as to the combination of prior art references.

2.1.3.1. US Patent Law: The Standard of Non-Obviousness in the Aftermath of KSR

The impropriety of an 'obvious-to-try' standard in biotechnological cases has been accepted since *In re O'Farell* and *In re Deuel*.[394] It was decided that a general incentive or the existence of a method will not render the result obvious because the application of biotechnological methods is generally unpredictable and even the smallest alterations can have unexpected results which increases the likelihood of failure of a project.

Recently, however, the standard for non-obviousness has been discussed again when the Supreme Court demanded a return to the Graham factors instead of the rigorous application of the TSM test.[395] An 'obvious-to-try' standard as applied in *KSR* could also yield different results in patent cases involving biotechnologically produced pharmaceuticals. A bioprospecting project and the subsequent R&D activities using resources discovered with the

392 Eger/Ebermann/Ramanujam, Incremental Innovation and Patent Protection for Pharmaceutical Products in India, in Babu et al, Economic Analysis of Law in India, 128, 135, 136.

393 Conforto, Traditional and Modern-Day Biopiracy: Redefining the Biopiracy Debate, 19 J. Envtl. L. & Litig. 357, 366.

394 Supra notes 306 and 307.

395 Supra Part 2:1.2.3.1.c.

help of traditional medical knowledge could well be 'obvious-to-try' in the sense of *KSR*[396] and *Graham*.[397] The claimed patents for the pharmaceutical end product provide solutions for a technical problem and satisfy a market demand. They often combine different prior art references, namely the knowledge of the use of a plant and the application of a biotechnological method to extract the active agent. The results of the application of such methods are, on the other hand, often unpredictable.

It stands to reason whether the unpredictability of the result and the unreliable expectation of success will be considered sufficient to render a project non-obvious under the revived standard. It has yet to be established which effects the *KSR* decision will have on patenting in the pharmaceutical arts at all. If subsequently applied to pharmaceutical and biotechnological cases, *KSR* has some influence on how high the threshold for non-obviousness will be.[398]

There are some arguments against the application. First of all, patent law regulates versatile subject matter and must accord to different demands in the respective industries and markets. Patent law is therefore technology-specific and the assessment of non-obviousness must take this into consideration.[399] The Supreme Court's judgment in *KSR* relates to a mechanical patent and is thus not *per se* a binding precedent in biotechnological and pharmaceutical patent cases. The further developments are yet unclear. Preceding *KSR*, the decision of the Federal Circuit in *Pfizer, Inc. v Apotex, Inc.* implied a more lenient approach to establish a *prima facie* case of obviousness in a biotechnological case.[400] The decisions of the Federal Circuit in *Takeda Chemical Industries, Ltd. v Alphapharm Pty.*[401], on the other hand, points in a different direction holding that even if the selection of a certain compound for drug development has been suggested by the prior art obviousness would only be given if there was a reasonable expectation of success that modifications would result in beneficial improvements.[402] The court still demands some reason that would have led a chemist to work with a compound suggested by the prior art and to modify it in order to render the result of the modification obvious. In ethnopharmacological bioprospecting cases the traditional medical knowledge disclosure provides

396 Id.

397 Supra Part 2:1.2.3.1.a.

398 Wegner, Chemical and Biotechnology Obviousness in a State of Flux, 26 Biotechnolgy L. Rev. 437, 459.

399 Richardson, Back to the Graham Factors: Nonobviousness after *KSR v Teleflex*, in Takenaka, Patent Law and Theory, 414, 416 438; Burk/Lemley, Is Patent Law Technology-Specific? 17 Berkeley Tech. L.J. 1155, 1160ff.

400 *Pfizer v Apotex* 480 F.3d 1348 (2007); Mueller, Chemicals, Combinations, and 'Common Sense': How the Supreme Court's KSR Decision Is Changing Federal Circuit Obviousness Determinations in Pharmaceutical and Biotechnology Cases, Legal Studies Research Paper Series Working Paper No 2008–7.

401 492 F.3d 1350 (2007).

402 Id at 1360–1362; Trask, 'Obvious to Try': A Proper Patentability Standard in the Pharmaceutical Arts? 76 Fordham Law Rev., 2625, 2655 – 2657.

some reasons but the decisive question will be whether the biotechnological method is suggested by the prior art.

At present, no cases have been decided finding a biotechnological enhancement of a plant resource that has been discovered with the help of an indigenous group obvious. This has two main reasons. Firstly, under US patent law the closest prior art will usually not be the traditional medical knowledge since this frequently stems from abroad and thus does not form part of the state of the art under the domestic approach. The second argument in favor of patentability is that the complexity and unpredictability of biotechnological techniques and the implied difficulty and length of the research usually provide the grounds for inventiveness. The fact that a plant and its particular uses, activities and effects are known is certainly very helpful when developing a new drug. However, the process of isolating the active agent does not follow automatically once the plant is known. A lot of scientific skill and additional inventive contribution by the developer is required for such a R&D project to be successful.[403] The process of isolating compounds in their pure form is difficult. Certain types of bacteria may secrete isolated genetic information such as proteins into a culture medium but the concentration of the protein from this solution is quite complicated.[404] The results are largely empirical and unpredictable and a reasonable expectation of success is usually not given in biotechnological cases.[405] Rather, the necessity of research, the length of time this research takes and the expenses speak for inventiveness.[406]

2.1.3.2. The Inventive Step Requirement in Europe: Neem and Hoodia

Under European patent law traditional medical knowledge has better chances to be considered as the closest prior art. The step taken to process the so found biological resource, however, will hint at inventiveness due to the length and difficulty of research. The application of the 'could-would test' also suggests that some motivation or reason to pursue a certain path is required in order to prove a lack of inventiveness. The unimaginative worker will often not pursue a certain research path due to the fact that biotechnological research endeavors rely on complicated and unreliable processes.

Exemplary in regard to inventiveness findings by the EPO in regard to products derived from traditional knowledge are the *Neem* and *Hoodia* cases.

---

403 Supra Part 1:1.2.2; Huft, Indigenous Peoples and Drug Discovery Research: A Question of Intellectual Property Rights, 89 Nw. U. L. Rev. 1678, 1725.

404 Grubb/Thomson, Patents for Chemicals, Pharmaceuticals and Biotechnology, 232.

405 Ducor, Patenting the Recombinant Products of Biotechnology and Other Molecules, 30; Hamburger/Hostettmann, Bioactivity in Plants. The Link Between Phytochemistry and Medicine, 30 Phyto 3864, 3872; Burk/Lemley, Is Patent Law Technology-Specific? 17 Berkeley Tech. L.J. 1155, 1157.

406 Schulte, Patentgesetz, §4 note 87.

a. The Decision of the EPO in the *Neem* and *Hoodia* Patent Cases

In its decision in the *Neemfungicide* proceedings[407] the EPO made it clear that it considers traditional knowledge in the context of inventiveness rather than within *ordre public* or morality considerations. This is certainly a good approach as the concepts of *ordre public* or morality are vague and uncertain. Inventiveness, on the other hand, is – at least in theory – a well-defined concept.

The Appeal Board considered the claimed invention to be obvious because the publication that was considered to be the closest prior art disclosed the method of solvent extraction to extract *Neem* oil from the seeds. The Board concluded that the isolation of natural products from plants was commonly undertaken by means of solvent extraction and solvent elution. Once the method of solvent extraction was known it was obvious for a person skilled in the art to try a different solvent.

Another patent case before the EPO concerning prior use by traditional groups is the *Hoodia* patent case.[408] The *Hoodia* patent by the South African Council for Scientific and Industrial Research (CSIR) concerns the use of an extract from the *Hoodia* cactus as an appetite suppressant. The South African San people have used *Hoodia* to suppress hunger since ancient times. They used to eat the plant when going on hunting expeditions which allowed them to take fewer provisions and thus to transport more captured animals.[409] The observed effect that eating the plant removed hunger feelings has been documented in a number of publications. In this case the Appeal Board found that the submitted claims involved an inventive step and upheld the patent of CSIR. Although the evidence suggested that the San have used certain plants to suppress hunger, the Appeal Board found nevertheless, that a person skilled in the art could not obviously derive from this disclosure that an extract from the plant could be used for the manufacture of an appetite-suppressant, anti-obesity medicament. The Board followed the reasoning of the appellants who argued that the hunger suppressing properties could also be due to the filling of the stomach from eating the plant especially since the *Hoodia* cactus is a succulent that stores large amounts of water.[410]

b. Discussion of the Decisions

The different outcomes of the cases have been criticized on the basis that the quality of the traditional knowledge contributions in the cases must be

407 T 416/01; supra Part 2:2.1.2.1.

408 T 543/04.

409 Dolder, Traditional Knowledge and Patenting: The Experience of the Neemfungicide and the Hoodia Cases, 26 Biotechnology L. Rep. 583, 587.

410 T 543/04.

considered to be equal.[411] The reasoning in the *Neem* case is certainly comprehensible. For a person skilled in the art it would indeed be obvious to try a different solution in order to solve the technical problem of quick perishing of the oil. Similarly, in the *Hoodia* case the inventive step by CSIR appears doubtful. Dolder finds that the connection between suppressing hunger and treating obesity can be drawn even by someone not skilled in the art and the conclusion that certain compounds of that plant could be used in an anti-obesity medication is not that ingenious and argues that the consumption of the contents of *Hoodia* by the San represents itself as a selection of the plant most efficiently serving their needs which constitutes the decisive inventive step and largely outweighs the subsequent contribution in isolation and purification by the patent applicants.[412] Moyer-Henry attributes the findings to policy considerations and states that the San people felt exploited by CSIR because they had provided the necessary knowledge that made further research possible. When accused of biopiracy, CSIR offered a settlement to the San for the use of their knowledge which the San accepted. In case of the *Neem* patent the Indian Government made it quite clear that they would not accept the exploitation of the *Neem* tree and that opposition to the patent would not end until the patent was revoked.[413] Other authors see the cases as examples of the unpredictability of decisions of the EPO.[414]

The facts of the cases, however, justify the different treatment. In case of the *Neem* tree the prior use already provided a method of extraction the oil. It is the logical next step to use a different medium to perform the extraction. The reduction to practice by the San people, on the other hand, consisted merely of consuming the plant. Finding that a certain plant suppresses hunger is a discovery. This effect can have various reasons. The plant may contain a certain compound that suppresses hunger feelings. It could also be the case that the plant is more nutritious than other plants. In the latter case, it would not be suitable to treat obesity. These considerations may already have discouraged the unimaginative worker to try for the development of a medication based on the

411 Dolder, Traditional Knowledge and Patenting: The Experience of the Neemfungicide and the Hoodia Cases, 26 Biotechnology L. Rep. 583ff.; Moyer-Henry, Patenting Neem and Hoodia: Conflicting Decisions Issued by the Opposition Board of the European Patent Office, 27 Biotechnology L. Rep. 1ff.

412 Dolder, Traditional Knowledge and Patenting: The Experience of the Neemfungicide and the Hoodia Cases, 26 Biotechnology L. Rep. 583, 588.

413 Moyer-Henry, Patenting Neem and Hoodia: Conflicting Decisions Issued by the Opposition Board of the European Patent Office, 27 Biotechnology L. Rep. 1, 8.

414 The failure to develop a consistent body of case law under the EPC has already been discussed by Ho, Building a Better Mousetrap: Patenting Biotechnology in the European Community, 3 Duke J. Comp. & Int'l L. 173. She concludes that the unpredictability of decisions is especially problematic for the biotechnological sector as such research is expensive and requires assurance of the option to recoup the investment by securing patent protection. See also: Czmus, Biotechnology Protection in Japan, the European Community, and the United States, 8 Temp. Int'l & Comp. L.J. 435, 442f.

observation of the San people. Consequently, the isolation of the active ingredient is the inventive step undertaken by CSIR. This step had already been undertaken by Indian farmers in the *Neem* tree case. Although the argumentation of the Board of Appeal may be somewhat misleading, the result is in line with the concepts developed in regard to inventiveness requirements in case of improvements of biological resources.

2.2. ANALYSIS OF THE RESULTS

The patentability of biotechnological inventions is nowadays accepted in the US as well as in the EU. This is to a fair extend attributable to policy decisions manifested in case law and the enactment of the Biotechnology Directive.

An important limitation to patent law is that fundamental ideas and phenomena of nature cannot be the subject of a patent. Biological resources and processes seem to be discoveries rather than inventions as they already exist in nature and are merely uncovered. Many biotechnological inventions concern the use of a new method to produce a known thing.[415] This implies at first sight that while the process is certainly patentable the product should not be. On the other hand, one can clearly distinguish between a discovery in the true sense of the word and a discovery of a molecular structure which is by no means obvious and was not available to the public before.[416] In biotechnology science, products are produced that have in this state not previously existed in nature. The reward in form of the patent is given for the isolation and purification of a substance. Research activities in this field meet specific criteria inherent in the definition of inventions as they adopt a natural discovery to social needs. The input activity differs considerably in degree and kind from the activity applied by a traditional knowledge group and justifies a different treatment.

2.2.1. THE IMPORTANCE OF PATENTS FOR PHARMACEUTICAL R&D

A closer look at the benefits of pharmaceutical research shows that patents are essential in this field.

The justification for patent protection is that such protection generates incentives to invest in the development of valuable innovation that would without a protective system be appropriable with the consequence that

---

415 Burk, Biotechnology and Patent Law: Fitting Innovation in the Procrustean Bed, 17 Rutgers Computer & Tech. L. J. 42.

416 Sena, Directive on Biotechnological Inventions: Patentabiliy of Discoveries, IIC 1999, 731, 734.

investments in the development would be commercially unprofitable as the creations would be non-tradable public goods. This reasoning is not uniformly applicable but depends on factors that differ between sectors and industries. These factors include the cost of R&D, the cost and speed of imitation, the availability of alternative rewards and the importance of continued innovation.[417]

Biotechnology plays an important role in today's pharmaceutical industry. Pharmaceutical biotechnological R&D provides many advantages. It has contributed much to the field of medicine in diagnosis, treatment of diseases and vaccination and promises to find new or more effective remedies for many diseases. Modern biotechnological techniques were initially developed as research tools but it became soon apparent that they have an immense commercial value.[418] R&D conducted by the pharmaceutical industry has contributed greatly to the development of curative and preventive purposes for a vast array of human diseases and promises further benefits to society thereby making investment and innovation in this area clearly desirable.[419]

Biotechnology is a key industry with great potential. It is one of the fastest-growing areas of scientific, technical and industrial innovation.[420] However, the sector bears certain features that seem to make it sensitive to trade policy, regulation and patent law.

The modern pharmaceutical industry is a high-risk, high-return industry that develops and sells innovative high-value added products in a tightly regulated market.[421] R&D in the field of biotechnology is costly and time-consuming. The basic research, e.g. the isolation of a valuable genetic compound, and the development of a marketable product are difficult, expensive and lengthy in time due to the unpredictability of the outcome of complex processes. This results in projects frequently not coming to a successful end. There are also administrative obstacles such as clinical trial phases and time-consuming approval procedures.[422] R&D in the biotechnological sector requires large financial inputs. Returns are only expected after several years once the product can be marketed. With regard to the overall R&D expenditures, pharmaceutical companies invest a higher proportion of sales in R&D than most other industries.[423] However, in case of successful marketing, the returns can be

417 Burk/Lemley, Policy Levers in Patent Law, 89 Va. L. Rev. 1575, 1577, 1581ff.

418 Burk, Biotechnology and Patent Law: Fitting Innovation in the Procrustean Bed, 17 Rutgers Computer & Tech. L. J. 15.

419 Correa, Trade Related Aspects of Intellectual Property, 275; Burk, Biotechnology and Patent Law: Fitting Innovation in the Procrustean Bed, 17 Rutgers Computer & Tech. L. J. 22, 85.

420 Bauer/Gaskell, Biotechnology, 5.

421 Burk/Lemley, Policy Levers in Patent Law, 89 Va. L. Rev. 1575, OTA, Biotechnology in a Global Economy, 7.

422 Supra notes 56, 57.

423 Kate/Laird, The Commercial Use of Biodiversity, 47.

expected to be high during the time the new drug can be marketed exclusively due to patent protection.

As a consequence of the high costs involved in the development process the private sector plays a dominant role in conducting pharmaceutical R&D. The businesses found in the biotechnology sector include technology providers, information providers, research firms and biotechnological firms.[424] Biotechnological R&D, especially in the pharmaceutical sector, is wanted by society and incentives need to be set. The standard economic theory on public goods applies here. The fixed costs for the research and development of a new drug are very high, the marginal cost including those of imitation are comparably low.[425] The economic rationale behind the patentability of biotechnological inventions is the enhancement of innovative productivity in this sector. Regulation is indicated because an unregulated market will produce undersupply due to the public good characteristics of information. This is especially true in the pharmaceutical and biotechnological sector. Several empirical studies have shown that the pharmaceutical industry is especially sensitive to patent law and policy.[426] The pharmaceutical sector is an area in which the trade-off must be considered to be efficient. Consequently, patents are an important tool to induce innovation in this area.

2.2.2. THE PREDICTABILITY OF THE OUTCOMES OF PATENT PROCEEDINGS

It has been pointed out so far that patent proceedings can have different outcomes depending on whether the patent is applied for in the US or the EU. This is not *per se* optimal because in a globalized world legal rules should be uniform. Clearly, the goals of the TRIPS agreement have not been reached yet.

From the discussed cases the conclusion can be drawn that there is some uncertainty in regard to the interpretation of the novelty and non-obviousness requirements. In the *Neemfungicide* proceedings, the EPO allowed oral evidence but avoided to base its ruling on the oral evidence but rather considered a printed publication to be the closest prior art.[427] Nevertheless, a patent applicant cannot rely on the relevance of published prior art sources alone. It makes it more difficult to predict the outcomes of patent proceedings if it is not clear what will be considered to be the closest prior art. In regard to the inventive step some

424 Dutfield, Intellectual Property, Biogenetic Resources and Traditional Knowledge, 15, 16.

425 Landes/Posner, The Economic Structure of Intellectual Property Law, 313; Merges/Nelson, On the Complex Economics of Patent Scope, 90 Colum. L. Rev. 839, 897.

426 Mansfield, Patents and Innovation: An Empirical Study, 32 Management Science 173; Mansfield, Intellectual Property Protection, Foreign Direct Investment and Technology Transfer, World Bank Discussion Paper No. 19.

427 Supra Part 2:2.1.2.2.

authors claim that the EPO is producing an inconsistent body of case law.[428] In US patent case law, new uncertainties were introduced by the Supreme Court's decision in *KSR*.[429]

Unpredictability of decisions and lack of clearly defined rights constitute impediments to bargaining. Especially the biotechnology industry needs the assurance that investments can be recouped and strongly relies on patent protection. It can be anticipated that a private company will be reluctant to invest in R&D when – in addition to the risk of failure to develop the product in itself – it has to consider the uncertainty of success in the patent application process or the danger of opposition proceedings.

Firms act as profit maximizing entities. They want to create information and innovation at the lowest possible cost. Research can be undertaken in two ways, either in the form of the search for new knowledge or by relying on existing knowledge which can be used as a starting point for developing a new and/or improved product. From society's point of view the research path that can be undertaken at the lowest costs is preferable. The second option, reliance on existing knowledge, is the scenario of using traditional medical knowledge as an input for follow-on research. Existing knowledge can reduce the costs of developing an innovative product. The novelty requirement in patent law thereby ensures that knowledge in the public domain is excluded from the scope of patent protection.

A strict novelty requirement will avoid distortion of a firm's incentives to conduct independent searches in cases in which the search of existing knowledge would yield the same information at lower costs.[430] Uncertainty as to the extent of the prior art has the consequence that a firm may find it hard to predict whether prior existing traditional knowledge will be considered as invalidating prior art and whether the step from the prior knowledge to the final product will be considered to be obvious. In such a scenario the incentives of the firm to search for existing knowledge are distorted. It is likely that the firm will rely on investment in new knowledge even if the costs are higher. This can especially be anticipated for the pharmaceutical sector that depends on the effectiveness of patents.

---

428 E.g. Ho, Building a Better Mousetrap: Patenting Biotechnology in the European Community, 3 Duke J. Comp. & Int'l L. 173.

429 Supra note 312.

430 Merges/Duffy, Patent Law and Policy, 418.

CHAPTER 3
THE RIGHTS OF THE PROVIDERS OF TRADITIONAL MEDICAL KNOWLEDGE

Ethnopharmacological bioprospecting relies to a large extent on the input from traditional knowledge groups. The existence of such knowledge has been discussed in regard to its relevance as prior art that could destroy the novelty of the final product or render the invention obvious or lacking an inventive step, respectively.

The contribution of the local groups can furthermore be discussed in regard to its autonomous patentability. In this part the rights of the providers of the traditional medical knowledge are analyzed which includes the question of whether the contribution of the group qualifies them to be owners of a patent or at least joint inventors of the final product.

3.1. THE PATENTABILITY OF TRADITIONAL MEDICAL KNOWLEDGE

Due to its intrinsic characteristics traditional knowledge encounters several obvious problems in meeting the patent requirements. Especially the requirements of invention, novelty and non-obviousness provide thresholds which are not easily met.

3.1.1. PRODUCTS OF NATURE

Patent law is designed to protect innovations as opposed to discoveries. Natural occurring substances do not enjoy the status of inventions unless human intervention leads to a substantial alteration of the natural substance. In US patent law this problem is discussed under the 'products of nature doctrine'. The US courts have determined that natural substances are not patentable but allow exceptions to this rule for substances that are purified and do in this pure form not occur in nature provided that the pure form yields a greater value than the natural occurring product.[431] Under European patent law naturally occurring substances may be the basis for a patent if isolated from their natural environment or produced by means of a technical process.[432]

Traditional medical knowledge relies on naturally occurring substances. Finding a plant that cures a specific disease is firstly a discovery. As already mentioned, however, the distinction between discovery and invention is not clearly determined. A discovery becomes an invention once it is reduced to practice in order to satisfy social needs. In case of plant-derived medication this refers to processing the plant. In a traditional knowledge community this is done to a degree that satisfies the needs of the group. The human intervention lies in the application of methods like boiling or grinding and is minimal.

This kind of intervention is comparable to the intervention examined in *Funk Bros Seed Co v Kalo Inoculant Co*[433], *Cochrane*[434] and *Ex parte Latimer.*[435] Purification or isolation of a product into a form that does in this altered state not occur in nature as it has, for example, been established in *Parke Davis*[436] is frequently not undertaken by the traditional and local groups. Their intervention does not alter the plant substantially. Consequently, the application of the products of nature doctrine will frequently yield traditional medical products unpatentable under US patent law.

European patent law does not deny patentability merely on the grounds that a product does occur in nature as long as it has been isolated by means of a technical process. Clear rules in regard to what constitutes a technical process, however, are yet to be developed. At the very least one must require a process that contains one step that is not thinkable without human intervention and considerably influences the result.[437] Under this definition traditional medical knowledge applications of plant resources could theoretically overcome the classification to be a discovery 'as such'. Cases in this regard have not been decided yet.

3.1.2. NOVELTY AND NON-OBVIOUSNESS

The products must furthermore meet the requirements of novelty and inventiveness. Given that patentability applies only to subject matter that is novel one could assume that traditional knowledge can, by definition, not fit this requirement for patentability. This interpretation, however, would

431 Supra Part 2:1.2.1.1.
432 Article 3 (2) of the Biotechnology Directive.
433 Supra note 257.
434 Supra note 261.
435 Supra note 263.
436 Supra note 264.
437 Kraßer, Patentrecht, 127.

misunderstand what traditional knowledge really encompasses. Traditional must not be understood in the sense of 'ancient' or 'old'. Much of the knowledge of local and indigenous people is not ancient but a vital and dynamic part of the contemporary lives of many communities.[438] 'Traditional' rather refers to the method of creating traditional knowledge, to the way the knowledge is acquired and used. It is developed, sustained and passed on within a traditional community, between generations, sometimes through specific customary systems of knowledge transmission. The term traditional does not refer to the nature of the knowledge but rather to its relationship with the community and its creation according to the traditions and beliefs in the community.

The concept of novelty determines that prior art invalidates a patent. It excludes all subject matter that is already part of the public domain from patentability and prevents the grant of a patent for something known to have been invented already.[439] But the transmission of the knowledge within the community creates problems. The knowledge of local and indigenous groups is frequently passed down from generation to generation. This, however, implies that much of the knowledge is already in the public domain. In addition, in case prior art is determined on a global scale much of the innovative activity of a traditional knowledge community forms part of the prior art and thus invalidates any patent claim.[440]

This holds at least true for knowledge that is available to a larger number of people, e.g. an entire local group or a majority of a community. Cases in which traditional medical knowledge is held exclusively by selected members of a group, as for example, the shaman healer who monopolizes his knowledge by undertaking certain rituals, may require a different assessment. As stated above[441], knowledge that is only available to a limited number of people does not form part of the state of the art provided that it is impossible for the information to leak out. The standard here is the 'public at large'. A scientist who observes the shaman and can distinguish the rituals and the use of the plant, however, gains access to the knowledge. It follows from this that the monopolization of the knowledge as undertaken by traditional peoples is generally not sufficient to keep it out of the public domain.

With regard to non-obviousness or inventiveness it can be assumed that the changes undertaken by a traditional knowledge community will be considered to be trivial. The achievement lies in the realization that a certain plant cures a specific disease. This, however, is a discovery. The next step, the reduction to practice by putting it in a form that can be consumed by humans or applied to

438 Supra Part 1:1.1.3.2; WIPO, Intellectual Property and Traditional Knowledge, 6.

439 Landes/Posner, The Economic Structure of Intellectual Property Law, 303.

440 Wei, Fitting Biological Products within the Intellectual Property Framework, in Ong, Intellectual Property and Biological Resources, 69; see below Part 3:1.1.1.2 for a proposal to exclude the innovative activity of the traditional knowledge group from the public domain.

441 Part 2:1.2.2.2.

the body, will be obvious to a person skilled in the art because the methods used are generally simple and well-known.

3.1.3. FORMAL REQUIREMENTS

Beside the intrinsic incompatibility of traditional knowledge with substantive patent standards, problems arise also in regard to meeting the formal requirements of a patent application. A traditional knowledge invention can often not be defined clearly as it develops over time and improves from one generation to the next.[442] Therefore it is difficult and often even impossible to name an identifiable act of invention and describe it properly as would be required to meet the rules on specification. In addition, patent specifications must be written in a technical way. An indigenous group that attributes some of the effects to rituals and supernatural forces may find it difficult to comply with the formal rules.

In conclusion, a patent will frequently not be available to traditional knowledge holders themselves. The indigenous culture is not coherent with the underlying perceptions of patenting; the patent laws are not designed to match the social and economic conditions of indigenous groups.[443]

3.2. THE OWNER OF THE PATENT: THE CONCEPT OF JOINT INVENTORSHIP

So far it has been found that traditional medical knowledge will usually not qualify as a patentable invention. The biotechnological enhancement, on the other hand, often will. The next question is whether the contribution of the indigenous group will at least be sufficient to award them the status of joint inventors.

In the old days inventions occurred as the 'flash of the genius' to a single person. Patent law was designed to reward this single inventor. This proposition became quite complex when the single inventor was no longer the norm but the exception. Today, a greater degree of sophisticated inventions that are the result of collaboration of different people with different skills are produced. In response to this development many patent laws have introduced the concept of joint ownership which allows rewarding the cooperative endeavors of several individuals.

---

442 Gervais, Traditional Knowledge & Intellectual Property: A TRIPS-Compatible Approach, Mich. St. L. R. 2005, 137, 141.

443 Latorre Quinn, Protection for Indigenous Knowledge: An International Law Analysis, 14 St. Thomas L. Rev. 287, 295; Bratspies, The New Discovery Doctrine: Some Thoughts on Property Rights and Traditional Knowledge, 31 Am. Indian. L. Rev. 315, 320.

The joint ownership concept could be applicable to cases in which a patent is granted on a biotechnological pharmaceutical product which has been developed with some help of an indigenous group.

3.2.1. LEGAL DEFINITION OF JOINT INVENTORSHIP

3.2.1.1. Requirements for Joint Inventorship in US Patent Law

A joint invention is the product of a collaboration of two or more people working together to solve the problems addressed. The concept of joint inventorship is embedded in Section 116 of the US Patent Act which has been amended to remedy the increasing technical problems involved when research teams cumulatively work on complex inventions.[444] The section states that two or more persons who have made an invention jointly shall apply for the patent jointly. The statute, however, does not set forth a minimum quality or quantity of the contribution required for joint inventorship. It merely provides a negative definition by providing that joint inventorship is not barred if the inventors did not work together at the same place or time, made unequal contributions or did not each contribute to every claim of the patent.[445]

In order to fill the gap, case law has elaborated two principal requirements that need to be fulfilled for two inventors to be considered to be co-inventors. Firstly, each inventor must contribute to the inventive concept. Secondly, the joint inventors must collaborate with each other.

Each inventor has to contribute to the inventive concept. In the leading case *Monsanto Co. v Kamp*[446] the court established the principal requirement for joint invention. It stated that

> '[...] a joint invention is the product of collaboration of the inventive endeavours of two or more persons working toward the same end and producing an invention by their aggregate effort' in the form that 'each of the inventors work[s] on the same subject matter and make[s] some contribution to the inventive thought and the final result.'[447]

Courts have repeatedly stated that inventorship is predominantly determined by conception and defined conception to be the completion of the mental part of the inventive act, e.g. the formation of a definitive and permanent idea in the

444 Lange/LaFrance/Myers, Intellectual Property, Cases and Materials, 575.

445 Section 116: '*When an invention is made by two or more persons jointly, they shall apply for patent jointly and each make the required oath, except as otherwise provided in this title. Inventors may apply for a patent jointly even though (1) they did not physically work together or at the same time, (2) each did not make the same type or amount of contribution, or (3) each did not make a contribution to the subject matter of every claim of the patent. [...]*'.

446 *Monsanto Co. v Kamp*, 269 F. Supp. 818, 154 U.S.P.Q. 259 (1967).

447 *Monsanto*, id at 824.

mind of the inventor in the sense that the invention is complete and operable and can be applied by one skilled in the art without extensive research or undue experimentation.[448] Required is more than a general idea or a research plan but it does not have to go as far as actually reducing the invention to practice and proving that the idea works.[449] Conception thus has two elements, the definite and permanent idea of the inventor and the enablement of a skilled person to reduce the invention to practice.

The contribution of the inventors must not be of equal quality or importance for the invention as long as it affects the conception. It has been found that joint inventorship may even be given if the conception of the entire device may be due to one inventor but the other one makes suggestions of practical value and thereby assisted in working out the main idea.[450] Subsequent cases have elaborated on the quality of the contribution finding that while an inventor need not by himself undertake all the steps to reduce the invention to practice, merely supplying background knowledge or general information to an invention is not sufficient to become an inventor.[451]

Secondly, joint inventors must collaborate. It can be derived from the statute and the cases dealing with collaboration that the standard of collaboration is rather low. Joint inventorship does neither require that the inventors worked together at the same time[452] nor that they have collaborated on each claim of a patent.[453]

3.2.1.2. Joint Inventorship Under the EPC

In regard to the requirements for joint inventors the EPC stays silent as well. The European Court of Justice did not have to decide any cases broaching the requirements for joint inventorship.

The right to a European patent is covered by Article 60 EPC which states in the first paragraph that the patent shall belong to the inventor. While the provision also mentions inventions of employees it does not refer to joint inventors. Despite this lack of reference it is apparent that joint inventors are entitled to a European patent. This can clearly be derived from Article 59 EPC which recognizes the joint application by two or more inventors.

---

448 *Burroughs Wellcome Co. v Barr Laboratories, Inc.*, 40 F.3d 1223, 1228, 1230 (1994); *Sewall v Walters*, 21 F.3d 411, 415 (1994); Lange/LaFrance/Myers, Intellectual Property, Cases and Materials, 559.

449 *Burroughs Wellcome* id at 1228.

450 35 USC Section 116 (2); *Monsanto* id at 824.

451 *Idacon, Inc. v Central Forest Products, Inc.*, (not reported in F.Supp.) 1986 WL 15837, 14 (1986).

452 35 USC Section 116 (1); *Shields v Halliburton Co.*, 667 F.2d 1232, 1235 (1982).

453 35 USC Section 116 (3); *Ethicon, Inc. v United States Surgical Corporation*, 937 F.Supp. 1015, 1036 (1996).

The silence in regard to joint inventors raises the question whether the determination of the quality of the contribution of each inventor that constitutes co-inventorship has been left to national law.

The negotiation history of the EPC supports this assumption. The earlier drafts of the EPC used to contain a provision that deemed the right to a European patent in case of a joint invention to belong to the co-inventors jointly.[454] The said provision has been abandoned with the explanation that this would interfere with national law.[455] From this the conclusion can be drawn that the determination of joint inventors was purposely left to national law.

Such a conception, however, appears to be unsystematic in the context of the European Patent Convention. The EPC governs the grant of a European patent. National laws, on the other hand, regulate the scope of the patent once it has been granted. The interpretation of who is the inventor is systematically part of the granting process and thus regulated by the EPC. The regulation on the inventions of employee's supports this argument. According to Article 60 (1) EPC the law of the State of the employee's main activity is applicable in case of inventions of employees. This, however, is clearly conceptualized as an exception to the general rule. It can be derived from the materials to the EPC that the concept of the inventor is not to be determined by national laws but to be interpreted autonomously within the Convention.[456] The right to the patent is part of the granting process and hence covered by the EPC. The submission of inventions by employees to the national laws as an exception to this rule was incorporated due to the differing concepts prevailing in the Member States. The materials do not contain any further reference to this issue and in particular no explanation why an interference with national law was feared in cases of joint inventors but not in cases of a sole inventor.

Conceptually joint inventorship must be seen as a subcategory of inventorship if one wants to interpret it within the scope of Article 60 EPC. A different treatment of 'inventorship' and 'joint inventorship' can hardly be justified. In consequence, the requirements of joint inventors are to be derived from the Convention itself while national laws, court decision and scientific opinions can be relied on in the process.[457] Consent among the Contracting States is given in as far as that some sort of collaboration has taken place. In regard to the quality of the contribution the standard is similar to the US. This entails an intellectual contribution to the inventive concept resulting from an own initiative; mere handicraft contributions are not sufficient to establish joint

454 Article 17 II HE 1961/1962 Dok. IV/3076/62; Cronacher, Das Recht auf das Patent im Europäischen Patentübereinkommen, 142, 143.

455 Dok. IV/3076/62-D, 145; Cronacher, Das Recht auf das Patent im Europäischen Patentübereinkommen, 143.

456 Singer/Stauder, Europäisches Patentübereinkommen, Article 60 note 5.

457 The same conclusion is drawn by Singer/Stauder, Europäisches Patentübereinkommen, Article 60 note 8.

inventorship.[458] This does not mean that each contribution has to satisfy the patent requirements on its own as long as the contribution influences the solution.[459] Equal weight of the contributions is not required. Generally, it appears that the requirements for joint inventorship under the EPC do not differ greatly in the Contracting States and that the given consensus can be used to interpret joint inventorship in accordance with the EPC. The European jurisprudence is also quite similar to the US practice.

3.2.2. JOINT INVENTORSHIP OF TRADITIONAL KNOWLEDGE GROUPS AND PHARMACEUTICAL COMPANIES

Joint inventorship requires some sort of collaboration between the joint inventors.

The level of interaction between the traditional knowledge groups and companies that use their knowledge and apply it in R&D activities and follow-on innovation varies. In an ethnopharmacological bioprospecting project, the pharmaceutical company's field team or intermediaries interact with local and indigenous groups with the intention to use their knowledge in order to find pharmacologically active plants. In this case sufficient collaboration that satisfies the US as well as the EU standard is certainly given.

It is not a bar to joint inventorship that the contribution of the local groups occurs prior to the research endeavors of the bioprospectors. As stated in Section 116 (1) of the US Patent Act and subsequently in *Shields v Halliburton Co*[460] the joint inventors must not work at the invention at the same time. The court explicitly stated that a patent for a joint invention is not invalidated by the fact that one of them first perceived the crude form of the elements and the possibility of adaptation to accomplish the desired result.[461] In this sense, the contribution of the traditional knowledge group in discovering the plant and applying it as a cure to a specific disease can constitute collaboration. In European patent law equal weight of the respective contributions is not required. In regard to the timing of the contributions this implies that it is not harmful, if one joint inventor provides his contribution prior to the other inventor.

The second question is whether the quality of a contribution is sufficient to confer to the traditional knowledge group and the pharmaceutical company the

---

458 E.g. BGH GRUR 1978, 583 – *Motorkettensäge*, BGH GRUR 1966, 558 – *Spanplatte*; Hacon/Pagenberg, Concise European Patent Law, EPC 2000, Article 60 note 3; Benkard-*Melullis*, Europäisches Patentübereinkommen, Article 60 note 15.

459 E.g. BGH GRUR 2001, 226, 227 – *Rollenantriebseinheit*; Benkard-*Melullis*, Europäisches Patentübereinkommen, Article 60 note 16.

460 Supra note 452.

461 *Shields*, id at 1235.

status of joint inventors. As stated by the US courts, joint invention requires contribution to the conception, e.g. the complete and permanent idea that allows for the invention to be put into practice without undue experimentation. This corresponds with the requirement of an intellectual contribution under European patent law. The contribution of the pharmaceutical company, e.g. the people engaged in the R&D process in isolating the active agent, overcomes the hurdle of requiring undue experimentation and constitutes an independent intellectual contribution of some weight. They reduce the idea to practice. This contribution is inventive as it involves more than routine application of known methods due to the unpredictability of biotechnological processes.

Depending on the individual facts of the case a substantive contribution by the traditional knowledge group may be given. Patents claiming a process for isolating a compound will very rarely be attributable to such contribution but it may be possible to find a contribution in case of product and use patents.

Idacon v Central Forest determined that it is insufficient to claim joint inventorship if the contribution lays only in the provision of background knowledge or general information other than the information that makes the invention differ from the prior art.[462] This implies that information that is an essential compound of the conception, without which the invention would not have been accomplished, should suffice to give joint inventor status to its supplier.[463] Similarly, under the European standard an intellectual contribution arising from an own initiative is necessary.

Once a pharmaceutical drug is derived from the use of a certain plant that has been identified with the help of members of a traditional knowledge community, an active contribution to the invention is given. The traditional group has developed their medication due to their own needs. It therefore constitutes a contribution that is in itself valuable. This contribution is essential to the development of the final drug. Without the contribution the development of the drug would probably not have taken place or the development would have been delayed considerably. The development of the exact same drug by other means, e.g. mass or random screening, is unlikely and would – if at all – occur at considerably higher costs.

Although it appears that the concept of joint inventorship is applicable to the cases several problems remain. While the contribution must not extend to all elements of the final claim, a contribution to the inventive concept is only given if information that makes the invention differ from the state of the art is provided. Otherwise the contribution would amount to the provision of background knowledge only. As the state of the art encompasses the knowledge of the local groups, a contribution to the conception of the invention can

462 *Idacon vs Central Forest*, supra note 451, at 14, 15.

463 Huft, Indigenous Peoples and Drug Discovery Research: A Question of Intellectual Property Rights, 89 Nw. U. L. Rev. 1678, 1710.

therefore only be given if knowledge that is exclusively held by certain members of the group, e.g. shamans who are prepared to keep it a secret, is shared. The problems that arise in regard to the scope of the state of the art have already been discussed.[464]

Where the claimed invention consists of the use of the active compound of a plant the link between the final result and the traditional knowledge contribution is visible. In these cases, joint inventorship may be given. In many other cases the traditional knowledge contribution leads a bioprospector to a research path that results in the development of a pharmaceutical with no visible link to the initial hint.[465] In these cases it appears quite doubtful whether the traditional knowledge provider could be joint inventor under current standards.

The next problem is the allocation of knowledge and rights to a single inventor. Intellectual property protection in the form of patent protection usually applies to an identifiable inventor, an identifiable invention and a defined restricted act[466] whereas traditional knowledge is often not assigned to an individual holder or a single inventor. Although individual ownership is a concept found in traditional knowledge communities, e.g. a shaman monopolizing his knowledge of healing by using rituals, the majority of traditional communities rely on collectively held ownership. Due to this aspect of traditional knowledge it will be quite difficult to assign the traditional knowledge to one identifiable inventor. Very often groups or even states are the stakeholders. This has the consequence that there are no identifiable inventors who could claim inventorship or joint inventorship.[467] Local and indigenous peoples are generally not in a position to claim patents for their knowledge. The collective nature of traditional knowledge hardly fits into contemporary ownership conception.

So far, no cases show the application of the joint ownership concept to traditional medical knowledge contributions. It appears overall that the cases in which joint inventorship of traditional knowledge groups or, more precisely, members of such groups and developers of final products is given will be quite rare.

---

464 Supra Part 2:3.1.2.

465 Carvalho, From the Shaman's Hut to the Patent Office: A Road Under Construction, in McManis, Biodiversity and the Law, 241, 250.

466 Gervais, Spiritual but not Intellectual? The Protection of Sacred Intangible Traditional Knowledge, 11 Cardozo Int'l & Comp. L. 467, 467, 485.

467 Hahn, Traditionelles Wissen indigener und lokaler Gemeinschaften zwischen geistigen Eigentumsrechten und der *public domain*, 171; Gervais, Spiritual but not Intellectual? The Protection of Sacred Intangible Traditional Knowledge, 11 Cardozo Int'l & Comp. L. 467, 481, 485ff (with emphasis on copyright and communal authorship but also referring to patents).

3.3. ANALYSIS OF THE RESULTS

Cases in which traditional medical knowledge will provide a patentable invention or at least a contribution which allows the local and indigenous groups to claim joint inventorship status are practically non-existent. The patent system and its design are not compatible with the traditional knowledge systems and consequently this kind of knowledge frequently remains unprotected.

3.3.1. THE PUBLIC GOOD PROBLEM

Knowledge that is not protected by an intellectual property mechanism can be freely accessed and used. It is non-rival in consumption and non-excludable. Traditional medical knowledge bears these characteristics because the lack of protection has the consequence that the knowledge holders cannot exclude others from the use of their knowledge once they have gained access. Such knowledge cannot be traded on the market but freely appropriated and used. The providers of the knowledge are not in a position to negotiate the use of their knowledge. In consequence, traditional medical knowledge is a non-tradable public good.

Intellectual property regimes address these problems. Patent law, however, rewards innovations, not discoveries. Economic theory does not support the creation of intellectual property rights for information that is already in the public domain. The non-depletability of informational resources implies that it is economically inefficient to afford exclusive rights in information that is publicly available. The marginal cost of sharing something existing is low. Patent law demands some level of inventiveness. If patents are granted for ideas that are so obvious that people skilled in the art could develop them without much effort, then the incentives provided by the patent system would be unnecessary to generate the idea. In such circumstances the patent would have social costs because it imposes an output restraint on production without necessarily having social benefits because others would have developed the idea even without the incentive to a patent.[468] Traditional medical knowledge is from a technical point of view simple and easy to copy. Its main value stems from a discovery.

These considerations speak against protecting traditional knowledge and support the current status. One might even conclude that it would only harm the free market flow of knowledge from 'preliterate' societies to 'modern' societies which could make better use of it without constraints imposed by intellectual

[468] Merges/Duffy, Patent Law and Policy, 614.

property protection such as disclosure or higher prices.[469] On the other hand, in the absence of a protective system, disincentives to invest in knowledge creation and innovation may be the result. The holders of the knowledge might chose to keep it a secret. Unwillingness to share knowledge can result in an undersupply of knowledge creation and innovation.[470]

3.3.1.1. Suboptimal Rate of Innovation

Economic theory argues that a market for unprotected public goods tends to be inefficient because an undersupply of the respective good is caused. The incentive-to-invest theory sees the economic justification of intellectual property rights in the creation of incentives to invest in the generation of new knowledge. From a dynamic efficiency point an argument against protection is that traditional knowledge is created as a result to the needs faced by a traditional knowledge community and that those communities have created knowledge for thousands of years. Thus, there seems to be no need for the creation of incentives; the communities would not have the dynamic efficiency of promoting new knowledge.[471] On the other hand, it has been noted that traditional knowledge is not static but to a certain extent innovative. Traditional knowledge groups rely to a large extent on existing knowledge but they also create new knowledge.

Intellectual property protection is not only about the creation of new knowledge but also about the dissemination of knowledge. The crucial point is not the creation of incentives to generate the knowledge in the first place but rather to share it and make it available for further research activities. There is an equal danger that the lack of protection results in undersupply of innovation. In this sense there is no difference between the creation of new knowledge and the disclosure of existing but yet undisclosed knowledge. In both cases the availability of the knowledge for the public is the crucial concern. At least it can be anticipated that innovation occurs at higher cost if innovators rely on searching for new knowledge rather than building upon existing knowledge.

In the current systems it is likely that the traditional knowledge groups will keep their knowledge secret.[472] New technologies bring information to the remotest corners of the world. Once the respective local groups learn how their knowledge is used and which profits are generated while at the same time they see their habitats being diminished it is rational to assume that they will demand a share of the profits which could, for example, be used to preserve their

---

469 Carvalho, From the Shaman's Hut to the Patent Office: A Road Under Construction, in McManis, Biodiversity and the Law, 241, 245.

470 Supra Part 1:3.1.1.2.

471 Carvalho, From the Shaman's Hut to the Patent Office: A Road Under Construction, in McManis, Biodiversity and the Law, 241, 245.

472 Kadidal, Subject-Matter Imperialism? Biodiversity, Foreign Prior Art and the Neem Patent Controversy, 37 IDEA 371, 388.

environment. In traditional knowledge communities, means to keep knowledge secret already exist, e.g. the shaman who protects his knowledge by combining its application with the conduction of a ritual.[473] While these mechanisms might not be an effective bar for scientific researchers other means to ensure secrecy will evolve and lead to the unavailability of traditional medical knowledge for follow-on research.

3.3.1.2. Free-Riding

It can be observed that patents on biotechnological inventions in the pharmaceutical sector are essential to secure research and innovation in this field. It can furthermore be concluded that R&D activities relying on traditional medical knowledge are more efficient than projects that concentrate on generating new knowledge. Pharmaceutical R&D and traditional medical knowledge both contribute to social welfare. The use of traditional medical knowledge as an initial input for pharmaceutical R&D without compensating the providers of the knowledge, however, is a form of free-riding. The concept of free-riding refers to scenarios in which the creative work of someone else is copied and sold at costs that are lower than the marginal costs of producing it. In the bioprospecting cases the proprietor invests himself but he takes advantage of the knowledge and thereby reduces his costs.

This constitutes an externality because the patent holder does not bear all the costs of the invention although he appropriates all the profits. A part of the external costs that are located to the traditional knowledge community that provides the knowledge as well as to the source countries that provide the biological resources.

3.3.2. ALLOCATION OF RESOURCES

Most of the world's biodiversity is found in an inverse proportion to technological and industrial wealth.[474] The developing countries in the South are home to the majority of biological diversity and plant genetic resources. The technologies to transfer these resources into marketable products, however, are frequently found in the developed world.

In such a scenario bargaining needs to take place and should ideally lead to the allocation of resources to the mutual benefit of the bargaining parties. It can be observed, however, that access to genetic resources and traditional knowledge is still largely unregulated and free whereas the technologies as well as the

473 Supra Part 1:1.1.3.3; Suchman, Invention and Ritual: Notes on the Interrelation of Magic and Intellectual Property in Preliterate Societies, 89 Colum.L.Rev. 1264.

474 Macilwain, When Rhetoric hits Reality in Debate on Bioprospecting, 392 Nature 535.

improved products and processes are subject to patent protection in the WTO Member States. As a result little technology transfer takes place and the developing source countries frequently face high monopoly prices for pharmaceutical products. This is a dilemma that has been recognized by the CBD and is supposed to be addressed.

In application of the Coase theorem, efficient allocation of resources takes place if rights are clearly defined and transaction costs are low. The *Hoodia* case[475] demonstrates that successful bargaining is possible and private contracts can provide a solution to conflicts. However, cases in which bargaining fails prevail. There are considerable obstacles to private bargaining. Conflicts arise especially in scenarios in which a transnational firm files a patent application without informing the traditional knowledge community about this and – consequently – without offering monetary compensation. The obstacles to private bargaining in these cases are caused by unequal bargaining power and information asymmetries that arise due to the fact that private information is concerned. The parties have different cultural backgrounds and intentions. This results – in the worst case – in mistrust. Contracts work well in scenarios where parties have equal bargaining power. Most developing countries are in a weak bargaining position as they lack scientific and technological capacity to identify and capture the full potential economic benefit that can be extracted by pharmaceutical R&D.[476] As a consequence it is likely that the negotiated royalties are inadequate. Beside different bargaining power and incomplete information, a lack of clearly defined rights is another major obstacle to bargaining. To the extent that the traditional knowledge communities do not hold any clearly defined rights licensing of their innovations cannot take place. In conclusion, both requirements of the Coase theorem are not given. The rights are not clearly defined and the different backgrounds and intentions of the groups lead to high transaction costs.

Although consumer demand for nature-derived products is high the market is inefficient. This concerns both the market for plant derived pharmaceuticals and the market for R&D inputs in this area. The contribution from traditional communities possessing medical knowledge increases the success rate and makes searches and R&D undertakings more efficient. Without inputs from traditional knowledge communities a number of developments in the specific R&D sectors are possible. Firstly, the firms could still proceed on undertaking R&D in this area and achieve positive results. These results, however, would come at higher cost. Secondly, the R&D endeavors in this area could come to an end because the activities turn out to be unprofitable either because the search does not yield any results at all or because the costs of the search are too high to

475 Supra Part 2:2.1.3.2.

476 Dutfield, Intellectual Property, Biogenetic Resources and Traditional Knowledge, 8.

be recouped in the period the final product enjoys exclusive protection. Both developments are inefficient.

3.3.3. IMPLEMENTATION OF THE CBD

The CBD obliges members to provide protection for traditional knowledge and demands for the approval and involvement of the holders of traditional knowledge, innovations and practices and for benefit-sharing. These obligations are set out in Article 8 (j) of the Convention. Disclosure of the source of biological materials and associated traditional knowledge used in an invention are useful to monitor compliance.

3.3.3.1. Prior Informed Consent

Proof of prior informed consent is not required in a patent application. The patent laws in their current form do not provide for any prior informed consent of the providers of the genetic resources and the related knowledge. The approach taken in the US that holds anything under the sun made by man patentable encourages the patentability of altered naturally occurring biological material. The Biotechnology Directive also allows the patenting of altered materials, although somewhat narrower than the approach taken in the US. As a consequence of these concepts anyone who has access to biological material may use them and incorporate them in a patentable invention.[477]

In those rare cases in which a traditional knowledge group holds a patent, infringing activities by third parties will rather result in *ex post* action, e.g. claims for omission or licensing than in prior consent.

3.3.3.2. Benefit Sharing

Benefit sharing regulations are also not implemented under current patent law. The current concept does not induce the negotiation of benefit-sharing agreements. An appropriation of the benefits derived from the utilization of traditional knowledge can be the result of a licensing agreement. This, however, requires a position of the holders of traditional knowledge in which they have room for bargaining, e.g. a right they can license. Beside this, the bargaining power of the groups and the source countries is generally weak. They are often not in a position to develop marketable products themselves because they are often lacking the know-how and the technologies to do so.[478]

---

477 Latorre Quinn, Protection for Indigenous Knowledge: An International Law Analysis, 14 St. Thomas L. Rev. 287, 301.

478 Supra Part 2:3.3.2.

3.3.3.3. *Disclosure of the Origin of the Source*

In regard to the disclosure requirement it can be concluded that disclosure of the source of knowledge and material used is not a mandatory element in the patent application processes. Although patent laws require disclosure of the invention, it does not go as far as to the disclosure of the source of traditional knowledge or the biological material used. Disclosure requirements in patent law ensure the publicity of the invention. Disclosure is required only to the extent as the information is necessary in order to understand how the invention works and to repeat it.

Disclosure of biological material is requested in the Biotechnology Directive.[479] This provision, however, is drawn up in voluntary terms and applies only when disclosure is possible and appropriate. Specification requirements relate only to the invention, not to its background or motivation. Consequently, disclosure in this regard is also only mandatory to the extent that it is necessary to understand how an invention works.

In conclusion, it must be stated that the CBD objectives are not implemented under TRIPS and the patent laws of the United States and the European Union.

3.4. SUMMARY OF THE MAIN RESULTS OF PART 2

The analysis has shown that the evaluated patent regimes do generally not confer rights to countries or indigenous and local communities over naturally occurring genetic resources originating within their territories. The systems rather confer rights over genetic materials that have been altered and such alteration has led to the development of a novel and sufficiently inventive product in the sense that the new product constitutes an improvement of the original remedy.

It is erroneously claimed that companies can import traditional knowledge and patent it as 'new' while a traditional knowledge group cannot. Such practice would contravene the products of nature doctrine. A traditional knowledge group cannot patent because its use is the use of a product as it appears in nature which is barred from patentability as it does not comply with the requirements of invention, novelty and non-obviousness or inventiveness. A foreign company cannot patent a natural product for the same reason. A patent claim requires some form of modification and improvement of the natural occurring substance which can be achieved by applying biotechnological methods and processes.

The position of a traditional knowledge group to claim a patent right for its knowledge or its medical products is therefore weak. Property rights for the end product frequently lie with the company that has developed an altered and

479 Supra Part 2:1.3.1.2.b.

improved product. The patent claim encompassing this final product is furthermore often not invalidated by the prior knowledge or use. Even under a global novelty requirement anticipation is not likely because the groups cannot identify the active agent of the plants they use. The patent claim, however, encompasses exactly the chemical structure of the compound.

The effect of the application of patent laws to traditional medical knowledge and follow-on innovation, however, is not – as claimed by some critiques of the system – that the indigenous groups are deprived of the use of the indigenous biological resources because they face high monopoly prices as a consequence of patenting.[480] The monopoly applies to the altered product only. Another point of argument that seems to be overlooked by the proponents of the 'biopiracy' perspective is that biotechnological R&D involves a lot of scientific ability, inventive contribution and the input of large resources on side of the developers and increases social welfare.

The system as it currently stands nevertheless creates negative externalities. The biotechnological industry enjoys the benefits that arise from the use of traditional medical knowledge but it does not bear all the costs. These are partly allocated to the traditional knowledge communities and source countries which provide access and knowledge without achieving compensation or participating in the derived benefits.

Another severe shortcoming of the current treatment of traditional knowledge and related biotechnological inventions is that the outcomes of patent cases are to some extent unpredictable which may be attributable to policy being decisive rather than clearly applicable rules. Different concepts in the US and the EU lead to different outcomes of patent claims as the *Neem* patents clearly show.[481] But even within one jurisdiction the concepts are not entirely objective and the outcome of cases consequently unpredictable or at least conceived to be so.

The rapid developments in the biotechnological sector have challenged the legal system and put the adaptability of the patent system at issue. While the interaction by the local groups is often not sufficient to establish a patentable product, the knowledge is an important source that provides inputs for the development of valuable biotechnological inventions which increase social welfare. Economic theory suggests that it is efficient to rely on existing knowledge when conducting R&D based on plant genetic resources because such an approach is more likely to yield results than random or mass screening and reduces the costs of research and development considerably. Consequently, incentives need to be set in order to get access to the knowledge and resources. In case traditional knowledge and biological resources are appropriated without

480 Shiva, Global Trade and Intellectual Property: Threats to Indigenous Resources, in Krimsky/Shorett, Rights and Liberties in the Biotech Age, 98, 104.

481 Supra Part 2:2.1.2.2.

adequate acknowledgement and compensation, however, it can be anticipated that access will not be granted. This development runs contrary to what would be beneficial from a welfare point of view.

The US and EU systems as they stand today do not implement the obligations set out in Article 8 (j) of the CBD. They neither require prior informed consent nor induce benefit sharing. Disclosure of the source requirements could be useful to find out about traditional medical knowledge use in patented products. Beside a voluntary disclosure of the source requirement in the Biotechnology Directive, however, disclosure in patent laws is limited to what is necessary to understand how an invention works which does not extend to prior use in a traditional knowledge setting.

Traditional knowledge provides important and valuable input for pharmaceutical R&D. Yet, it is neither protected *per se* nor can a legal basis be found that provides for compensation. Licensing, for instance, can only occur if there is a right that can be licensed. Instead, traditional medical knowledge is non-excludable because the patent system does not confer a patent right on it. It has been shown that under the current conception, incentives are solely set for the pharmaceutical firm that develops a medical product. These firms gain an advantage in the form of reduced search costs of bioprospecting projects. Patents put firms in a position to charge prices above marginal cost during the term of the patent. The traditional knowledge contribution, on the other hand, is not rewarded. There are no incentives for traditional knowledge groups to share their knowledge beside pure altruism. On the long term, secrecy and undersupply can be anticipated.

Intellectual property and especially patents (should) provide important means for strengthening the range of incentives that local communities need for conserving genetic resources and associated traditional knowledge. The ultimate test for any incentive system is whether it can nurture and augment the spirit of experimentation, exploration and sharing.[482]

This is the dilemma that needs to be solved. Pharmaceutical R&D is socially desirable, but so is the use of traditional medical knowledge as an input to such R&D. Biotechnological patenting is essential to ensure an optimal amount of R&D in this sector. Protection of traditional knowledge is indicated and must be taken up in order to work against existing and expected market failures. The necessity to take measures in this regard has been recognized and found its way into international law as the mandate of the CBD. Implementation action, however, has yet not been taken.

---

[482] Gervais, Traditional Knowledge & Intellectual Property: A TRIPS-Compatible Approach, Mich. St. L. R. 2005, 137, 138.

PART 3

PROTECTING AND REWARDING TRADITIONAL MEDICAL KNOWLEDGE CONTRIBUTIONS UNDER PROPERTY AND LIABILITY REGIMES

A number of countries have joined international treaties and thereby put themselves under a legal obligation to protect traditional knowledge. Legal obligations follow in particular from the CBD. Difficulties may arise due to the circumstance that the signatories to the CBD and the Members of the WTO are not congruent groups. Utilitarian reasons dictated by economic considerations justify the assumption that traditional knowledge protection is indicated. The economic reasons that support the protection of traditional medical knowledge include local, national and even global economic and welfare benefits that result from correcting the present market failures and the thereby established incentives to provide access as well as contribution to sustainable use of biological diversity and its conservation.[483] These reasons apply to all countries and not only the signatories of the CBD. Finally, moral obligations are often cited such as an obligation towards indigenous groups to protect their knowledge and to prevent biopiracy. Equity considerations might call for an adequate, fair and equitable sharing of the benefits derived from the use of biological resources and traditional knowledge. To a certain extent these obligations have found their way into the international treaties.

Economic considerations can give guidance as to the adequateness and extent of legal intervention. Generally, free and restricted competition is the favored approach in most of today's economies and is considered to lead to a socially optimal equilibrium in markets but certain market failures can demand for regulation by laws. Such market failures include monopolies, externalities, public goods or severe information asymmetries.[484] Market failures caused by the non-excludability of others from using traditional knowledge, the existence of information asymmetries as barriers to efficient bargaining and the uncertainty of rights distort the equilibrium in the area of traditional knowledge.[485] In order to assure an efficient use of the resource 'traditional knowledge' these problems must be addressed.

Article 8 (j) of the CBD obliges Member States to respect, preservation and maintenance of traditional knowledge, innovation and practices relevant to biodiversity conservation. The sharing of benefits derived from the utilization of traditional knowledge and the relevance of the consent of the providers are included in the provision.

In the next chapter, possible shapes of a protective and compensation systems are presented. One approach to traditional medical knowledge protection is a positive protection regime under which the traditional knowledge holders have an intellectual property right in their invention. An alternative to a property right is a liability-based regime that provides for compensation and benefit sharing. Instead of exclusively protecting the traditional knowledge innovation

483 Supra Part 1:2.3; Part 2:3.3.

484 Cooter/Ulen, Law & Economics, 43ff.

485 Supra Part 2:3.3; Part 2:2.2.2.

per se this approach focuses on the regulation of its use. The introduction of disclosure and prior informed consent requirements will be discussed as well.

The following analysis includes a discussion of the economic effects and the degree to which the different approaches can be anticipated to implement the objectives of the CBD and set the desired incentives. From an economic perspective the crucial concern is which effects any action will have on economic development. In the case of traditional medical knowledge this concerns the impact of protection on follow-on innovation in pharmaceuticals.

CHAPTER 1
THE PROPERTY RIGHTS-BASED APPROACH TO PROTECTION

Under a property rights-based approach the traditional knowledge providers receive an enforceable intellectual property right for their knowledge and innovations. This approach addresses the problem of non-excludability of second comers and free-riding. In theory, the grant of a property right puts the owner in a position to prevent others from using the protected knowledge because the use is contingent to the consent of the rights holder. This provides for a bargaining position and allows the owner to negotiate the use of his rights.

1.1. THE CONSTRUCTION OF TRADITIONAL KNOWLEDGE RIGHTS

Protection of traditional knowledge by awarding the traditional knowledge holders a property right for their knowledge can be undertaken by adapting the existing legal framework on patents or by establishing effective *sui generis* rights. A subset of an intellectual property right would be a solution that is based on joint ownership.

1.1.1. NOVEL INTERPRETATION OF EXISTING NORMS

It has been proposed that the existing patent framework is interpretable as to benefit traditional knowledge holders. Lewinski recalls the principle of non-discrimination embodied in the TRIPS Agreement and demands a neutral approach to the patentability of traditional knowledge. Such knowledge must not pre-emptively be judged as being less patentable than knowledge from other sources.[486]

[486] Lewinski, Indigenous Heritage and Intellectual Property, 96.

1.1.1.1. *Invention*

Traditional medical knowledge often presents itself as a discovery of the healing properties of a plant resource. This is an argument against patentability under the product-of-nature doctrine.[487] However, under contemporary patent law the distinction between discovery and invention is blurred to a great extent. Much of what is patented in the area of biotechnology can be considered to be a discovery rather than an invention. This concept has also found its way into European patent law which does not exclude biological materials *per se* from patentability. It has been held that an extension of this line of argument provides a case for the patentability of purified natural substances by indigenous peoples.[488] A less stringent application of the products-of-nature doctrine to traditional medical knowledge may be a viable way to include traditional medical knowledge in the realms of patent law.

1.1.1.2. *Novelty and Inventive Step*

Much of the knowledge of traditional communities is already in the public domain and thus fails to meet the novelty and non-obviousness or inventive step requirements.[489]

A more distinct approach to the assessment of which knowledge is part of the public domain may provide a solution for the perceived disadvantages traditional knowledge communities are exposed to as compared to Western companies. It has been suggested to distinguish between the 'background' of collectively-held knowledge and the 'foreground' of the developments within a traditional knowledge community that constitute specific innovation and individual contributions in response to a changing environment and social needs.[490] The latter should be considered innovative in the patent sense.

Another approach questions the application of the public domain concept to traditional knowledge groups in principle with multifaceted reasons. One argument against the inclusion of traditional medical knowledge in the public domain is that traditional knowledge – while forming part of the state of the art – can still be considered to be novel because it stems from a different knowledge system that is unrelated to and independent from the developments in the formal system.[491] Suchman observes that preliterate societies use magic as a way to monopolize ideas and inventions and concludes that these rituals remove their

---

487 Supra Part 2:1.2.1; Part 2:3.1.1.

488 Mgbeoji, Patents and Traditional Knowledge of the Use of Plants: Is a Communal Patent Regime Part of the Solution to the Scourge of Bio Piracy? 9 Ind. J. Global Legal Stud. 163, 180.

489 Supra Part 2:3.1.2.

490 Lewinski, Indigenous Heritage and Intellectual Property, 96.

491 Biber-Klemm/Cottier, Rights to Plant Genetic Resources and Traditional Knowledge, 246.

inventions from the public domain.[492] Graham notes that different scientific systems should not be prejudiced because they do not follow the Western model.[493] Mgbeoji compares the dissemination of knowledge in a traditional knowledge community with a huge laboratory complex in a developed nation in which many people know about an invention which does not lead to that knowledge falling in the public domain.[494] In case a traditional knowledge community is clearly partitioned from the general public the knowledge cannot be considered to be in the public domain because 'public domain' by definition requires access for more than a restricted group of people.[495] It shows that there are several attempts to a different definition of the public domain under which traditional medical knowledge can be considered to be outside the public domain and thus novel.

These proposals have in common that they attempt to stay in line with the patent concepts. The rationale of patent protection is the creation of incentives to innovate and disseminate new knowledge. At the same time the exclusive protection of knowledge and information causes a deadweight loss and impedes follow-on innovation. The trade-off is hence only efficient if the monopoly applies to new knowledge that was not available to the public before. The novelty and non-obviousness requirements are supposed to ensure this. A patent on traditional medical knowledge and practices cannot be obtained for knowledge that is already widely available. Patent protection can only be discussed if the knowledge is restrictively held. This may be the case if knowledge is monopolized within the community, e.g. by shamans who keep their knowledge secret by the use of rituals or if the community is small and distinctively separated from mainstream civilisation.

1.1.2. SUI GENERIS SYSTEMS – DEFINITION OF NEW RIGHTS FOR INDIGENOUS PEOPLES

Conventional intellectual property rights, however, may not satisfy the interests of the traditional knowledge holders. The concept of private intellectual property is unfamiliar to many indigenous groups. Traditional knowledge often dates back for generations and is handed down to future generations. The groups may have an interest in unlimited protection, e.g. in case the knowledge is considered

492 Suchman, Invention and Ritual: Notes on the Interrelation of Magic and Intellectual Property in Preliterate Societies, 89 Colum.L.Rev. 1264, 1274.

493 Dutfield, TRIPS-related Aspects of Intellectual Property Law, 33 Case W. Res. J. Int'l L. 233, 242.

494 Mgbeoji, Patents and Traditional Knowledge of the Use of Plants: Is a Communal Patent Regime Part of the Solution to the Scourge of Bio Piracy? 9 Ind. J. Global Legal Stud. 163, 179.

495 Hahn, Traditionelles Wissen indigener und lokaler Gemeinschaften zwischen geistigen Eigentumsrechten und der *public domain*, 165; supra Part 2:1.2.2.2.

to be sacred which is not provided for by contemporary patent law.[496] There are furthermore problems in regard to the enforcement of the rights. It is the concern of the patent holder to enforce his rights which requires knowledge of intellectual property laws and activities in the scene, financial and technical means as well as capacity and capability, all of which might not be present in a traditional knowledge society.[497] Finally, the administrative costs of application and enforcement are high.

This may lead to the conclusion that the patent systems can not be modified to incorporate traditional medical knowledge and provide for its protection. An alternative approach proposes the definition of new rights in the form of the creation of *sui generis* rights for traditional knowledge innovation designed as communal intellectual property rights that specifically accommodate the interests of traditional knowledge groups.[498]

A *sui generis* system would have to be carefully designed and poses numerous questions. This concerns foremost the subject matter of protection. Here it is already critical to decide whether to favor one regime covering all manifestations of traditional knowledge.[499] Given that the subject matter is diverse and complex specific regimes designed to cover components of traditional knowledge might be more adequate. Multiple systems could focus on subcategories like artistic creations, expressions and folklore, plant genetic resources for food and agriculture and associated traditional knowledge and traditional medicine.[500] Further components of a *sui generis* system that need to be regulated are the requirements for protection, the content and duration of the conferred rights and questions of ownership. Finally, procedural questions like the mode of acquisition of the rights and enforcement mechanisms need to be addressed.[501] Obviously, the design of a *sui generis* system is a complex task; putting multiple systems at work even increases the complexity. Such a body of law may be difficult to manage and interferences with existing regimes will certainly arise.

---

496 Sahai, ICTSD 2002, 16.

497 Biber-Klemm/Cottier, Rights to Plant Genetic Resources and Traditional Knowledge, 159, 160; Roht-Arriaza, Of Seeds and Shamans: The Appropriation of the Scientific and Technical Knowledge of Indigenous and Local Communities, 17 Mich. J. Int'l L. 919, 957.

498 Mgbeoji, Patents and Traditional Knowledge of the Use of Plants: Is a Communal Patent Regime Part of the Solution to the Scourge of Bio Piracy? 9 Ind. J. Global Legal Stud. 163, 174ff; Mashelkar, Intellectual Property Rights and the Third World, 81 Current Science 955, 957; Cottier/Panizzon, Legal Perspectives on Traditional Knowledge: The Case for Intellectual Property Protection, Journal of International Economic Law, 7 JIEL 371, 387ff.; Bratspies, The New Discovery Doctrine: Some Thoughts on Property Rights and Traditional Knowledge, 31 Am. Indian. L. Rev. 315, 322, 323.

499 Cottier/Panizzon, Legal Perspectives on Traditional Knowledge: The Case for Intellectual Property Protection, Journal of International Economic Law, 7 JIEL 371, 387.

500 Correa, Traditional Knowledge and Intellectual Property: Issues and Opinions surrounding the Protection of Traditional Knowledge, 14.

501 Sahai, ICTSD 2002, 17ff.

With regard to traditional knowledge and due to the ways it is frequently held in communal rights must be available as well as individual ownership.[502] The appropriate content and duration of such rights will be very difficult to determine. A general objection to unlimited protection is that this is at odds with the underlying economic rationale for intellectual property law which demands full disclosure and ultimately puts the knowledge in the public domain after the right expires.[503] Knowledge that is publicly available adds to the stock of knowledge that can be used to build upon. Follow-on research is thereby initiated and sufficiently different products are patentable. A right conceptualized to the needs of traditional knowledge communities, on the other hand, might restrict access and is possibly adverse to the fundamental concept of patent law that the patent is awarded only in exchange for the publicity of the invention.

It can be concluded that the development of a *sui generis* system poses considerable questions and difficulties. Especially the relationship with and impact on existing regimes must be carefully examined which clearly is a long-term task. The creation of a new system should therefore be a solution of last resort. It is preferable to find out why an existing system does not work and adapt it than to put a new system in place for any new problem that does not comfortably fit into existing regimes as there is the obvious danger that one is unable to anticipate its impact on the existing system. With every new *sui generis* system the body of law becomes more complex and error-prone. *Sui generis* intellectual property systems have a tendency of generating social costs which outweigh the aspired social benefits.[504] In the area of intellectual property these costs include a distortion of sharing of know-how and technologies, the blocking or slowing of follow-on innovation, negative effects on access to innovation, increased transaction costs and litigation costs as well as high duplication costs because follow-on innovation must work around the protected subject matter.[505] Finally, the development of a set of new rules to treat the issue of traditional knowledge will take considerably longer than finding ways to solve the problems within the existing rules.

502 Cottier/Panizzon, Legal Perspectives on Traditional Knowledge: The Case for Intellectual Property Protection, Journal of International Economic Law, 7 JIEL 371, 388; Mgbeoji, Patents and Traditional Knowledge of the Use of Plants: Is a Communal Patent Regime Part of the Solution to the Scourge of Bio Piracy? 9 Ind. J. Global Legal Stud. 163, 183, 186.

503 Apart from trademark law, however, which has a different economic justification.

504 Gervais, The Internationalization of Intellectual Property: New Challenges From the Very Old and the Very New, 12 Fordham Intell. Prop. Media & Ent. L.J. 929, 970; Reichman, Of Green Tulips and Legal Kudzu: Repacking Rights in Subpatentable Innovation, 53 VNLR 1743, 1751ff.

505 Reichman/Lewis, Using Liability Rules to Stimulate Local Innovation in Developing Countries: Application to Traditional Knowledge, in Maskus/Reichman, International Public Goods, 337, 341.

1.2. IMPLEMENTATION OF ARTICLE 8 (J) CBD THROUGH TRADITIONAL KNOWLEDGE RIGHTS

Article 8 (j) of the CBD requires prior informed consent and the sharing of the benefits derived from the utilization of traditional knowledge, innovation and practices. Provided that the mentioned practical problems can be overcome, an intellectual property right for the providers of traditional medical knowledge could satisfy these demands. There are several proposals as to the implementation of these objectives, such as a patent right for traditional knowledge provided that the patentability standards are modified in order to encompass traditional medical knowledge or a *sui generis* right that accommodates for the concerns for the traditional knowledge groups. The objections to a newly designed right have been discussed. The analysis below is therefore restricted to the effects of a patent.[506]

A patent confers a bundle of rights. The patent holder is put in a position to use and sell his invention or to prohibit use by third parties. This implies that the use of the protected knowledge will be contingent to the consent of the owners of the right who could demand the omission of use in case a biotechnological invention infringes traditional medical knowledge. The sale or negotiation of a license would result in a partial allotment of the benefits of follow-on applications of the knowledge to the original providers.

The extent of those rights is determined by the breadth of the patent. The value of a patent depends on how much competition the owner faces from substitutes. It must first be determined whether a biotechnologically enhanced product with basically the same function as the indigenous product would infringe the patent for the original product. The approach to determine infringement is exemplified on the examples of US and European patent law.

1.2.1. INTERPRETATION AND INFRINGEMENT

Infringement of a patent is governed by Section 271 of the US Patent Act and Article 69 EPC. An invention is infringing when it falls within the literal meaning of a patent claim. An invention is also infringing if it constitutes a close substitute that performs essentially the same function as the patented invention thereby depriving the patentee of the benefit of his invention. This form of infringement is treated under the 'doctrine of equivalents'.

[506] The reasoning will, however, be largely applicable to *sui generis* right systems provided that they were designed similarily to a patent right.

1.2.1.1. *Literal Infringement*

Literal infringement describes cases in which an invention complies precisely with the patent claim.

The interpretation of the claim starts with an assessment of the ordinary meaning of the words. Evidence from outside the bounds of the patent itself such as dictionaries, encyclopedias or expert testimony can be used.[507] The interpretation is not limited to the dictionary meaning of the terms but includes a new meaning the inventor may create for his invention. The patent specification serves as a dictionary for the claim language.[508]

The main difference between US and European patent law in regard to claim interpretation is the extent to which the prosecution history can be taken into account. In most European countries remarks and acts of the applicant in the course of the examination procedure are not consulted when interpreting the claims.[509] Interpretation of the patent claim in the US, on the other hand, starts with interpreting the claim language based on the intrinsic evidence in the patent specification as well as the prosecution history and the prior art.[510]

1.2.1.2. *The Doctrine of Equivalents*

Patent protection expands to close substitutes under the doctrine of equivalents which has a long tradition in US case law and found its way into European law by means of Article 2 of the Protocol on the Interpretation of Article 69 EPC.

a. US

The doctrine of equivalents in US patent law goes back to early Supreme Court patent cases such as *Winans v Denmead*[511] and was explicitly recognized in the decision in *Graver Tank v Linde Air Products.*[512] The Supreme Court noted that '*imitation of a patented invention which does not copy every literal detail*' is

507 Merges/Menell/Lemley, Intellectual Property in the New Technological Age, 216ff.; Fisher, M., Fundamentals of Patent Law, 174.

508 In the US: *Vitronics Corp. v Conceptronic Inc.*, 90 F.3d 1576, 1582 (1996); in the EU: e.g., BGH IIC 1999, 932 – *Spannschraube* (Germany); Paris Court of Appeal, PIBD 1994, 563, III – *Suspa v Morel* (France); Hacon/Pagenberg, Concise European Patent Law, EPC 2000, Article 69 note 5.

509 E.g.: BGH IIC 2002, 302 – *Kunststoffrohrteil* (Germany); *Bristol-Myers Squibb v Baker Norton*, [1999] RPC 253 (UK); *Kirin-Amgen Inc. v Hoechst Marion Roussel Ltd.* [2005] RPC 9 (UK); *Contacts Lens Liquid*, Hoge Raad, [1998] O.J. EPO 142 (Netherlands). A proposal to change this rule has been rejected at the Diplomatic Conference for the adoption of the EPC; see Hacon/Pagenberg, Concise European Patent Law, EPC 2000, Article 69 note 6.

510 *Vitronics Corp. v Conceptronic Inc.*, supra note 508; Mueller, An Introduction to Patent Law, 275.

511 56 U.S. 330 (1893).

512 339 U.S. 605 (1949).

possible and would '*convert the protection of the patent grant into a hollow and useless thing*' because such conducts would set incentives for copyists to make trivial and unsubstantial changes in order to circumvent the protection conferred by a patent and discourage in consequence disclosure thereby working to the detriment of the primary function of the patent system.[513] Hence, the rationale for the doctrine of equivalents are economic and fairness considerations. On the other hand, the doctrine of equivalents has some negative effects on the public notice function of patent claims because the scope of a patent may not be clear in advance to competitors who rely on the patent claims.

The application of the doctrine of equivalents is subject to some limitations, the most important defense to infringement being prosecution history estoppel which provides that a patentee may not attempt to cover by means of claiming equivalency any subject matter he has surrendered in order to obtain the patent by narrowing his claim down.[514] Courts are furthermore limited by the prior art when interpreting the scope of the patent and determining equivalency.[515]

US case law shows some inconsistency in regard to scope and application of the doctrine of equivalents. In *Hughes Aircraft Co v United States* the Court of Appeal expanded the doctrine by introducing the 'as the whole' test under which the patentee does not need to show infringement of every element of his claims but of the invention 'as a whole'.[516] In the 1980s the doctrine was narrowed down in *Pennwalt Corp. v Durand-Wayland Inc.*[517] where the Court abolished the 'as a whole' approach but required that all elements of an invention must appear in an accused device to find infringement. The Supreme Court took position in regard to the doctrine of equivalents in *Warner-Jenkinson Co, Inc. v Hilton Davis Chemical Co.*[518] It confirmed the determination of equivalence on an element-by-element basis and emphasized the public notice function of the claims which demanded for a narrower application of the doctrine of equivalents. The different conceptions in regard to claim drafting have some influence on the standards. Since every element of a claim is essential and material to that claim under peripheral claim drafting, '*the doctrine of equivalents must be applied to individual elements of a claim, not to the invention as a whole*'.[519] Equivalence occurs if there are no substantial differences in the function each element performs, or in the way it performs that function.[520] The court stated in regard to prosecution history estoppel that in case the patent record does not reveal the

513 *Graver Tank*, id at 607.

514 Fisher, M., Fundamentals of Patent Law, 192; Mueller, An Introduction to Patent Law, 298ff.

515 Merges/Nelson, On the Complex Economics of Patent Scope, 90 Colum. L. Rev. 839, 860.

516 717 F.2d 1351 (1983).

517 833 F.2d 931 (1987).

518 520 US 17 (1997).

519 *Warner-Jenikson*, id at 30.

520 Lemley, The Economics of Improvement in Intellectual Property Law, 75 Tex. L. Rev. 989, 1006.

reasons for amendment of a claim the burden of proof is on the patent owner to show that the amendment did not relate to patentability. If he failed to do so '*prosecution history estoppel would bar the application of the doctrine of equivalents as to that element*'.[521] This rule has been confirmed and further expanded in *Festo Corp v Shoketsu Kinzoku Kogyo Kabushiki Co.* commonly referred to as *Festo II*.[522]

b. European Patent Law

The extent of protection conferred by a European patent is determined by the claims under consideration of the description and the drawings, Article 69 (1) EPC. The principal rule is that the claims determine the extent of protection. According to Article 1 of the Protocol on the Interpretation of Article 69[523], Article 69 does not imply that the extent of protection is limited to the strict, literal meaning of the terms of the claim. Rather the patent is to be interpreted in a manner that confers fair protection on the patentee while at the same time providing a reasonable degree of legal certainty for third parties.

The doctrine of equivalents has been incorporated into European patent law by means of Article 2 of the Protocol on the Interpretation of Article 69 which includes equivalents when determining the extent of protection. Consequently, protection is not limited to embodiments infringing the invention as defined in the strict meaning of the claims. The patentee does not have to show that every element of his invention is embodied in the competing invention in order to prove infringement but only that all the material or essential elements, the essential integers, have been copied.[524]

Under the doctrine of equivalents the solution to the problem by the invention and the alleged infringing device are compared. The German Supreme Court has developed a method for determining equivalence which presumes infringement if a modified element performs substantially the same function and produces substantially the same result; it is obvious to a person skilled in the art that the same result that is achieved by means of the invention can be obtained by means of the modified element; and finally that a person skilled in the art would consider the modified claim feature as an equivalent to the feature in the original claim.[525] Recently some change can be observed in the German jurisprudence in regard to determining equivalence which appears to narrow down the scope of application of the doctrine of equivalence. The Federal Supreme Court decided two cases in which the patent description disclosed several alternatives to achieve a technical solution but only one of these

521 *Warner-Jenikson*, id at 30.

522 522 U.S. 735, 122 S.Ct. 1831 (2002).

523 In the following Interpretation Protocol.

524 Seville, EU Intellectual Property Law and Policy, 103.

525 BGH IIC 2003, 197 – *Custodial II*; BGH IIC 2002, 873 – *Cutting Blade I*.

alternatives was incorporated in the patent claim.[526] The court decided that there was no infringement in grounds of equivalence if the attacked embodiment made use of a disclosed solution that found no explicit expression in the claim as this solution was not within the scope of protection.[527] Equivalence could only be assumed if the alternative solution, while having the same technical result as the claimed solution, also shows differences from that solution that are on a par with the differences between the claimed and the disclosed alternative solution.[528]

The English practice differs from the practice of the continental Contracting States which all apply the doctrine of equivalents. It does not refer to equivalents but determines whether modified devices infringe by undertaking a 'purposive construction' of the patent claims which allows for construing the scope of the claims widely enough to fit the objectively assessed purpose of the claims. Originally, British Courts relied on the *Catnic*-test and distinguished between essential elements of the claim and elements which were not essential.[529] As this classification turned out to be unsatisfactory in a number of respects the test was subsequently modified and is in its current form known as the 'Protocol questions'. Applying this approach, courts ask the following questions: Does the variant have a material effect upon the way the invention works? If yes, the variant is outside the claim. If no, would this (i.e. no material effect) have been obvious for the skilled person at the publication date? If no, the variant is outside the claim. If yes, would the skilled person have understood from the language of the claim that the patentee intended that strict compliance with the primary meaning was an essential requirement of the invention? If yes, the variant is outside the claim.[530]

1.2.1.3. Implications for the Right of Traditional Knowledge Providers

A biotechnologically enhanced product would infringe a traditional knowledge property right under the doctrine of equivalents if it performed essentially the same function and achieved the same result as the original remedy in the same way. However, the changes undertaken by the biotechnological companies can be quite substantial. The characteristics of the original remedy are in many cases improved in regard to the efficiency, the reduction of side effects, the manner of application or the durability. It is therefore questionable whether the enhanced product is an equivalent as to each element of the claim that performs essentially the same function and achieves the same result. In case the efficiency of a

526 BGH X ZR 16/09 – *Okklusionsvorrichtung*; BGH X ZR 69/10 – *Diglyzidverbindung*.
527 BGH X ZR 16/09 – *Okklusionsvorrichtung*.
528 BGH X ZR 69/10 – *Diglyzidverbindung*.
529 House of Lords, [1969] RPC 367, 391.
530 See: *Improver v Remington* [1990] FSR 181, 189; Fisher, M., Fundamentals of Patent Law, 305, 309, 310; Hacon/Pagenberg, Concise European Patent Law, EPC 2000, Article 69 note 16.

medical remedy is improved or the method of application to the human body is altered it cannot be said that the result is achieved in the same way. In other cases there may not even be a direct link between the remedy the traditional group used and the final product because the traditional medical knowledge merely indicated a research path making the assumption of infringement even more difficult.

The proposed traditional knowledge right provides a bundle of rights which can be exerted to exclude others from using the protected subject matter. This puts the holders in a position to demand omission of the use or to bargain benefit-sharing agreements. This, however, works in theory only, if the traditional knowledge right is sufficiently broad in scope. Only then will a development using traditional knowledge infringe the right with the consequence that a license must be obtained. It follows from this that a patent for traditional medical knowledge would have to be very broad in scope in order to cover follow-on applications and to work efficiently towards the implementation of consent and benefit sharing. Otherwise the pharmaceutical end product from a competitive company would constitute a non-infringing substitute. On the other hand, the effects of a broad right for the providers of traditional medical knowledge might be adverse on the innovation process.

1.2.2. ECONOMIC ANALYSIS – THE EFFECTS OF PATENTS IN CUMULATIVE INNOVATION SCENARIOS

The breadth of a patent determines which products infringe and influences how much competition an innovator faces. A broad patent protects the patentee from competition through substitutes, enables him to license and thereby gives him market power.[531]

1.2.2.1. Optimal Allocation of Rights and Division of Profits

The patent mechanism and the scope of patents influence the allocation and distribution of rights between the first and second generation innovation. The scope of the first patent determines which second generation improvements will infringe. As a general rule it can be stated that the broader the first patent the more likely there will be an infringement by a follow-on invention with the consequence that licenses need to be obtained in order to use or market the new product.[532] A narrow first patent, on the other hand, allows for improvements

531 Scotchmer, Innovation and Incentives, 103.

532 Fisher, M., Fundamentals of Patent Law, 143; Green/Scotchmer, On the Division of Profits in Sequential Innovation, 26 RAND J. Econ., 20, 21; Scotchmer, Standing on the Shoulders of Giants: Cumulative Research and the Patent Law, 5 JEP, 29, 30.

that are patentable thereby stimulating R&D in second generation products. This, however, comes at the price of disincentives for first generation innovations.[533]

Improvements to basic inventions are often useful and wanted by society. Generally, the more innovators are engaged the greater are the chances that valuable improvements are developed. The holder of the pioneer patent cannot be expected to undertake all the research, develop all possible improvements or even to pursue the different approaches towards the achievement of one solution which may have independent social values.[534] Consequently, cooperation between different inventors is necessary. Agreements in regard to the use of a protected invention can be concluded, either before any improvement is made and no costs have been incurred yet (*ex ante* agreement) or alternatively, after sunk costs have been incurred and the product is found to be infringing (*ex post* license).

Broad patents for the first innovation may induce *ex post* licensing. Kitch argues that the prospect function of patents supports the case for broad patents on the initial knowledge. According to Kitch, such broad patents would firstly provide incentives for efficient development as they allow the patent holder who owns the prospect of his invention to appropriate the entire benefits. Secondly, Kitch claims that a broad patent on the initial invention encourages coordination between first and second generation inventions and reduces wasteful duplicate research because it allows the patent holder to coordinate research efforts efficiently.[535]

Licensing in the area of intellectual property, however, can be costly and uncertain. It will also not provide fully efficient incentives. Negotiations at this stage will typically concern the incremental value of the second innovation (the willingness of consumers to pay for the improvement) but typically not include the sunk research costs incurred.[536] Furthermore, while the incentives for the second innovator demand that he gets the entire incremental value, the compensation for externalities or spillover the first innovator provides, requires that part of the surplus is allocated to him which results in double marginalization.[537] The assumption that broad patents on the initial knowledge provide for the optimal coordination of research efforts does not take into

533 Scotchmer, Standing on the Shoulders of Giants: Cumulative Research and the Patent Law, 5 JEP, 29, 30.

534 Merges/Nelson, On the Complex Economics of Patent Scope, 90 Colum. L. Rev. 839, 873; Rai, Fostering Cumulative Innovation in the Biopharmaceutical Industry: The Role of Patents and Antitrust, 16 Berkeley Tech. L.J. 813, 825.

535 Kitch, The Nature and Function of the Patent System, Journal of Law and Economics, 20 JLE 265, 276, 278.

536 Scotchmer, Standing on the Shoulders of Giants: Cumulative Research and the Patent Law, 5 JEP, 29, 32; Green/Scotchmer, On the Division of Profits in Sequential Innovation, 26 RAND J. Econ., 20, 23.

537 Scotchmer, Standing on the Shoulders of Giants: Cumulative Research and the Patent Law, 5 JEP, 29, 34.

account that the transaction costs in intellectual property licensing can be considerably high. The subject matter is complex, transactions may involve the assignment of partial legal rights, the parties engage in long-term relationships which require monitoring and the separate values of the first and second generation of innovators as well as the future value of an invention are often difficult to determine.[538] Once coordination is not successful the broad patent on the initial knowledge hinders subsequent research.

There are basically two cases in which broad patents on the original invention are indicated. Firstly, basic inventions with a high stand-alone value and secondly, basic inventions with a low stand-alone but a high value of expected improvements provide cases in which exclusive protection of the basic invention is efficient. The incentives to invest in the basic invention are in these cases indicated due to the large spillovers and the combined welfare effects from the basic and the follow-on inventions.[539]

To sum up, economic theory implies that broad patents stimulate investment in basic research and primary innovation but stifle competition and delay subsequent innovation.[540] Licensing of technologies to improvers can be a way out of this problem. Hence, the more absolute the patent right for the first inventor is, the more critical is effective licensing to subsequent innovation and the more sensitive the industry to market failures in licensing.[541] Impediments to licensing therefore provide a case for more narrow patents.[542] A narrow patent, on the other hand, is less profitable for an innovator as it allows for the marketing of substitutes. As a consequence narrow patents support subsequent research.

1.2.2.2. Hold-up and Anticommons

The conclusion that broad patent protection on first inventions stimulates fundamental research while at the same time discouraging investment in follow-on innovation is not always true as a fundamental research product can have little stand-alone value leading to the situation that its value is not sufficient

538 Lemley, The Economics of Improvement in Intellectual Property Law, 75 Tex. L. Rev. 989, 1053; Rai, Fostering Cumulative Innovation in the Biopharmaceutical Industry: The Role of Patents and Antitrust, 16 Berkeley Tech. L.J. 813, 831.

539 Eger/Ebermann/Ramanujam, Incremental Innovation and Patent Protection for Pharmaceutical Products in India, in Babu et al, Economic Analysis of Law in India, 128, 151; Cooter/Ulen, Law & Economics, 126.

540 Correa, Managing the Provision of Knowledge: The Design of Intellectual Property Laws, in Kaul et al, Managing Global Public Goods, 417.

541 Lemley, The Economics of Improvement in Intellectual Property Law, 75 Tex. L. Rev. 989, 998, 999.

542 Gallini/Scotchmer, Intellectual Property: What is the Best Incentive System? Innovation Policy and the Economy, 2 Innovation Pol'y and the Economy 51, 69.

to cover its costs. As noted by Scotchmer[543] and further developed in the model of Green and Scotchmer[544] production of such inventions will only take place if the producer has the prospect of appropriating (some of) the profits of follow-on inventions (option value).

This provides a case for broad patent protection on the first invention. Second generation innovators, on the other hand, are dependent on the conditions imposed by the holder of the first patent – if the second innovation infringes – and will not invest if they cannot recoup their investment. If no investment in improvements can be anticipated, the first innovator will not invest either since this would be inefficient leading to the economic problem of hold-up.[545] In consequence even socially beneficial innovations would not be developed. As nicely put by Scotchmer, the challenge is to reward first innovators for the foundations they provide to later innovators and ensure also adequate rewards for follow-on innovators for their improvements.[546]

Much knowledge is cumulative and efficient creation of new works and inventions requires access to and use of prior works.[547] Patents at an early stage of the R&D process may be an obstacle to downstream research and commercialization. As Heller and Eisenberg argue in their anticommons model, the underuse of scarce resources occurs once too many entities hold rights thereby putting constraints on each other.[548] Too many patents can also cause a situation commonly referred to as blocking of patents. This may occur if a broad patent on a basic invention and a narrower patent on an improvement held by different owners are related in the sense that the improvement patent is subservient to the original patent. The improvement cannot be executed without infringement of the other patent and the owner of the subservient patent can in turn prohibit the use of the improvement leading to a situation in which the patent owners are blocking each other.[549]

In consequence, there is the concern that a greater number of intellectual property rights may inhibit future innovation and lead to the development of fewer useful products.

543 Scotchmer, Standing on the Shoulders of Giants: Cumulative Research and the Patent Law, 5 JEP, 29, 31.

544 Green/Scotchmer, On the Division of Profits in Sequential Innovation, 26 RAND J. Econ., 20ff.

545 Green/Scotchmer, On the Division of Profits in Sequential Innovation, 26 RAND J. Econ., 20, 22ff.; Lévêque/Ménière, Economics of Patents and Copyright, 39.

546 Scotchmer, Standing on the Shoulders of Giants: Cumulative Research and the Patent Law, 5 JEP, 29, 30.

547 Lemley, The Economics of Improvement in Intellectual Property Law, 75 Tex. L. Rev. 989, 997; Merges/Nelson, On the Complex Economics of Patent Scope, 90 Colum. L. Rev. 839, 908.

548 Heller/Eisenberg, Can Patents Deter Innovation? The Anticommons in Biomedical Research, 280 Science 698ff.

549 Merges/Nelson, On the Complex Economics of Patent Scope, 90 Colum. L. Rev. 839, 860, 861; Rai, Fostering Cumulative Innovation in the Biopharmaceutical Industry: The Role of Patents and Antitrust, 16 Berkeley Tech. L.J. 813, 833.

1.2.2.3. *Conclusion*

A traditional knowledge right would essentially constitute a right in the basic invention and would have to be broad in scope in order to allow the traditional knowledge holders to appropriate its value. Traditional medical knowledge, however, does not have a high stand-alone value. From society's point of view, subsequent biotechnological research is wanted. This is due to the fact that the traditional knowledge remedies are generally crude and in this form not eligible for marketing, transport, storage and sale and cannot be used to the benefit of other people. Even if it is patented it is still unlikely that the local and indigenous communities can make profits with this right by marketing the protected product themselves.

The combination of the basic invention and subsequent innovation, however, is valuable. Economic theory supports the protection of the basic invention in this case in order to set incentives to invest under consideration of the large spillovers of the basic invention and the expected large welfare gain of the combination of the primary and secondary innovation.

Traditional knowledge groups, however, do not need strong incentives to invest in innovation. They innovate for their own sake and survival. The incentives that need to be set concern granting access to knowledge, not generating the knowledge in the first place. In addition, it needs to be considered that the model that argues for the patent on the basic invention in light of the expected welfare gains of the combined primary and secondary inventions works only if successful licensing takes place. The negotiation of licenses, however, can cause high transaction costs. The unfamiliarity of the engaged parties and different cultural backgrounds certainly pose difficulties in bargaining situations. The parties may also have different ideas as to the outcome of negotiations. A pharmaceutical company can be expected to act upon profit maximizing considerations. The motivation of the traditional knowledge group may be quite different as non-economic incentives may play a role. They might consider the conservation of their environment or bring beliefs in the negotiations, e.g. in case a sacred plant is used. Unfamiliar groups usually have higher transaction costs when negotiating an agreement. The different cultural backgrounds and intentions make the outcomes of negotiations unpredictable. Overall, there is a high risk that no agreement is found which reduces the incentives for the follow-on innovator to invest in R&D.

Traditional knowledge holders are themselves not in a position to undertake further research and develop medical products but could control their knowledge and exclude other inventors who are capable of developing the improvements. In this scenario the value of the follow-on application is also the value of the initial knowledge and neither party can use its innovation or the improvement, respectively, without the consent of the other which is the classic problem of hold-up. In either case, the resource will not be efficiently used. It appears that in case of traditional knowledge broad patents on the basic invention would rather inhibit future innovators to undertake follow-on research and are not indicated despite the fact that the combined primary and innovation provide for a large welfare gain.

A property right for traditional knowledge may have some advantages for providers of this knowledge. The trade-off can nevertheless overall not be considered to be efficient.

1.3. CO-OPERATION BETWEEN INDIGENOUS GROUPS AND PHARMACEUTICAL COMPANIES AND JOINT INVENTORSHIP

An alternative to a right on the traditional medical knowledge *per se* – be it in the form of a patent or a *sui generis* right – could be provided by the joint inventorship concept.

1.3.1. MODIFICATION OF THE REQUIREMENTS

Under the current rules of collective inventions and joint inventorship there are two distinct problems that prevent an efficient regulation of the use of traditional medical knowledge in biotechnological R&D.

Firstly, the traditional knowledge holders are often not in a position to claim a right in their knowledge and innovations because the invention is in many cases not a clearly defined act attributable to a single inventor but rather the result of cooperative endeavors of the community, developed over time and held collectively. In case the knowledge is monopolized by members of the group, e.g. shamans, these can claim the right. In other cases, the group would have to be considered to be the owner. The law would have to recognize this concept. Here, an amendment of the legal rule would be necessary that allows for traditional knowledge groups to claim the right.

The second problem is the required standard of the quality of the contribution. Frequently the contribution of the groups will be too small to manifest their status as joint inventors as concurrently defined. In order to be duly commensurate to the problem an adaptation of the legal concept would be required under which the requirements as to the contribution and especially collaboration are lowered and clearly defined. Prior informed consent could serve as proof of collaboration.[550] Disclosure requirements could help to include

550 Biber-Klemm/Cottier, Rights to Plant Genetic Resources and Traditional Knowledge, 245.

those contributions that merely indicate a research path but are not directly visible in the final project.

1.3.2. THE RIGHTS OF JOINT INVENTORS

There are several possibilities to adapt the law or modify its interpretation, respectively, with the result that many of the contributions of traditional knowledge groups to pharmaceutical developments would fit within a joint inventorship concept. In a next step, the effects of such an adaptation need to be evaluated. The suitability and effectiveness of this approach to regulate the issue of traditional medical knowledge protection depends on which rights joint inventorship encompasses.

There are different ways joint owners can shape their legal relationship. The most convenient results will be reached if the joint inventors come to an agreement. If this is not possible, a legal rule applies. Two different legal rules can be found in US and German patent law.[551]

The rights of joint inventors include the rights in regard to the utilization of the invention and the distribution of any profits derived from use, sale or licensing activities.

1.3.2.1. Use of the Patented Invention

The right of each inventor to use the patented joint invention is influenced by the extent of the rights of the other inventor. Joint ownership can be conceptualised in the sense that each co-inventor has full access to the patented invention and may employ it as he sees fit. As opposed to this, the owners may be obliged to take their mutual interests into consideration which may go as far as demanding mutual consent. US patent law follows the former, German law the latter concept.

Property rights including ownership are attached to patents as a whole, not to the individual claims. Consequently, in case of joint inventorship each of the inventors presumptively owns a pro rata undivided interest in the entire patent regardless of whether he holds joint inventorship in only one claim.[552] Section 262 of the US Patent Act accords to each of the joint owners to a patent the right to make, use, sell or offer to sell the patented invention if the joint

551 There is no common legal concept to joint inventorship in Europe. The rights of joint inventors are subject to national law in Europe, supra Part 2:3.2.1.2. The EPC regulates the grant of the patent. The content of the conferred right is a matter of the national jurisdictions. German law has been chosen because it follows a different conception than US patent law and provides a good basis for a discussion of the effects of different rules.

552 Merges/Locke, Co-Ownership of Patents: A Comparative and Economic View, 72 J. Pat. & Trademark Off. Soc'y 586, 589.

owners have not agreed otherwise.[553] Consent of the other joint inventor(s) is not required by the legal rule. This applies regardless of how small the size of a co-owner's undivided interest is.

German patent law does not contain any detailed rules in regard to the distribution of rights between joint inventors. In the absence of an agreement between the joint owners, civil law applies. These are the rules regulating partnerships, §§705 or joint ownership, §§741ff of the German civil code.[554] According to the rules each joint inventor has the right to use the invention but must take the rights of other owner(s) into consideration.[555] The denial of consent deprives each inventor of the possibility to license the invention.

1.3.2.2. Sharing of Profits

The underlying assumption of the legal rule is that the joint inventors have contributed equally to the invention. Accordingly they hold an equal share of the rights which translates in a right to an equal distribution of the created surplus between the inventors.[556] However, it can be established between the parties that one owner has contributed a larger part to the invention. This individual determination precedes the legal rule but obviously comes at some costs as it may be difficult to establish the weight of the individual contributions.

1.3.2.1. Discussion

The requirement of mutual consent puts each owner in the position to prevent the use of the patented invention by the other owner(s). This way, the same negative effects a property right confers can occur. As the engaged groups have different cultural backgrounds and intentions it can be expected that difficulties in undertaking negotiations and achieving consent arise.[557] Consequently each owner can block the utilization by the other owner. As opposed to this, if each joint owner can execute the patent rights without consent of the other owners, these effects are to some extent moderated.

---

553 35 U.S.C. Section 262 reads: '*In the absence of any agreement to the contrary, each of the joint owners of a patent may make, use or sell the patented invention without accounting to the other owners.*'

554 The application of the rules for partnerships (§§705ff BGB, Gesellschaft bürgerlichen Rechts) requires some sort of agreement between the parties in the sense of working for a collective purpose.

555 §§743 S. 2, 747 S. 2 German Civil Code (BGB); Kraßer, Patentrecht, 357; Mes, Patentgesetz, §6 note 26.

556 §742 German Civil Code (BGB); Merges/Locke, Co-Ownership of Patents: A Comparative and Economic View, 72 J. Pat. & Trademark Off. Soc'y 586, 588; Chakraborty/Tilmann, Nutzungsrechte und Ausgleichsansprüche einer Mehrheit von Erfindern, in Ann, FS für König, 63, 73.

557 Supra Part 3:1.2.2.3.

With regard to the distribution of profits the legal rule does not frequently lead to satisfactory results. In the traditional knowledge scenario it will generally not be the case that the contributions of the parties are equally valuable. The pharmaceutical company invests in R&D and carries the costs as well as the risk of failure. Consequently, they must get a larger share of the generated surplus. The value of the contributions must be determined for each individual case which increases the costs of bargaining.[558]

As a result the joint ownership approach bears the danger of being inefficient because it requires bargaining and entails high transaction costs.

1.4. CONCLUSION ON THE PROPERTY RIGHTS APPROACH

The property rights approach addresses the problem of non-excludability of second comers to access and use knowledge that is not sufficiently innovative to enjoy exclusive protection under contemporary patent law. A patent or a right designed similarly to a patent gives the holders a bundle of rights including the right to use their knowledge exclusively and to prevent the use by others. At first sight, the property rights approach contains an obvious solution to the problem of free-riding by addressing the problem of non-excludability of traditional knowledge. But while it implements Article 8 (j) CBD to the extent that the proposed 'approval' of the providers of traditional knowledge, innovations and practices will be required it can be expected to limit its 'wider application'.

A positive right for the providers of traditional medical knowledge is beneficial from the point of view of the traditional knowledge groups. There are good reasons for the notion that the providers of traditional knowledge have a legitimate interest in enjoying exclusive protection. The main argument in support is that the current rules allow free-riding and lead to a market failure that causes an undersupply of knowledge that can be used in pharmaceutical R&D. The main drawback of the property rights approaches, however, is that they effectively fail to solve this problem. In order to work for the traditional knowledge providers and enable them to influence the use of their knowledge and extract profits from its utilization the right would have to be sufficiently broad in scope. This would, on the one hand, constitute implementation of the requirement of approval of the groups and put them in theory in a position to license their knowledge, thereby working towards the sharing of benefits from the utilization of their knowledge.

On the other hand, economic reasoning poses the legitimate concern that a positive right would impede subsequent follow-on R&D to the detriment of the

558 Dolder, Patente auf der Grundlage traditioneller Kenntnisse indigener Gemeinschaften, in Ann, FS König, 96.

public at large because broad patents on the initial knowledge require successful licensing in order to allow for the efficient development of innovation. The transaction costs of licensing, however, are high due to the unfamiliarity of the parties, different cultural backgrounds and intentions. A broad patent would take traditional knowledge out of the public domain but not incite follow-on developments using this knowledge. This would be inefficient from society's point of view. Intellectual property rights limit the use of ideas and innovations and thereby create social costs. This is from an economic perspective only justified if they overall encourage enough creation and dissemination of new knowledge to offset these costs. This, however, cannot be anticipated.

A broad intellectual property right on the traditional knowledge, the importance of successful licensing and the probable possibility of failure of negotiations are important arguments against the creation of a traditional knowledge right.

The best solution within the property rights approaches is proposed by a joint inventorship construction as conceptualized in US patent law. The advantage is that the joint owners do not depend on each other's consent to use an invention. While this avoids that blocking occurs, problems in regard to the distribution of profits remain.

In the following alternatives to a property right are discussed.

CHAPTER 2

BENEFIT-SHARING AGREEMENTS AND LIABILITY RULES

At the heart of the CBD lies the idea of benefit sharing. The sharing of the benefits derived from the utilization of elements of biological diversity is addressed in several places of the Convention. First and foremost it is contained in Article 1 of the Convention as one of the objectives. Article 8 (j) CBD speaks of sharing of benefits derived from the utilization of traditional knowledge, innovations and practices and Article 15 (7) CBD extends the principle to the sharing of results of research and developments as well as benefits arising from the utilization of genetic resources between the users and the source countries. Article 19 CBD deals with the distribution of benefits of biotechnological research activities based on genetic resources provided by Contracting Parties.

The purpose of benefit-sharing agreements is to address the problem of missing or inadequate rewards for the use of genetic resources and traditional knowledge contributions. Benefit sharing is ideally reached as a consequence of private bargaining. Private bargaining is preferable to a legal rule because the parties are in a better position to determine the value of their contributions. Generally speaking, private contracts are more flexible than legal rules. Ideally, the legal environment ensures that private bargaining can take place. Experience shows that traditional medical knowledge which serves as a basis for the development of pharmaceutical products does not receive adequate compensation. There are cases in which royalties are paid to the community that provided the knowledge, e.g. in case of the San.[559] However, these cases constitute the exceptions rather than the rule and they all involve voluntary agreements. From a legal perspective the position of a local or traditional community to achieve adequate compensation is weak because the laws do not give them enforceable rights. This implies that other means to ensure that the sharing of profits takes place need to be found.

Benefit sharing can be the result of a legal rule. It has been proposed to implement benefit sharing by imposing an obligation on the patentee to provide proof of a fair and equitable agreement when applying for a patent. An alternative is a liability regime that provides for compensation.

[559] Supra Part 2:2.1.3.2.a.

2.1. MANDATORY BENEFIT-SHARING AGREEMENTS AS CONDITIONS TO PATENTABILITY

Agreements between providers of initial knowledge and improvers can be concluded *ex ante* before the second innovator invests in improvements or *ex post* after the investment has been made. The conclusion of *ex ante* agreements in cumulative innovation scenarios is preferable because at this stage there are no sunk research costs yet and it is ensured that a project is only undertaken if it increases the joint profit. This point of view is notably argued by Scotchmer.[560] The conclusion of *ex post* licenses, on the other hand, neglects the sunk costs.

Requirements to provide proof of a benefit-sharing agreement may induce *ex ante* negotiations. It would be reasonable for a follow-on innovator to conclude such agreements before he invests in his research. On the other hand, the value of the respective contribution is unsure at that time. This, however, is not the only problem that a benefit sharing obligation poses.

The introduction of a requirement overcomes the lack of a bargaining position of the providers of traditional medical knowledge. This implies that proof of evidence of a benefit-sharing agreement must be designed as a condition of patentability in the sense that non-compliance results in the rejection of the patent application in order to be effective. Within the contemporary patent law framework the implementation would require an adaptation of the patent laws by requiring the patent applicant to provide proof of a benefit-sharing agreement when filing his patent application. The obligation to fulfill the requirements must be on the follow-on innovator because he has the relevant information and can act at the lowest costs.

With regard to the content of such agreements it is obvious that the opinions on what is fair and equitable will probably differ. It may also be difficult for a follow-on inventor to identify the person or group that is to be compensated. This is in particular a relevant concern once knowledge in the public domain is used. If the provision of a benefit-sharing agreement was a condition to patentability, the burden to determine the equity of the agreement and the examination of whether the agreement has been concluded between the entitled parties would be on the patent officer which may well be beyond his remit and capability. This implies that such a rule would be error-prone and inefficient.

Furthermore, the conclusion of a benefit-sharing agreement still requires bargaining. This puts a considerable burden on the applicant. Firstly, bargaining between the parties can involve high costs because many parties are involved. The parties that might claim a right in the final drug due to their contributions

---

560 Scotchmer, Standing on the Shoulders of Giants: Cumulative Research and the Patent Law, 5 JEP, 29, 32; Green/Scotchmer, On the Division of Profits in Sequential Innovation, 26 RAND J. Econ., 20, 23.

in the development process include the source country, the collaborating indigenous traditional knowledge group, intermediaries such as the collecting institution and the drug developing company.[561] As explained above, the unfamiliarity of the groups, the different cultural backgrounds and possibly different goals with regard to the direction of the research and the outcomes of negotiations constitute impediments to bargaining.[562] Secondly, the subject of the negotiations is mainly private knowledge. Delayed exchange is an issue as well as the problem as to how to assess the value of the initial contribution. This value is unsure at the time the contribution is made and the weight of the respective contributions may well be valued differently by the groups. Finally, the traditional knowledge groups may be reluctant to reveal information which is then not protected. A pharmaceutical company, on the other hand, needs to gain access to the knowledge before concluding an agreement. The contributor will be reluctant to share the knowledge if it is unsure which benefit will flow back; follow-on innovators will not be willing to make a commitment without knowing the value of the contribution.

The introduction of a mandatory benefit sharing provision will not change the situation. Bargaining still entails high transaction costs and may fail. The effect will then be discouragement of follow-on innovation because the firm cannot rely on securing their future profits. The consequence in case no agreement is found is that the use of traditional knowledge will not be possible.

2.2. BENEFIT SHARING UNDER A LIABILITY-BASED APPROACH

The classic alternative to a property right is a liability rule. Liability rules regulate use and provide for compensation for the use of a resource. Contrary to property rules they do not give the owner the right to exclude others. Under a liability rule the use of a resource is allowed without the authorization of the owner on the condition that compensation is paid afterwards. Liability rules are typically used in tort law and aim at deterring infringement.[563] Legal rules compensating for infringing activities are disgorgement of unjust enrichment, payment of lost profit or injunctions.[564]

The determination of the value of an entitlement that is protected by a property right is undertaken by the parties. The advantage of a property rule is that the parties are often best suited to determine the value according to their

561 Horton, Protecting Biological Diversity and Cultural Diversity under Intellectual Property Law, 10 J of Envt'l Law and Litigation 1, 9, 10.

562 Supra Part 3:1.2.2.3.

563 Kaplow/Shavell, Property Rules versus Liability Rules, 109 Harv. L. Rev. 713, 715ff.

564 Cooter/Ulen, Law & Economics, 322ff; Schankerman/Scotchmer, Damages and Injunctions in Protecing Intellectual Property, 32 RAND J. Econ. 199, 200.

preferences. On the other hand, the determination of the value causes assessment costs. Once these costs are too high and negotiations unlikely to be undertaken or to succeed, property rules might prevent economically desirable transactions leading to a welfare loss and a liability rule may lead to economically more satisfying results.[565] Under a liability regime the value of a resource or an entitlement is determined by a court or a jury. As a general rule, a liability rule is to be preferred over a property rule when transaction costs are high and private negotiations are unlikely to succeed.[566]

Liability rules have recently received some attention in the area of intellectual property law.[567] As opposed to the status quo, a liability regime that provides for compensation if traditional knowledge is used constitutes an improvement. A liability regime confers an entitlement to the holders and puts an end to free use.

2.2.1. CONDITIONS OF A COMPENSATORY LIABILITY REGIME

The idea of a compensatory liability regime for small-scale innovation – that is innovation that is not patentable – is discussed by Reichman[568] and Reichman and Lewis.[569] They argue that a properly designed liability regime that allows the use of an innovation under specified conditions will help stimulating local innovation in developing countries and can also be used to enhance traditional knowledge protection.[570] The conditions include the manner of use of an innovation, the period for which it may be employed, the kind of compensation and provisions to modify the terms of use by mutual agreement.[571] Under such a

565 Calabresi/Melamed, Property Rules, Liability Rules, and Inalienability: One View of the Cathedral, 85 Harv. L. Rev. 1089, 1106; Landes/Posner, The Economic Structure of Tort Law, 31.

566 Calabresi/Melamed, Property Rules, Liability Rules, and Inalienability: One View of the Cathedral, 85 Harv. L. Rev. 1089, 1106; Merges, Of Property Rules, Coase and Intellectual Property, 94 Col. L. Rev. 2655, 2663.

567 See for example: Reichman, Of Green Tulips and Legal Kudzu: Repacking Rights in Subpatentable Innovation, 53 VNLR 1743ff.; Merges, Contracting Into Liability Rules: Intellectual Property Rights and Collective Rights Organizations, 84 Cal. L. Rev. 1293ff.; Schankerman/Scotchmer, Damages and Injunctions in Protecing Intellectual Property, 32 RAND J. Econ. 199ff.

568 Reichman, Of Green Tulips and Legal Kudzu: Repacking Rights in Subpatentable Innovation, 53 VNLR 1743ff.

569 Reichman/Lewis, Using Liability Rules to Stimulate Local Innovation in Developing Countries: Application to Traditional Knowledge, in Maskus/Reichman, International Public Goods, 337ff.

570 Id.

571 Reichman, Of Green Tulips and Legal Kudzu: Repacking Rights in Subpatentable Innovation, 53 VNLR 1743, 1781; Reichman/Lewis, Using Liability Rules to Stimulate Local Innovation in Developing Countries: Application to Traditional Knowledge, in Maskus/Reichman, International Public Goods, 337, 348, 349.

rule first innovators, in this case the traditional knowledge communities, can appropriate a part of the second innovator's profit. Reichman and Lewis further suggest that the first innovator can exclude second comers from competing in the same market with a wholesome duplication of the invention and gain the right to use the improvements in order to make further improvements on his own.[572]

As opposed to a property right the use of knowledge that is regulated by a liability rule is not contingent on the consent of the providers. The use is allowed but compensation has to be paid. It must be seen that a liability rule can only be considered to be the second best solution as the groups may still feel disadvantaged if their knowledge can be used without their consent. Nevertheless, introducing a liability regime is an improvement to the current situation because the entitlement of local and traditional peoples in their knowledge is recognized which increases respect and esteem for their knowledge, innovation and practices. This approach has the potential to address the problem of undersupply. At first sight, it appears that monetary compensation may not provide efficient incentives to traditional knowledge groups. On the other hand, financial means put them in a position to preserve their environment and sustain their habitats. Furthermore, a compensatory regime shows that traditional knowledge is valued. This might increase the willingness of young members of indigenous groups to engage in the traditional lifestyle and thereby prevent the erosion of the groups by migration to the cities. Overall, compensation can be anticipated to set efficient incentives for traditional knowledge groups to share their knowledge, innovation and practices.

The main problem will be the determination of the value of the respective contributions.

2.2.2. DETERMINATION OF THE VALUE

Obviously, the proposed liability regime can only work if the compensation is set at an adequate value. If it is too high, deterrence will occur and second generators find the use of the knowledge unattractive. If the value is set too low, the main goal, adequate sharing of benefits has not been reached. From an economic perspective, adequate is the amount that sets efficient incentives for the holders of traditional knowledge to share their knowledge without deterring the incentives of the follow-on innovators.

The main difficulty in applying a liability rule will thus be the determination of the value. Generally, liability rules require setting an external objective standard of value for an entitlement.[573] Property rules, on the other hand, leave difficult valuation problems to the parties.

572 Id at 349ff.

573 Calabresi/Melamed, Property Rules, Liability Rules, and Inalienability: One View of the Cathedral, 85 Harv. L. Rev. 1089, 1106, 1108.

The determination of value under a liability rule can take different forms and be undertaken by different institutions.

2.2.2.1. Statutory Rules

The value of the initial contribution can be determined by a statutory rule that provides for a fixed amount that has to be paid to the traditional knowledge group. Possible ways to determine this amount are a lump-sum upfront payment, a certain percentage of the generated value or royalties. The problem with an upfront payment is the valuation of the contribution at that point. A more suitable alternative is the payment of a constant royalty that can be elevated on the profits and should extend to the length of the patent term. For reasons of simplicity the introduction of certain percentages for certain improvements which could be divided in groups of minor, medium and large contributions has been suggested.[574]

While this approach reduces the transaction costs entailed in private bargaining it is ill-fitted to accommodate to the individual case. The initial contributions and the follow-on investments to develop the final product will generally have different weight and value in each individual case. A statutory rule is also quite static. Even if it was possible to set adequate royalty rates, statutory rules are usually slow in adapting to changes in the industry and may be subject to lobbying which could result in inadequate and inequitable royalties.[575]

2.2.2.2. Collective Rights Organizations

The alternative to a statutory rule is the establishment of a collective rights organization that evaluates the contribution and determines the amount that has to be transferred to the providers of the initial knowledge.

In light of the complexity of the subject matter and the different groups involved, the requirements for the organization that is in charge of determining the value of the respective contributions and set the amount of compensation to be paid are high. The respective organization must be trustworthy to both pharmaceutical companies and traditional knowledge groups. It is clear that it will be very difficult to reconcile the opposing interests and to avoid extensive lobbying to the detriment of a group.

This entails a committee of experts with different backgrounds and nationality. Each party that has interests in the final products and claims to

574 Reichman, Of Green Tulips and Legal Kudzu: Repacking Rights in Subpatentable Innovation, 53 VNLR 1743, 1784; Lemley, The Economics of Improvement in Intellectual Property Law, 75 Tex. L. Rev. 989, 1007ff.

575 Merges, Contracting Into Liability Rules: Intellectual Property Rights and Collective Rights Organizations, 84 Cal. L. Rev. 1293, 1299.

compensation must find itself represented in the organisation. Obviously, the institution has to have access to the relevant information. The institution monitors the use of traditional knowledge, issues licenses and distributes fees to right-holders to the extent their knowledge is used.[576] Given that the relations are international the institution needs to be supranational in order to be considered neutral.

The determination of the benefit to be exchanged takes time and could delay the application process. Furthermore, such an institution could only act after the R&D has been conducted because it would require information as to the weight of the contribution, e.g. the costs of the R&D process and knowledge of the expected profits before coming to a decision. However, if all parties irrevocably commit themselves to the decisions of the institution a postponement of the execution of benefit-sharing could even be independent from the patent application.

2.2.3. IMPACT OF BENEFIT SHARING ON RETAIL COSTS OF PHARMACEUTICALS

There are some arguments in favor of a liability-based compensatory regime. Under a liability regime second comers can access and use the knowledge without permission subject to paying adequate compensation. The clear advantage of a liability rule is that such a regime avoids some of the problems imposed by intellectual property regimes such as blocking, slowing or even inhibiting of follow-on innovation by exclusion of second comers. Since compensation is provided for under a liability rule this does not constitute a free access regime which is an improvement to the current situation. Possibly, a liability rule would even induce private bargaining. A properly designed legal rule which seeks to remove the impediments to private bargaining and is backed up by a subsidiary liability rule that applies in cases in which no agreement is found or in which such an agreement is not fair and equitable has the advantage of inciting private bargaining while avoiding unfair agreements.[577]

In economic terms, the introduction of mandatory benefit-sharing rules will lead to an increase in prices as producer of drugs can be expected to add the additional costs of a benefit-sharing agreement to the retail price.

The marginal cost of innovation is high while the marginal cost of sharing something that already exists is low which generally speaks against the indication of benefit-sharing in such scenarios. It can furthermore be objected

[576] Dutfield, Intellectual Property, Biogenetic Resources and Traditional Knowledge, 117.

[577] Reichman, Of Green Tulips and Legal Kudzu: Repacking Rights in Subpatentable Innovation, 53 VNLR 1743, 1783, 1784; Dolder, Patente auf der Grundlage traditioneller Kenntnisse indigener Gemeinschaften, in Ann, FS König, 88.

that knowledge that has fallen in the public domain should remain free of charge. However, it cannot be disregarded that much of traditional knowledge in the public domain has come there by improper means. As Graham Dutfield notes, the description of a medical application of a plant by an ethnobiologist does not imply that the providing group has decided to abandon any rights they may have in their knowledge.[578] Similarly, methods for concealment of knowledge such as rituals or magical beliefs – albeit being ineffective to deceive a scientist – obviously prove that knowledge was not willingly revealed.

The implications of the failure in the market for R&D inputs through traditional medical knowledge support the introduction of benefit sharing rules. It can be observed that the market does not generate the reasonable and expected result. In a market with full information and in the absence of transaction costs the efficient allocation of resources will take place regardless of the initial allocation and without state intervention (Coase theorem). In this scenario it can be assumed that an efficient allocation of resources takes place regardless of the original assignment of rights. This implies, however, that the assignment of property rights matters and affects the efficient use of resources in situations where the transaction costs are not zero.[579] In a market with full information, potentially valuable knowledge would be sold to the company that seeks it as an input for the development of a new drug. Due to the nature of knowledge and R&D the company would/could not offer a fixed price as it would not know the value of the knowledge as the success of developing a new drug cannot be anticipated. The providers of the knowledge would not give it away for free knowing that the company will possibly make profits out of it. The reasonable solution in this situation is an agreement that gives the providers of the knowledge a fraction of the generated profit in accordance to the value of the contribution in the final product. This outcome would be efficient. However, the market does not generate this result. Instead, much knowledge is appropriated without adequate returns.

As a result of benefit sharing the costs for those that have so far freely used the resource traditional knowledge will certainly increase. On the other hand, this result appears to be merely a reallocation of costs and goes hand in hand with the provision of incentives to contribute to environmental and cultural preservation, sustainable use of biodiversity and generation of new knowledge.

Requiring benefit sharing in some form has the obvious effect of increasing the costs for the patentee. However, these costs arise in any case. In the present scenario – without compensation – the costs are allocated to the providers of resources and knowledge. If they are shifted to the patentee this can be considered to be merely a reallocation of costs which leaves the net sums (costs, profits) unaffected. This is Kaldor Hicks optimal.

---

578 Dutfield, Intellectual Property, Biogenetic Resources and Traditional Knowledge, 118.

579 Cooter/Ulen, Law & Economics, 95.

2.3. CONCLUSION ON BENEFIT SHARING

Benefit sharing is a central objective of the Convention on Biological Diversity. One argument that may indicate that the solution to achieve benefit sharing lies outside the intellectual property regimes is provided by Article 8 (j) of the CBD itself. Patent rights reward knowledge that is new and involves an inventive step whereas benefit sharing as proposed in Article 8 (j) refers to traditional knowledge, innovation and practices in general and is not limited to rewarding new knowledge outside the public domain. The provision does not refer to new knowledge but speaks of benefits arising from the utilization of knowledge. This includes knowledge that is new in the sense that it was not available to the public before as well as knowledge that is in the public domain but useful for further R&D.

It can be anticipated that benefit sharing will have beneficial impacts on traditional medical knowledge preservation, creation and disclosure once the knowledge receives an economic value, recognition and respect. Fair and equitable sharing of benefits would especially promote the interests of the traditional knowledge providers and developing countries who are currently less proficient in access to technology and bargaining. Benefit-sharing agreements give traditional knowledge and biological resources an economic value and increase recognition, esteem and respect for these assets which might ultimately increase the willingness to share them. Such agreements are furthermore indirectly beneficial to conservation issues as the receivers of royalties can be expected to contribute to conservation and sustainable utilization of resources.[580] The sharing of biotechnologies on a *quid pro quo* basis supports the economic development of developing and underdeveloped source countries.

The introduction of proof that a fair and equitable benefit-sharing agreement has been concluded as a condition to patentability, however, is not the optimal solution to implement benefit sharing regulation. This is due to the fact that bargaining between traditional knowledge communities and companies involves high transaction costs. In addition, the placement of such a rule into the patent laws would put the burden of evaluating the equity of the agreements on the patent officers. A liability-based regime accounts to these problems, especially if the determination of the value of a contribution is left to a collective rights organization. This has the clear advantage that the assessment of fairness and equity of an agreement is left to neutral experts. A subsidiary liability rule could even induce the conclusion of private agreements. It will certainly improve the situation of the traditional knowledge providers and help to implement the CBD objectives while at the some time avoiding the problems that occur under a property rights based approach.

---

580 Part 1:1.3.2.

But a liability rule addresses only the problem of denying a reward for the contribution of the traditional knowledge groups. It is an improvement to the current situation because it recognizes the entitlement of traditional knowledge providers in their knowledge. However, it constitutes only a second best solution because it cannot accommodate to cases in which a local group has a legitimate interest in preventing the use of its knowledge.

A liability regime can be used to address benefit sharing in cases in which the knowledge has been accessed by proper means, e.g. the use of knowledge in the public domain. The CBD furthermore demands the involvement and the approval of the holders of traditional knowledge, innovations and practices which is not necessarily provided under a liability rule. Benefit sharing also requires access to the information that traditional knowledge has been used. The introduction of disclosure requirements may be indicated. The next chapter discusses these problems.

CHAPTER 3

PRIOR INFORMED CONSENT AND DISCLOSURE REQUIREMENTS

A prior informed consent requirement provides for the implementation of the CBD mandate and is supposed to increase respect and recognition of traditional knowledge and uses. Prior informed consent requirements and disclosure requirements increase transparency and have the main objective to monitor traditional knowledge use in order to ensure compliance with benefit sharing obligations.[581]

3.1. THE CONTENT AND SCOPE OF THE REQUIREMENTS

Prior informed consent of the providers of traditional medical knowledge and biological resources as well as disclosure requirements as to the origin of the source of genetic material and knowledge used in an invention could be incorporated in the patent application process in the form that the patent applicant has to provide evidence of the compliance with the requirements. The effects and costs of the requirements depend on two factors: firstly, the extent of the requirement and secondly, the sanction in case of non-compliance.

3.1.1. PRIOR INFORMED CONSENT REQUIREMENT

Article 8 (j) of the CBD explicitly refers to the prior informed consent concept as it demands the wider application of the knowledge, innovation and practices of indigenous and local traditional knowledge communities *with the approval and involvement* of the holders of such knowledge. A prior informed consent provision is also contained in Article 15 (5) of the CBD in relation to access to genetic resources.

581 Report of the Commission on Intellectual Property Rights, 85; Carvalho, From the Shaman's Hut to the Patent Office: In Search of a TRIPS-Consistent Requirement to Disclose the Origin of Genetic Resources and Prior Informed Consent, 17 Wash. U. J.L.& Pol'y 111, 116; Carvalho, The TRIPS Regime on Patents, 259.

Different stakeholders could claim that their consent should be decisive, such as the sovereign source country hosting the genetic resources and the traditional knowledge communities or on a local level the traditional knowledge groups inhabiting the areas in which the genetic resources originate. Consequently, the prospector faces the problem to identify whose consent is required which increases his search and bargaining costs.

Knowledge that is widely spread can consequently practically not be subject to a prior informed consent requirement. This follows from the fact that it would be impossible to determine a stakeholder who could claim that his consent is required. Furthermore, consent may be implied once knowledge is in the public domain provided that the knowledge has come into the public domain by proper means.

3.1.2. DISCLOSURE REQUIREMENTS

Disclosure requirements oblige the patent applicant to disclose the source of biological material used in his invention. Disclosure of the origin of the source of biological material requirement is for example regulated in the Biotechnology Directive. Disclosure requirements could also extend to traditional knowledge used in the course of developing an invention in order to monitor traditional knowledge use.

Without disclosure requirements it will be very difficult to find out whether an invention is based on traditional medical knowledge. On the other hand, this also implies that omission to comply with an obligation to disclose the use of traditional knowledge will hardly be discovered. A patent officer will in most cases not have reason to suspect prior use.[582]

As with consent requirements, the extent of the required disclosure needs to be clear to the applicant.

3.1.3. EFFECTS AND COSTS OF PRIOR INFORMED CONSENT AND DISCLOSURE REQUIREMENTS

3.1.3.1. The Sanction in Case of Non-Compliance

Prior informed consent and disclosure of the origin of the source of biological material and traditional knowledge used in a claimed invention can be designed in different forms of intensity.

[582] Dutfield, Intellectual Property, Biogenetic Resources and Traditional Knowledge, 113; Dolder, Patente auf der Grundlage traditioneller Kenntnisse indigener Gemeinschaften, in Ann, FS König, 93.

In a weak form, compliance with the requirements is voluntary and non-compliance does not affect the validity of the rights of the patentee. A voluntary disclosure requirement is contained in the Biotechnology Directive. Mandatory requirements differ as to the legal consequences of non-compliance. In their strongest form the requirements would be conditions to patentability. Non-compliance would result in the rejection of the application and provide grounds for opposition and revocation.

3.1.3.2. The Effects of Disclosure Requirements

Disclosure requirements are monitoring tools. If they are designed as voluntary rules the efficiency is doubtful. In case disclosure requirements are designed in a mandatory way it must be ensured that they do not put an undue burden on the applicant.

It appears that an applicant who has gained access to traditional medical knowledge in the course of a bioprospecting research project can comply with the disclosure requirements at low costs because he knows where he received the material and the knowledge. Pharmaceuticals often rely on a few single compounds. Tracing and declaring the sources of these compounds appears to be a manageable task.[583] It can furthermore be assumed that the source of the associated traditional knowledge is generally known in bioprospecting cases.

The point has been raised that new disclosure requirements – if mandatory and with legal consequences – could add uncertainties to the patent system and negatively effect innovation and economic development incentives of patents.[584] From the point of view of the patent applicant disclosure requirements may be problematic, however, if the biological material used is widely spread or knowledge is not held exclusively by a limited number of people. It will then be impossible for the patent applicant to be sure that he has fulfilled his obligation with the consequence that the success of his application is not reliably predictable. However, the objective of disclosure is to establish a link to prior traditional knowledge use. If the applicant indicates the immediate source he has gained the information from, the purpose will be fulfilled. It is not harmful if the information cannot be derived solely from the indicated source but that there are other sources that could offer the same information. Once disclosure of a source has established reason to suspect prior use in traditional knowledge settings, the onus to trace the providers who have rights to compensation is on the executive body of the liability regime. The patent applicant is under the obligation to disclose the source he got the information from. A requirement to

---

583 Report of the Commission on Intellectual Property Rights, 85; Dutfield, Intellectual Property, Biogenetic Resources and Traditional Knowledge, 113.

584 Santamauro, Reducing the Rhethoric: Reconsidering the Relationship of the TRIPS Agreement, CBD and Proposed New Patent Disclosure Requirements Relating to Genetic Resources and Traditional Knowledge, E.I.P.R. 2007, 91, 91.

disclose all possible sources would evidently be impractical especially with respect to knowledge that is in the public domain. It is crucial to design the disclosure rules clearly in order to add as little uncertainty as possible. Obviously, the danger of misuse and circumvention of disclosure requirements exists.

Finally it should be noted that the main costs are caused by the introduction of a liability regime under which compensation has to be paid for the use of traditional knowledge. The additional costs of disclosure requirements are necessary to implement the benefit sharing rules.

3.1.3.3. The Effects of Prior Informed Consent

Prior informed consent requirements may also perform the function of working towards benefit sharing but they have an additional different purpose than disclosure requirements. A prior informed consent requirement accounts also for the desire of the traditional knowledge groups to influence the appropriation of their knowledge and plays an important role in addressing the problem of misappropriation. If the denial of consent would inhibit the use of the knowledge, the providers of the consent would have effective means to prevent the use of their knowledge. A prior informed consent requirement therefore addresses the problem of non-excludability of follow-on innovators.

Requiring unanimous consent (no one can use a resource unless everyone agrees) can lead to tragic underuse (tragedy of the anticommons). In case denial of the consent by the providers of the traditional knowledge leads to an effective exclusion of the use of the resource at all, the result is inefficient use of the resource because second innovators could not use the resource. In consequence this leads to the same problems as granting a property right over the resource.[585]

The main difference to disclosure requirements is that the patent applicant is dependent on a third party to comply with an obligation. As part of a liability-based regime that aims at achieving the sharing of benefits without inhibiting the use of knowledge for further research, a mandatory prior informed consent requirement cannot be supported.

The introduction of a voluntary rule to provide consent, however, might still serve the purpose of increasing recognition and respect without having the said negative consequences.

3.2. COMPATIBILITY WITH TRIPS

The introduction of additional patent requirements in the national laws in order to protect traditional knowledge must be in accordance with the TRIPS Agreement.

---

585 Supra Part 3:1.2.2.

The TRIPS Agreement mentions disclosure requirements but stays silent in regard to prior informed consent requirements. As these are not mentioned in TRIPS which came into force well after the CBD, one could conclude that leaving out these objectives hints at their incompatibility with TRIPS. This view clearly disregards that the TRIPS agreement is a framework agreement that sets up general obligations but cannot deal with every single problem in the area of intellectual property. Thus, objectives not mentioned in TRIPS are not *per se* inadmissible. They rather may be implemented into national laws as long as they do not infringe the principle explicitly set out in the TRIPS Agreement.

3.2.1. PRIOR INFORMED CONSENT

The introduction of a rule that encourages the provision of prior informed consent in case traditional medical knowledge is used if designed as a voluntary rule without a sanction in case of non-compliance is unproblematic and may be implemented in national patent laws.

3.2.2. DISCLOSURE REQUIREMENTS

In regard to the introduction of disclosure requirements the introduction of a mandatory rule has been proposed. However, this may be incompatible with the TRIPS Agreement and require an amendment.

3.2.2.1. Substantive or Formal Requirements

The incorporation of substantial requirements that are not provided for in the TRIPS Agreement constitutes a violation of the Agreement. Additional formal requirements can be introduced by the Member States provided that they comply with Article 62 TRIPS.

Substantive requirements are those that concern the nature of the invention, namely novelty, non-obviousness and utility. Formal requirements refer to the form in which the invention is presented to the Patent Office. The specification of the invention is the main formal requirement.

Disclosure requirements are formal requirements in this sense because they concern the mode in which the invention is presented.

3.2.2.2. Article 29 TRIPS

Formal conditions to patentability are contained in Article 29 TRIPS. Article 29 TRIPS obliges patent applicants to disclose the invention.[586] To the extent

586 Supra Part 1:3.2.2.3.

disclosure of traditional knowledge used in an invention is necessary to understand the invention, disclosure is already mandatory for an applicant. Generally, the disclosure requirement as discussed under the CBD, however, will not be covered by Article 29 TRIPS as this disclosure requirement has a different objective. It is intended to facilitate monitoring and enforcement of benefit sharing regulations and thus refers to knowledge that gave an initial hint in the inventive process but is not relevant to understanding how the final invention works. This is different from the disclosure patent law requires as part of the fundamental trade-off. Thus, the disclosure requirements cannot be implemented on the basis of Article 29 TRIPS.

3.2.2.3. Article 62 TRIPS

Conditions not incorporated in Article 29 TRIPS can be implemented by the Members in their national laws provided that they comply with Article 62 TRIPS. Article 62 (1) TRIPS requires formal conditions to be reasonable in accordance with the provisions of the TRIPS Agreement.

Reasonable are formal conditions that help patent officers to assess whether an invention meets the substantive requirements for patentability. Disclosure of the source and of prior knowledge used in an invention is reasonable because it is essential to conduct a proper prior art search and to determine novelty and non-obviousness of an invention.[587] Viewed like this, the introduction of such a requirement cannot be considered to discriminate against those WTO members that did not ratify the CBD. The assessment of novelty and non-obviousness is a general concern. Consequently, disclosure requirements that identify traditional knowledge contributions may well be considered reasonable in the sense of Article 62 TRIPS and can be implemented in national patent laws as a formal condition to patentability.

National level action may set a positive example.[588] International action is certainly preferable because traditional knowledge and biological resources are used across borders and the territorial limitations of patents would set the positive effects off and cause an unbalance. Due to the uncertainties in regard to the coverage by Article 29 TRIPS and the general advantages of having a uniform international rule, it would indeed be preferable to implement the requirement within the TRIPS Agreement.

---

587 CIEL, Biodiversity and Intellectual Property Rights, 21.

588 Dolder, Patente auf der Grundlage traditioneller Kenntnisse indigener Gemeinschaften, in Ann, FS König, 88.

3.3. CONCLUSION ON DISCLOSURE AND PRIOR INFORMED CONSENT REQUIREMENTS

In order to support a compensatory benefit sharing regime disclosure requirements need to be incorporated in the patent laws. Such requirement should extend to the disclosure of the source of biological material and traditional medical knowledge used in an invention. The requirement would best be placed in the patent laws, preferable on an international level by incorporation in the TRIPS Agreement. It is crucial to define the extent of the required disclosure clearly and not put an undue burden on the applicant which might impede his incentives to invest. Efficiency considerations, on the other hand, speak for a sanction in case of non-compliance.

The introduction of a prior informed consent requirement, on the other hand, can only be supported in a voluntary form.

3.4. SUMMARY OF THE RESULTS OF PART 3

In this part the effects of a property rights-based approach as opposed to the effects of a liability-based approach were analyzed in regard to their potential to implement the protection of traditional medical knowledge, innovations and practices and their economic effects on pharmaceutical follow-on research that relies on biological resources and incorporates traditional medical applications in order to increase the efficiency of such R&D projects.

The property rights approach aims at the establishment of a positive right on the traditional knowledge which may be achieved either within the patent laws or by the establishment of a *sui generis* regime. In theory, an exclusive right on their innovations allows the holders of the knowledge to control its use and to negotiate agreements under which they can appropriate a share of the profits of follow-on inventions that employ this knowledge. This concept thereby implements the objectives of Article 8 (j) CBD, namely the approval and involvement of the traditional knowledge groups and the sharing of benefits derived from its utilization. A liability-based regime, on the other hand, provides only for benefit sharing. It may be backed up by a prior informed consent requirement and disclosure of the source of genetic material and traditional knowledge used in the laws regulating patentability.

Economic considerations provide arguments against the granting of a property right for traditional knowledge. These are based on the observation that such a right would necessarily have to be broad in scope in order to allow the holders to exploit it. There are general concerns, however, that broad patents on basic knowledge act as impediments to follow-on research. Successful licensing becomes crucial and failure results in inefficient outcomes in which second generation innovation is slowed down or, in the worst case, entirely prevented. There are obstacles that make failure to bargain likely. At the same time, the low stand-alone value of traditional knowledge prevents the holders from exploiting the right and undertaking further research on their own.

Liability rules allow the use of traditional knowledge but provide for the payment of compensation. This avoids the problems caused by the right to exclude conferred by a property right and improves the status quo because the entitlement of the traditional knowledge groups is recognized. The valuation of the contribution by a collective rights organization that consists of experts and represents all involved parties thereby ensures that the sharing of benefits is fair and equitable. Such a liability rule should be subsidiary to private agreements, the conclusion of which might be incited by a back-up rule. Compensation confers recognition and respect and is an improvement to the current situation. Liability rules can furthermore extend to knowledge in the public domain and need not be limited to new knowledge because they are not subject to the rationale underlying intellectual property.

A liability rule must be supported by requirements to disclose the use of biological resources and associated traditional knowledge which would most efficiently be designed as mandatory requirements to patentability. The introduction of disclosure requirements supports monitoring of compliance with the benefit sharing obligation. They must be designed carefully in order not to impose too high a burden on the patent applicant which may have the effects of disinciting R&D. Implementation on an international level is clearly preferable because it provides for uniform rules and overcomes barriers to trade as the consequence of the territorial component of patents.

A liability rule does not implement the requirement of approval of traditional knowledge holders as provided for in Article 8 (j) CBD. This is the disadvantage of such a regime. An obligation of the patent applicant to provide proof of prior informed consent might provide a solution. A rule that results in the rejection of the patent application or provides ground for opposition in case of non-compliance, however, cannot be justified on the grounds of economic theory because it has the same negative effects as a positive right. With regard to prior informed consent the CBD is inconsistent. On the one hand, the approval of traditional knowledge groups is proposed. On the other hand, the CBD supports the application of traditional knowledge, innovation and practices in follow-on innovation. It has been shown that these two goals are likely to contravene each other.

CONCLUSION

THE RESULTS OF THE ANALYSIS AND THE IMPLICATIONS FOR FUTURE DISCUSSIONS

This work has analyzed the role patents can play in implementing the protection of traditional medical knowledge as set out in Article 8 (j) of the Convention on Biological Diversity. The analysis relied on the methods of analyzing the law from an economic perspective. The result is that patents are only to a very limited extent suited to solve the problems. Liability rules appear to be more promising. Measures within the patent system can be used to monitor compliance under the liability rule.

The first part of the work introduced the problem, clarified the subject matter and provided background information necessary to the discussion.

It has been explained that traditional medical knowledge is one form of knowledge held by local and indigenous communities that live in a traditional way often separated from mainstream civilization. These communities have over generations developed medical remedies based on medically effective plants. At the same time they contribute to the preservation of their environment through their sustainable lifestyles. Their knowledge has been discovered to be of great value in modern pharmaceutical R&D. Plants have always played an important role in medicine. The potential to develop effective medication from plant origin has considerably increased with the advances in the biotechnological sector. Biotechnological methods can be employed to isolate and purify the medically active compounds and to reproduce them. The technology is applied on a molecular level and can be undertaken using only small samples of a resource. The inputs for biotechnological R&D stem from biological genetic resources. Valuable leads can be found by mass or random screening but given the large variety of species the hit rate is low. The use of traditional medical knowledge can considerably increase the chances to develop a medical remedy from plant origin because the application indicates a plant that contains an effective agent as well as a method of treatment. The use may also indicate a promising research path in a different direction.

Biotechnological R&D is a complex process. The employed methods are frequently unreliable and the results unpredictable. Small alterations can have unexpected results. The costs of a research project are high, success of a project is not reliably predictable, the time it takes to develop a medical product is long and marketing requires compliance with further time-consuming clinical and administrative approval procedures.

Much research and development is undertaken in the private sector which requires means to ensure that investments can be recouped. The patent system provides these means. A patent confers an in time limited monopoly to the owner which enables him to exclude others from using the protected invention and to charge a monopoly price during the protection term. The rationale underlying patenting is that intellectual creations are non-excludable and often easy to copy. This implies that a creator who has invested time and effort in developing an invention cannot exploit it in the absence of a protective system because once the invention is revealed others could reproduce it at a lower cost. The patent provides an incentive to invest in the creation of innovation. It limits the use of knowledge during the lifetime of the patent and excludes those from using the innovation that are not willing to pay the monopoly price thereby causing a deadweight loss. At the same time, the patent is only rewarded in exchange for the publicity of the invention which ensures that the public at large gains access after the patent expires.

It is this mechanism that links biotechnological pharmaceuticals, biological diversity and traditional knowledge. The final products are protected by patents. To the extent that they are derived from plant resources and associated traditional knowledge the question arises how the rights and the profits should be distributed between countries hosting the resources, traditional communities and the companies developing these final products. The free use of traditional knowledge in patentable inventions is often referred to as 'biopiracy' and there is a strong group condemning this practice as unfair exploitation. Controversial patent cases are manifold.

The Convention on Biological Diversity is an international agreement broaching the issue of loss of biological diversity and traditional knowledge protection. Its main objectives are the conservation and sustainable use of biological diversity and the sharing of benefits derived from the utilization of biological resources. It is based on the principle of national sovereignty and features the renunciation from the common heritage of mankind approach under which biological diversity is treated as an open source. The main problems in regard to biological diversity conservation is the fact that the products are not adequately priced as the market price does not include the costs that the loss of biodiversity creates. This is also an example of the tragedy of the commons. This theory states that open access to a physical resource leads to overutilization. Property rights can lead to a more efficient use. In regard to biological diversity which is mainly found in the developing countries the assignment of property rights gives the biological resources a commercial value which enables the source countries to exploit their resources and employ them to the benefit of their economic development.

In regard to the genetic information embodied in the biological resources and the traditional medical knowledge about the use of such resources, intellectual property rights are relevant. Intellectual property protection addresses the problem that knowledge and information are non-rival in consumption and easy to copy. They can be used by an unlimited number of people without being depleted. However, the use of traditional knowledge without adequate acknowledgement and compensation may lead to an unwillingness of traditional groups to share their knowledge and make it available for the benefit of all with the consequence of undersupply.

The CBD proposes intellectual property rights as one institution that can be used to implement its objectives. When talking about intellectual property rights the TRIPS Agreement becomes relevant as it provides substantial rules in regard to the protection of intellectual property on the international level. The negotiation of the TRIPS Agreement is the result of the tension between globalization and territoriality of intellectual property rights. As the world becomes more and more connected, information is available worldwide and companies are doing business across borders. One area in which markets are becoming increasingly global and international but regulation is still largely unharmonized despite many efforts to change this, is intellectual property protection. Intellectual property rights have a strong territorial component and different standards can create non-tariff barriers to trade. Opinions differ greatly as to the appropriate extent of protection between the developed countries in the North and the developing and underdeveloped countries in the South. The North is generally in favor of strong intellectual property protection. This view is based on the assumption that strong intellectual property regimes foster innovation which is considered to be the key to economic growth. Countries in the South oppose to this and argue that strong intellectual property regimes are detrimental to their economies. The integration of developing countries in the international trading community, however, led to increased intellectual property protection in the developing world – a trend that is continuing. Empirical studies show that while a country needs a certain level of development before it can extract benefits from intellectual property regimes. It appears that, despite the costs of implementation in the long term, developing countries will profit from the introduction of intellectual property protection.

The first part concludes with a closer look at Article 8 (j) of the CBD. The provision relates to traditional knowledge, innovation and practices relevant to the conservation and sustainable use of biological diversity and supports the wider application of such knowledge with the approval and involvement of the holders as well as the encouragement of the sharing of benefits arising from the utilization of such knowledge, innovation and practices. In regard to traditional medical knowledge it makes sense to evaluate the use of intellectual property rights to implement the objectives as knowledge and genetic information contained in plant resources are both potential subjects of intellectual property rights.

The second part evaluates the status quo of traditional medical knowledge and biotechnological inventions under current patent law in the United States and the European Union which are among the most active players in the biotechnology sector. The analysis starts with a comparative account of the patent laws in the United States and the European Union. Emphasis is thereby put on those requirements that are relevant in regard to patenting products derived from natural resources and based on traditional knowledge. These are the exclusion of discoveries, the scope of the state of the art and the assessment of non-obviousness or inventive step, respectively. In both jurisdictions natural products are not patentable. This is based on the products of nature doctrine in the United States and the exclusion of discoveries from patentability in European patent law. Biotechnological enhancements of natural substances, however, that are isolated from their natural environment, processed by means of a technical process and have a superior value are not barred from patentability. In regard to the relevant prior art the different concepts are explained. In US patent law the state of the art encompasses all printed publications but considers unpublished knowledge only if it originated within the US. This has an important consequence because traditional medical knowledge is often only orally transmitted and can hence not anticipate a patent in the US. European patent law, on the other hand, determines the state of the art on a global scale and includes unpublished knowledge from abroad. It nevertheless often leads to the same result because the revelation of traditional medical knowledge and applications does generally not extend to the structure of the effective compound. However, as this is the subject of the patent claim, anticipation does not occur because the disclosure is not technical in nature. Finally, the assessment of inventiveness and non-obviousness is analyzed. Here it is found that biotechnological products are often the results of unreliable processes with unpredictable result. This supports the case for an inventive step. The reduction to practice as undertaken in a traditional knowledge setting, on the other hand, is often simple and merely the next logical step after the usefulness of a plant has been discovered.

The analysis includes two case studies of controversially discussed patents, namely the *Neemfungicide* patent and the *Hoodia* patent. Overall, the application of the patent concepts as interpreted in the United States and the European Union comes to the conclusion that biotechnologically developed pharmaceuticals are patentable. Prior use by a traditional knowledge community does frequently not anticipate the patent claim but an inventive step may in particular cases be doubtful. Traditional medical knowledge, on the other hand, does generally not meet the requirements for patentability. The findings in the cases support the conclusion but they also show that there is some uncertainty as to the application of the patent concepts as well as disharmony as to the outcomes of patent proceedings in the different jurisdictions. Furthermore, it has been found that the contribution of the groups is often not even sufficient for them to claim the status of joint inventor.

Patents for the biotechnological products stay in line with the economic rational for the provision of patent protection. Private industries play an important role in R&D in the pharmaceutical sector. Development of new pharmaceuticals involves high costs but products are often easy to copy. On the side of the pharmaceutical firms incentives to invest in innovation are therefore necessary. They need an adequate option to recoup expenses of R&D which can be provided for by a patent. The classic patent trade-off applies. Society at large enjoys the benefits from improvements in pharmaceuticals and further research based on inventions can be undertaken after the patent expires.

Traditional medical knowledge, on the other hand, does not enjoy exclusive protection under the patent system and can be freely appropriated. The providers of such knowledge are therefore not in a position to exclude others and cannot negotiate about the use of their knowledge. This may eventually result in an unwillingness to reveal their knowledge and cause an undersupply in the market for plant-based pharmaceuticals. At the same time the use of knowledge in a pharmaceutical R&D project without providing for compensation is a form of free riding. A market failure demanding regulation can be observed. The objectives of the CBD have not been implemented so far.

Part 3 discusses the possible shapes of protective regimes and evaluates their economic effects. Protection within the intellectual property rights framework can either take the form of granting a positive property right for traditional medical knowledge or it can be implemented by incorporation of additional requirements into the patent laws, namely proof of prior informed consent and a fair and equitable benefit-sharing agreement. The economic analysis of patents in cumulative innovation scenarios supports the conclusion that a broad property right on traditional medical knowledge provides at first sight an obvious solution to the public good problem. It would also accommodate for the desire of traditional knowledge providers to control the use of their knowledge thereby implementing the required promotion of approval and involvement stated in Article 8 (j) CBD and Article 5*bis* of the Nagoya Protocol. The wider application of traditional medical knowledge in this case and the achievement of sharing of benefits arising from the utilization, however, cannot be expected. Economic reasoning rather leads to the conclusion that such an approach within the patent laws would provide serious obstacles to the employment of traditional medical knowledge in subsequent R&D. This is due to the fact that broad patents on the initial knowledge cause a necessity of successful bargaining. Failure of bargaining licenses for the use of broadly protected basic knowledge effectively hinders the use of the knowledge in second generation innovation. The existence of high transactions costs in the discussed scenarios makes failure likely and thereby implies that R&D in the pharmaceutical biotechnology sector will be inhibited or even prevented under such an approach despite the fact that the social welfare gains from the combined primary and secondary innovation can be expected to be high. The introduction of too many or unclear additional requirements on the option to receive a patent might increase costs for the firms and diminish to the willingness to invest in R&D.

It follows from this that the solution has to be found outside the patent system. The classic alternative to a property right is a liability regime. Under such a regime the use of a resource is allowed provided that compensation is paid afterwards. This is the main result of the work. The protection of traditional medical knowledge can only be supported to the extent that the benefits derived from the use are fairly and equitably distributed. This form of protection is an improvement to the current status. It provides for an efficient trade-off because on the one hand an entitlement of traditional knowledge providers is recognized while on the other hand follow-on applications of their knowledge are not impaired. A liability-based regime requires the creation of a supranational collective rights organization that represents all parties that have interests in the final product and monitors the use of traditional knowledge and values the respective contributions. The patent laws play a role as they provide the best possibility to implement monitoring devices by the introduction of disclosure requirements. The provision of proof of prior informed consent can from an economic perspective be justified within the patent laws only as a voluntary measure that has no effects on the validity of the rights.

A compensatory regime can apply to knowledge in the public domain which is in line with Article 8 (j) CBD that is not limited to newly created knowledge. Benefit sharing can be expected to lead to an increase in drug prices but this increase is not the result of new costs but rather a reallocation of costs from the traditional knowledge groups to the beneficiaries of the products that are developed with the help of this knowledge. This relocation of costs is efficient in terms of Kaldor-Hicks efficiency as the costs that are externalized without a benefit-sharing agreement (borne by the traditional knowledge group) are now internalized and borne by the group that can internalize them (the company that makes the profits and the end user who benefits from the final drug). Benefit sharing will likely positively influence the willingness of indigenous groups to make their knowledge available to follow-on researchers. Traditional knowledge communities are an integral part of the environment and contribute to the achievement of the goals set out in the CBD. If the reward is allocated to the local groups or even source countries it can be expected that it is used for protection of biological diversity and preservation of the habitats of the groups.

All these aspects constitute a welfare gain for society at large. The costs of benefit sharing can be traded-off with increased access to new and yet unknown knowledge and the positive effects for the conservation and sustainable use of biodiversity and the traditional knowledge groups.

For the developing countries it is important to invest in their own R&D capacities if they want to capture the benefits from their biological diversity. Regulation that enforces fair and equitable compensation for the export of genetic materials can only be a first step. Developing countries will not capture the entire possible benefits if they limit themselves to being exporters of the raw materials. First of all, without the ability to estimate the possible benefit from R&D the bargaining position is weak and it is likely that undercompensation occurs. Secondly, biodiversity is currently a valuable input for pharmaceutical R&D. However, the ethnopharmacological approach is by no means the only one. If access becomes too difficult and costly it is possible that other approaches will be used in the long run. Finally, bargaining is difficult where resources and knowledge are offered by several different suppliers. In case plant resources and traditional knowledge are not endemic or unique to one country, intra-country competition will provide severe obstacles to efficient access regulation and negotiations of adequate prices. This problem has, to some extent, been seen and is touched in Article 7*bis* and 8 of the Nagoya Protocol that requires cooperation in cross-border situations.

Innovation and development of advanced technologies contribute to economic growth. Biotechnology has the potential to contribute to the economic growth in developing countries. The implementation of the CBD can facilitate protection of biodiversity and traditional knowledge and sustainable development. The benefits transferred to a developing country also enable countries to invest in the development of their scientific and technological sector. Intellectual property rights are under these circumstances in the interest of developing countries as well.

The issues of access to biological resources and associated traditional knowledge and benefit sharing have just recently been addressed at the conference in Nagoya that successfully adopted the Nagoya Protocol which shall be implemented by 2012.

Overall, the results of the presented analysis imply that further research should be directed towards the shape and effects of a liability-based regime that awards compensation to traditional medical knowledge. It must furthermore be considered to which extent the prior informed consent requirement of Article 8 (j) CBD and Article 5*bis* of the Nagoya Protocol can be modified or must be abolished. Finally, it must not be overlooked that this work has undertaken the analysis on the example of traditional medical knowledge and plant genetic resources. There are, however, many other forms of traditional knowledge. Some bear economic potential and value, as for example measures that can be employed in environmental protection. Other forms of knowledge are more closely related to different forms of intellectual property and a positive approach to protection within a different intellectual property regime might be feasible there. Further research is necessary to decide whether different systems are needed to treat the different categories of knowledge or whether they all fit into one system.

BIBLIOGRAPHY

Abbott, Frederick M. and Gerber, David J. (Eds.), Public Policy and Global Technological Integration, London 1997.

Abbott, Frederick, Cottier, Thomas and Gurry, Francis, The International Intellectual Property System: Commentary and Materials Part I, The Hague 1999.

Abbott, Frederick, Cottier, Thomas and Gurry, Francis, International Intellectual Property in an Integrated World Economy, New York 2007.

Ann, Christoph et al (Eds.), Materielles Patentrecht: Festschrift für Reimar König zum 70. Geburtstag, Cologne 2003.

Arrow, Kenneth J., Economic Welfare and the Allocation of Resources for Invention, NBER Chapter in: The Rate and Direction of Inventive Activity: Economic and Social Factors, pp. 609–626 (1962).

Asebey, Edgar J. and Kempenaar, Jill D., Biodiversity Prospecting: Fulfilling the Mandate of the Biodiversity Convention, 28 Vand. J. Transnat'l L. 703 (1995).

Bauer, Martin W. and Gaskell, George (Eds.), Biotechnology – the Making of a Global Controversy, Cambridge 2002.

Benkard, Georg, Europäisches Patentübereinkommen, Munich 2002.

Biber-Klemm, Susette and Cottier, Thomas, Rights to Plant Genetic Resources and Traditional Knowledge: Basic Issues and Perspectives, Wallingford 2006.

Blakeney, Michael (Ed.), Intellectual Property Aspects of Ethnobiology, Perspectives on Intellectual Property Series Volume 6, London 1999.

Blakeney, Michael, The Protection of Traditional Knowledge under Intellectual Property Law, E.I.P.R. 2000, 251.

Bratspies, Rebecca M., The New Discovery Doctrine: Some Thoughts on Property Rights and Traditional Knowledge, 31 Am. Indian. L. Rev. 315 (2007).

Brinkmann, Stefan and Tilmann, Max. W., EPÜ-Handbuch, 2nd Edition, Cologne, Munich 2009.

Brush, Stephen B. (Ed.), Valuing Local Knowledge: Indigenous Peoples and Intellectual Property Rights, Washington DC 1996.

Burk, Dan L., Biotechnology and Patent Law: Fitting Innovation in the Procrustean Bed, 17 Rutgers Computer & Tech. L. J. 1 (1991).

Burk, Dan L. and Lemley, Mark A., Is Patent Law Technology-Specific?, 17 Berkeley Tech. L.J., 1155 (2002).

Burk, Dan L. and Lemley, Mark A., Policy Levers in Patent Law 89 Va. L. Rev. 1575 (2003).

Calabresi, Guido and Melamed, A. Douglas, Property Rules, Liability Rules, and Inalienability: One View of the Cathedral 85 Harv. L. Rev. 1089 (1972).

Pires de Carvalho, Nuno, From the Shaman's Hut to the Patent Office: In Search of a TRIPS-Consistent Requirement to Disclose the Origin of Genetic Resources and Prior Informed Consent, 17 Wash. U. J. L. & Pol'y 111 (2005).

Pires de Carvalho, Nuno, The TRIPS Regime on Patent Rights, 2nd Edition, The Hague 2005.

Chow, Daniel C.K. and Lee, Edward, International Intellectual Property: Problems, Cases and Materials, St. Paul, Minn. 2006.

Center for International Environmental Law (CIEL), Biodiversity and Intellectual Property Rights: Reviewing Intellectual Property Rights in the Light of the Objectives of the Convention on Biological Diversity, 2001.

Commission on Intellectual Property Rights (CIPR), Integrating Intellectual Property Rights and Development Policy, Report of the Commission on Intellectual Property Rights, London 2002.

Conforto, David, Traditional and Modern-Day Biopiracy: Redefining the Biopiracy Debate, 19 J. Envtl. L. & Litig. 357 (2004).

Cooter, Robert, Ulen, Thomas, Law and Economics, 5th Edition, Boston, Mass. 2008.

Cornish, William, Llewelyn, David, Intellectual Property: Patents, Copyright, Trademarks and Allied Rights, 3rd Edition Oxford, 2003.

Correa, Carlos M., Trade Related Aspects of Intellectual Property Rights: A Commentary on the TRIPS Agreement, Oxford, 2007.

Correa, Carlos M., The GATT Agreement on Trade-related Aspects of Intellectual Property Rights: New Standards for Patent Protection, E.I.P.R. 1994, 327.

Correa, Carlos M., Traditional Knowledge and Intellectual Property: Issues and Opinions surrounding the Protection of Traditional Knowledge, Discussion Paper, November 2001, available at: www.quna.org.

Cottier, Thomas and Panizzon, Marion, Legal Perspectives on Traditional Knowledge: The Case for Intellectual Property Protection, 7 Journal of International Economic Law 371 (2004).

Cottier, Thomas and Mavroidis, Petros C. (Eds.), Intellectual Property: Trade, Competition, and Sustainable Development, Michigan 2002.

Cronacher, Axel, Das Recht auf das Patent im Europäischen Patentübereinkommen, Dissertation Munich 1988.

Czmus, Akim F., Biotechnology Protection in Japan, the European Community, and the United States, 8 Temp. Int'l & Comp. L.J. 435 (1994).

Davis, Michael D., The Patenting of Products of Nature, 21 Rutgers Computer & Tech. L.J. 293 (1995).

Demsetz, Harold, Towards a Theory of Property Rights, 57 American Economic Review 347 (1967).

Dolder, Fritz, Traditional Knowledge and Patenting: The Experience of the Neemfungicide and the Hoodia Cases, 26 Biotechnology L. Rep. 583 (2007).

Ducor, Philippe G., Patenting the Recombinant Products of Biotechnology and Other Molecules, The Hague 1998.

Dutfield, Graham, Intellectual Property, Biogenetic Resources and Traditional Knowledge, London 2004.

Dutfield, Graham, TRIPS-related Aspects of Intellectual Property Law, 33 Case W. Res. J. Int'l L. 233 (2001).

Dutfield, Graham and Suthersanen, Uma, Global Intellectual Property Law, Cheltenham 2008.

Babu, P.G. et al (Eds.), Economic Analysis of Law in India, Theory and Practise, New Delhi 2010.

Farnsworth, Norman R. et al, Medical Plants in Therapy, 63 Bulletin of the World Health Organisation 965 (1985).

Fabricant, Daniel S. and Farnsworth, Norman R., The Value of Plants Used in Traditional Medicine for Drug Discovery, 109 Environmental Health Perspectives 69 (2001).

Falvey, Rod, Foster, Neil and Greenaway, David, Intellectual Property Rights and Economic Growth, Research Paper 2004/12, Leverhulm Centre 2004.

Falvey, Rod and Martinez, Reed, Trade and the Globalisation of Patent Right, GEP Research Paper No 02/12 (2002), available at http://ssrn.com/abstract=413263.

Fisher, Matthew, The Fundamentals of Patent Law – Interpretation and Scope of Protection, Oxford 2007.

Funder, Joshua V., Biology, Information and Property: The Legal Appropriation of Plant Biotechnology, 2001.

Gallini, Nancy, Scotchmer, Suzanne, Intellectual Property: What is the Best Incentive System?, 2 Innovation Policy and the Economy 51 (2002).

Garcia, Javier, Fighting Biopiracy: The Legislative Protection of Traditional Knowledge, 18 Berkeley La Raza L.J. 5 (2007).

Gehl-Sampath, Padmashree, Biodiversity Prospecting Contracts for Pharmaceutical Research: Institutional and Organisational Issues in Access and Benefit Sharing, Dissertation Hamburg 2003.

Gepts, Paul, Who Owns Biodiversity, and How Should the Owners be Compensated?, 134 Plant Physiology 1295 (2004).

Gervais, Daniel J., Traditional Knowledge & Intellectual Property: A TRIPS-Compatible Approach, Mich. St. L. R. 2005, 137–166, available at: http://works.bepress.com/daniel_gervais/3.

Gervais, Daniel J. (Ed.), Intellectual Property, Trade and Development: Strategies to Optimize Economic Development in a TRIPS-Plus Era, Oxford 2007.

Gervais, Daniel J., Spiritual but not Intellectual? The Protection of Sacred Intangible Traditional Knowledge, 11 Cardozo J. Int'l & Comp. L. 467 (2003).

Gervais, Daniel J., The Internationalization of Intellectual Property: New Challenges From the Very Old and the Very New, 12 Fordham Intell. Prop. Media & Ent. L.J. 929 (2002).

Gervais, Daniel J., The TRIPS Agreement: Interpretation and Implementation, E.I.P.R. 1999, 156.

Gervais, Daniel J., The TRIPS Agreement: Drafting History and Analysis, 3rd Edition, London 2008.

Ginarte, Juan C. and Park, Walter C., Determinants of patent rights: A cross-national study, 26 Research Policy 283 (1997).

Githaiga, Joseph, Intellectual Property Law and the Protection of Indigenous Folklore and Knowledge, 5 Murdoch University Electronic L. J. 1998, available at: www.murdoch.edu.au/elaw/issues/v5n2/githaiga52.html.

Gould, D.M. and Gruben, W.C., The Role of Intellectual Property Rights in Economic Growth, 48 Journal of Development Economics 323 (1996).

Green, Jerry and Scotchmer, Suzanne, On the Division of Profits in Sequential Innovation, 26 RAND Journal of Economics 20 (1995).

Grubb, Philip W. and Thomson, Peter R., Patents for Chemicals, Pharmaceuticals and Biotechnology: Fundamentals of Global Law, Practice and Strategy, 5th Edition, Oxford 2010.

Guellec, Dominique and van de la Potterie, Bruno, The Economics of the European Patent System: IP Policy for Innovation and Competition, Oxford 2007.

Hacon, Richard and Pagenberg, Jochen (Eds.), Concise European Patent Law, 2nd Edition, Alphen aan den Rijn 2008.

von Hahn, Anja, Traditionelles Wissen indigener und lokaler Gemeinschaften zwischen geistigen Eigentumsrechten und der public domain, Berlin 2004.

Halpern, Sheldon W., Nard, Craig A. and Port, Kenneth L., Fundamentals of United States Intellectual Property Law: Copyright, Patent, Trademark, 2nd Edition, Alphen aan den Rijn 2007.

Hamburger, Matthias and Hostettmann, Kurt, Bioactivity on Plants. The Link Between Phytochemistry and Medicine, 30 Phytochemistry 3864 (1991).

Hansen. Stephen A. and van Fleet, Justin W., Traditional Knowledge and Intellectual Property: A Handbook on Issues and Options for Traditional Holders in Protecting their Intellectual Property and Maintaining Biological Diversity, Washington DC 2003.

Hardin, Garett, Tragedy of the Commons, 162 Science 1243 (1968).

Heller, Michael A. and Eisenberg, Rebecca S., Can Patents Deter Innovation? The Anticommons in Biomedical Research, 280 Science 698 (1998).

Ho, Cynthia M., Building a Better Mousetrap: Patenting Biotechnology in the European Community, 3 Duke J. Comp. & Int'l L. 173 (1992).

Hoeckmann, Bernard M. and Kostecki, Michel M., The Political Economy of the World Trade Organisation, The WTO and Beyond, 3rd Edition, Oxford 2009.

Horton, Curtis M., Protecting Biological Diversity and Cultural Diversity under Intellectual Property Law, 10 J. Envtl. L. & Litig. 1 (1995).

Huft, Michael J., Indigenous Peoples and Drug Discovery Research: A Question of Intellectual Property Rights, 89 Nw. U. L. Rev. 1678 (1995).

Hwang, Eui, Masafumi, Kaneko, Ohnishi, Yasuo and Horinouchi, Sueharu, Production of Plant-Specific Flavanones by Escherichia coli Containing and Artificial Gene Cluster, 69 Applied and Environmental Microbiology 2699 (2003).

Janicke, Paul M., A Commentary on the New Patent Law in the United States, GRURInt. 2011, 887.

Johnson, Martha (Ed.), Lore: Capturing Traditional Environmental Knowledge, Hay River CA 1992.

Kadidal, Shayana, Subject-Matter Imperialism? Biodiversity, Foreign Prior Art and the Neem Patent Controversy, 37 IDEA 371 (1997).

Kalb, Claudia, Pharmacy Island, Newsweek, June 10, 2005.

Kaplow, Louis and Shavell, Steven, Property Rules versus Liability Rules, 109 Harv. L. Rev. 713 (1996).

Karjala, Dennis, Biotech Patents and Indigenous Peoples, 7 Minn. J.L. Sci. & Tech. 483 (2006).

ten Kate, Kerry and Laird, Sarah A., The Commercial Use of Biodiversity: Access to Genetic Resources and Benefit Sharing, London 1999.

Kaul, Inge, Grunberg, Isabelle and Stern, Marc A. (Eds.), Global Public Goods: International Cooperation in the 21st century, New York 1999.

Kitch, Edmund W., The Nature and Function of the Patent System, 20 Journal of Law and Economics 265 (1977).

Kraßer, Rudolf, Patentrecht, 6th Edition, Munich 2009.

Krimsky, Sheldon and Shorett, Peter (Eds.), Rights and Liberties in the Biotech Age, Lanham 2005.

Landes, William M., Posner, Richard A., The Economic Structure of Intellectual Property Law, Cambridge 2003.

Landes, William M. and Posner, Richard A., The Economic Structure of Tort Law, Cambridge 1987.

Lange, David, LaFrance, Mary and Myers, Guy, Intellectual Property, Cases and Materials, 3rd Edition, St. Paul, Mass. 2007.

Latorre Quinn, Miriam, Protection for Indigenous Knowledge: An International Law Analysis, 14 St. Thomas L. Rev. 287 (2001).

Lemley, Mark A., The Economics of Improvement in Intellectual Property Law, 75 Tex. L. Rev. 989 (1997).

Lerch, Achim, Intellectual Property Rights and Economic Resources – An Economic Analysis, Volkswissenschaftliche Diskussionsbeiträge, Universität Kassel, Nr. 08/00.

Lévêque, François, Ménière, Yann, The Economics of Patents and Copyright, 2004, available at: http://papers.ssrn.com/sol3/papers.cfm?abstract_id=642622.

Lévèque,Christian and Mounolou, Jean-Claude, Biodiversity, Chichester 2003.

von Lewinski, Silke, Indigenous Heritage and Intellectual Property, Genetic Resources, Traditional Knowledge and Folklore, 2nd Edition, Alphen aan den Rijn 2007.

Macilwain, Collin, When Rhetoric hits Reality in the Debate on Bioprospecting, 392 Nature 535 (1998).

Mansfield, Edwin, Patents and Innovation: An Empirical Study, 32 Management Science 173 (1986).

Mansfield, Edwin, Intellectual Property Protection, Foreign Direct Investment and Technology Transfer, International Finance Corporation; Discussion Paper Number 19, World Bank 1994.

Mashelkar, Raghunath A., Intellectual Property Rights and the Third World, 81 Current Science 955 (2001).

Maskus, Keith E., Intellectual Property Rights and Economic Development, 32 Case W. Res. J. Int'l L., 471 (2000).

Maskus, Keith E., The Role of Intellectual Property Rights in Encouraging Foreign Direct Investment and Technology Transfer, 9 Duke J. Comp. & Int'l L. 109 (1997).

Maskus, Keith E. and Reichman, Jerome H. (Eds.), International Public Goods and Transfer of Technology Under a Globalized Intellectual Property Regime, Cambridge 2005.

McManis, Charles, Biodiversity and the Law – Intellectual Property, Biotechnology and Traditional Knowledge, London 2007.

Merges, Robert P., Contracting Into Liability Rules: Intellectual Property Rights and Collective Rights Organizations, 84 Cal. L. Rev. 1293 (1996).

Merges, Robert P., Of Property Rules, Coase and Intellectual Property, 94 Col. L. Rev. 2655 (1994).

Merges, Robert P. and Duffy, John F., Patent Law and Policy: Cases and Material, 4th Edition, Newark 2007.

Merges, Robert P. and Locke, Lawrence A., Co-Ownership of Patents: A Comparative and Economic View, 72 J. Pat. & Trademark Off. Soc'y 586 (1990).

Merges, Robert P., Menell, Peter S. and, Lemley, Mark A., Intellectual Property in the New Technological Age, 4th Edition, New York 2006.

Merges, Robert P. and Nelson, Richard R., On the Complex Economics of Patent Scope, 90 Colum. L. Rev. 839 (1990).

Mes, Peter, Patentgesetz, Gebrauchsmustergesetz, 3rd Edition, Munich 2011.

Mgbeoji, Ikechi, Patents and Traditional Knowledge of the Use of Plants: Is a Communal Patent Regime Part of the Solution to the Scourge of Bio Piracy?, 9 Ind. J. Global Legal Stud. 163 (2001).

Moran, Katy, Health: Indigenous Knowledge, Equitable Benefits, IK Notes No. 15, World Bank, 1999.

Moyer-Henry, Kari, Patenting Neem and Hoodia: Conflicting Decisions Issued by the Opposition Board of the European Patent Office, 27 Biotechnology L. Rep. 1 (2008).

Mueller, Janice M., Chemicals, Combinations, and 'Common Sense': How the Supreme Court's KSR Decision Is Changing Federal Circuit Obviousness Determinations in Pharmaceutical and Biotechnology Cases, Legal Studies Reseach Paper Series Working Paper No. 2008–7, available at http://ssrn.com/abstract=1079118.

Mueller, Janice M., An Introduction to Patent Law, 2nd Edition, New York 2006.

Mugabe, John, Intellectual Property Protection and Traditional Knowledge – An Exploration in International Policy Debate (1999), available at www.wipo.int/tk/en/hr/paneldiscussion/papers/pdf/mugabe.pdf.

O'Driscoll, Gerald P. Jr. and Hoskins, Lee, Property Rights: The Key to Economic Development, 482 CATO Policy Analysis 1 (2003).

Odek, James O., Bio-Piracy: Creating Proprietary Rights in Plant Genetic Resources, 2 J. Intell. Prop. L. 141 (1994).

Oguamanam, Chidi, International Law and Indigenous Knowledge: Intellectual Property, Plant Biodiversity, and Traditional Medicine, Toronto 2006.

Organisation for Economic Co-operation and Development (OECD), Handbook of Biodiversity Valuation – A Guide for Policy Makers, Paris 2002.

Ong, Burton (Ed.), Intellectual Property and Biological Resources, Singapore 2004.

Paterson, Gerald, The European Patent System: The Law and Practise of the European Patent Convention, London 1992.

Posner, Richard, Intellectual Property: The Law and Economics Approach, 19 Journal of Economic Perspectives 57 (2005).

Primo Braga, Carlos A., Fink, Carsten and Sepulveda, Paz, Intellectual Property Rights and Economic Development, World Bank Discussion Paper No. 412 (2000).

Perez Putach, Meir (Ed.), The Intellectual Property Debate: Perspectives from Law, Economics and Political Economy, Cheltenham 2006.

Rai, Arti K., Fostering Cumulative Innovation in the Biopharmaceutical Industry: The Role of Patents and Antitrust, 16 Berkeley Tech. L.J. 813 (2001).
Rates, S.M.K, Plants as Sources of Drugs, 39 Toxicon 603 (2001).
Reichman, Jerome H., Of Green Tulips and Legal Kudzu: Repacking Rights in Subpatentable Innovation, 53 VNLR 1743 (2000).
Roht-Arriaza, Naomi, Of Seeds and Shamans: The Appropriation of the Scientific and Technical Knowledge of Indigenous and Local Communities, 17 Mich. J. Int'l L. 919 (1996).
Sahai, Suman, Protection of Indigenous Knowledge and Possible Methods of Sharing Benefits with Local Communities, International Center for Trade & Sustainable Development (ICTSD), Geneva 2002.
Santamauro, Jon, Reducing the Rhethoric: Reconsidering the Relationship of the TRIPS Agreement, CBD and Proposed New Patent Disclosure Requirements Relating to Genetic Resources and Traditional Knowledge, E.I.P.R. 2007, 91.
Sapp, Heather A., Monopolizing Medical Methods: The Debate over Patent Rights for Indigenous Peoples, 25 Temp. J. Sci. Tech. & Envtl. L. 191 (2006).
Schankerman, Mark and Scotchmer, Suzanne, Damages and Injunctions in Protecing Intellectual Property, 32 RAND Journal of Economics 199 (2001).
Schertenleib, Denis, The Patentability and Protection of DNA Based Inventions in the EPO and the European Union, E.P.I.R. 2003, 125.
Schulte, Rainer, Patentgesetz mit EPÜ, 8th Edition Cologne 2008.
Scotchmer, Suzanne, Innovation and Incentives, Cambridge 2005.
Scotchmer, Suzanne, Standing on the Shoulders of Giants: Cumulative Research and the Patent Law, 5 Journal of Economic Perspectives 29 (Winter 1991).
Sedjo, Roger A., Property Rights, Genetic Resources, and Biotechnological Change, 35 Journal of Law and Economics 199 (1992).
Sena, Guiseppe, Directive on Biotechnological Inventions: Patentability of Discoveries, IIC 1999, 731.
Seville, Catherine, EU Intellectual Property Law and Policy, Cheltenham 2009.
Shapiro, Robert J. and Hassett, Kevin A., The Economic Value of Intellectual Property, 2005.
Simpson, David R., Sedjo, Roger A. and Reid, John W., Valuing Biodiversity for Use in Pharmaceutical Research, 104 Journal of Political Economy 163 (1996).
Singer, Margarete and Stauder, Dieter, Europäisches Patentübereinkommen, Kommentar, 5th Edition, Cologne 2010.
Smarzynska Javorcik, Beata, The Composition of Foreign Direct Investment and Protection of Intellectual Property Rights. Evidence from Transition Economies, 48 European Economic Review 39 (2004).
Soejarto, D.D. et al, Ethnobotany/ethnopharmacology and Mass Bioprospecting: Issues on Intellectual Property and Benefit-sharing, 100 Journal of Ethnopharmacology 15 (2005).
Sutton, Victoria, Law and Biotechnology: Cases and Materials, Durham NC 2007.
Stenson, Anthony J. and Gray, Tim S., The Politics of Genetic Resource Control, London 1999.

Stenton, Gavin, Biopiracy within in the Pharmaceutical Industry: A stark Illustration of how Abusive, Manipulative and Perverse the Patenting Process can be towards Countries of the South, E.I.P.R. 2004, 17.

Suchman, Mark C., Invention and Ritual: Notes on the Interrelation of Magic and Intellectual Property in Preliterate Societies, 89 Colum. L. Rev. 1264 (1989).

Swanson, Timothy M. (Ed.), Intellectual Property Rights and Biodiversity Conservation: An Interdisciplinary Analysis of the Values of Medical Plants, Cambridge 1998.

Takenaka, Toshiko (Ed.), Patent Law & Theory: A Handbook of Contemporary Research, Cheltenham 2008.

Thomas, John R., Pharmaceutical Patent Law, Washington DC 2005.

Trask, Andrew V., 'Obvious to Try': A Proper Patentability Standard in the Pharmaceutical Arts?, 76 Fordham Law Rev. 2625 (2008).

Trebilcock, Michael J. and Howse, Robert, The Regulation of International Trade, 3rd Edition, London 2005.

Tritton, Guy, Intellectual Property in Europe, 3rd Edition, London 2008.

Turner, R. Kerry, Pearce, David and Bateman, Ian, Environmental Economics: An Elementary Introduction, New York 1994.

U.S. Congress, Office of Technology Assessment (OTA), Biotechnology in a Global Economy, Washington DC; 1991.

Van den Bossche, Peter, The Law and Policy of the World Trade Organization: Text, Cases and Materials, Cambridge 2005.

Walterscheid, Edward C., The Nature of the Intellectual Property Clause: A Study in Historical Perspective (Part I), 83 Pat. & Trademark Off. Soc'y 763 (2001).

Watal, Jayashree, Intellectual Property Rights in the WTO and Developing Countries, The Hague 2001.

Wegner, Harold C., Chemical and Biotechnology Obviousness in a State of Flux, 26 Biotechnology L. Rep. 437 (2007).

World Health Organisation (WHO), Factsheet on Traditional Medicine, Factsheet No 134, 2008 available at: www.who.int/mediacentre/factsheets/fs134/en/.

World Health Organisation (WHO), Traditional Medicine Strategy 2002–2005, Geneva 2002.

World Intellectual Property Organisation (WIPO), Intellectual Property and Traditional Knowledge, Booklet No. 2, WIPO Publication No. 920, Geneva 2008.

World Intellectual Property Organisation (WIPO), Intellectual Property Needs and Expectations of Traditional Knowledge Holders, WIPO Report on Fact-Finding Missions on Intellectual Property and Traditional Knowledge (1998–1999), Geneva 2001.

World Trade Organisation (WTO), The Relationship Between the TRIPS Agreements and the Convention on Biological Diversity, Summary of the Issues Raised and Points Made, Note by the Secretariat, Document IP/C/W/368/Rev.1., Geneva 2006.

World Trade Organisation (WTO), A Taxonomy on Country Experiences on International Technology Transfers, Document WT/WGTTT/W/3, Geneva 2002.

Yano, Lester I., Protection of the Ethnobiological Knowledge of Indigenous Peoples, 41 UCLA L. Rev. 443 (1993).

LIST OF CASES

EUROPEAN UNION CASES

T 1/80 - *Bayer/Carbonless copying paper* [1979–85] E.P.O.R. B250
T 24/81 - *BASF/Metal refining* [1979–85] E.P.O.R. B354
T 150/82 - *IFF/Claim Categorie* [1984] O.J. EPO 309
T 2/83 - [1984] O.J. EPO 265
T 14/83 - *Sumitono/Vinyl chloride resins* [1979–85] E.P.O.R. C737
T-144/83 - *Du Pont/Appetite suppressant* [1987] E.P.O.R. 6
T 292/85 - *Gentech* [1989] O.J. EPO 275
T 281/86 - *Unilever* [1989] O.J. EPO 202
T 301/87 - *Biogen* [1990] O.J. EPO 195
T 320/87 - *Lubrizol/Hybrid plants* [1990] O.J. EPO 3
T 611/89 - *Hüls Troisdorf AG* (not reported) cited in Hacon/Pagenberg, Concise European Patent Law
T 19/90 - *Harvard/Onco-mouse* [1990] E.P.O.R. 501
T 877/90 -*Hoopert/t-Cell Growth Factor* [1993] E.P.O.R. 6
T 267/91 - *Plus-Staufer AG* (not reported) cited in Hacon/Pagenberg, Concise European Patent Law
T 409/91 - *Exxon/Fuel oils* [1994] O.J. EPO 653
T 223/92 - *Genentech/HIF-Gamma* [2003] E.P.O.R. 10
T 356/93 - *Plant Genetic Systems,* [1995]O.J. EPO 545
T 39/93 - *Allied Colloids,* [1997]O.J. EPO 134
T 465/93 ABl 96, 32
T 0416/01 - *Neemfungicide*
T 543/04 - *Hoodia*
G 5/83 - *Eisai* [1985] O.J. EPO 64
G 2/88 - *Mobil/Friction reducing additive* [1990] O.J. EPO 93
G 1/92 - *Availability to the public* [1993] E.P.O.R. 241
C 34/10 - *Oliver Brüstle/Greenpeace e.V.* [2011] - not yet published
BGH GRUR 1966, 558 - *Spanplatte*
BGH X ZB 15/67 - *Rote Taube*
BGH GRUR 1978, 583 - *Motorkettensäge*
BGHz 103, 150 - *Fluoran*
BGH GRUR 1995, 330 - *Elektrische Steckverbindung*
BGHZ 98, 12 - *Formstein*
BGH IIC 1999, 932 - *Spannschraube*
BGH GRUR 2001, 226 - *Rollenantriebseinheit*
BGH IIC 2002, 302 - *Kunststoffrohrteil*

BGH IIC 2002, 873 – *Cutting Blade II*
BGH IIC 2003, 197 – *Custodial II*
BGH X ZR 89/07 – *Olanzapin*
BGH X ZR 16/09 – *Okklusionsvorrichtung*
BGH X ZR 69/10 – *Diglyzidverbindung*
VFG X ZR 39/95, GRUR 1998, 1003 – *Leuchtstoff*
Electrical and Musical Industries Ltd v Lissen Ltd 56 RPC 23 (1939)
House of Lords, [1969] RPC 367 – *Catnic*
House of Lords GRUR Int. 1993, 325– *Tumornekrosefaktor*
Court of Appeals GRUR Int 1998, 419 – *Hepatitis-C-Virus II*
Bristol-Myers Squibb v Baker Norton, [1999] RPC 253
Improver v Remington [1990] FSR 181
Kirin-Amgen Inc. v Hoechst Marion Roussel Ltd. [2005] RPC 9
Contacts Lens Liquid [1998] O.J.EPO 142
Tribunale di Milano GRUR Int. 1993, 249 – *Epilady XI*
Paris Court of Appeal, PIBD 1994, 563, III – *Suspa v Morel*

UNITED STATES CASES

Hotchkiss v Greenwood, 52 U.S. 248; 11 How. 248, 13 L.Ed. 683 (1850)
Seymour v Osborne, 78 U.S. 516 (1870)
Atlantic Works v Brady, 107 US 192; 2 S.Ct. 225, 27 L.Ed. 438 (1883)
Cochrane v Badische Anilin & Soda Fabrik, 111 U.S. 293 (1884)
Ex parte Latimer 1889 Dec. Comm'r Pat. 123 (1889)
Winans v Denmead, 56 U.S. 330 (1893).
Kuehmsted v Farbenfabrikanten of Elberfeld Co., 179 F. 701 (1910)
Parke-Davis & Co v H.K. Mulford & Co., 196 F.2d 641 (1929)
Funk Brothers Seed Co v Kalo Inoculant Co,. 76 U.S.P.Q. 280 (1948)
Cuno Engineering Corp., 314 US 84, 51 U.S.P.Q. 1 (1941)
Re Kepler, 132 F.2d 130 (1942)
Graver Tank v Linde Air Products, 339 U.S. 605 (1949)
Merck & Co Inc. v Olin Mathieson Chemical Corp., 253 F.2d 156 (1958)
Brenner v Manson, 383 U.S. 519, 148 U.S.P.Q. (BNA) 689; 86 S. Ct. 1033, 16 L.Ed.2d 69 (1966)
Graham v John Deere Company Kansas City, Calmar, Inc. v Cool Chemical Company, Colgate-Palmolive Company v Cool Chemical Company, 383 U.S.1, 86 S. Ct. 684, 15 L.Ed. 2d 545, 148 U.S.P.Q. 459 (1966)
Re Bridgeford, 537 F.2d 679 (1966)
Monsanto Co. v Kamp, 269 F. Supp. 818, 154 U.S.P.Q. 259 (1967)
Diamond v Chakrabarty 447 U.S. 303, 100 S. Ct. 2202, 65 L.Ed.2d 144 (1980)
Shields v Halliburton Co., 667 F.2d 1232 (1982)
Hughes Aircraft Co v United States, 717 F.2d 1351 (1983)
Idacon, Inc. v Central Forest Products, Inc., (not reported in F. Supp.) 1986 WL 15837, 14 (1986)

Pennwalt Corp. v Durand-Wayland Inc., 833 F.2d 931 (1987)
Spectra-Physics, Inc. v Coherent, Inc., 827 F.2d 1524 (1987)
O'Farrell, 853 F.2d 894 (1988)
Re Wands, 858 F.2d 731 (1988)
Christianson v Colt Industries Operating Corp., 820 F.2d 1992 cert. denied, 493 U.S. 822, 110 S. Ct. 81, 107 L.Ed.2d 47 (1989)
Newman v Quigg, 877 F.2d 1575 (1989)
Amgen, Inc. v Chugai Pharm. Co., 927 F.2d 1200 cert. denied, 502 U.S. 856 (1991)
Vas-Cath v Mahurkar, 935 F.2d 1555 (1991)
Re Vaeck, 947 F.2d 488 (1991)
Burroughs Wellcome Co. v Barr Laboratories, Inc., 40 F.3d 1223 (1994)
Sewall v Walters, 21 F.3d 411 (1994)
Re Deuel, 52 F.3d 1552 (1995)
Re Brana, 51 F. 3d 1560, 34 U.S.P.Q. 2d 1436 (1995)
Ethicon, Inc. v United States Surgical Corporation, 937 F.Supp. 1015 (1996)
Fujikawa v Wattansin, 93 F.3d 1559 (1996)
Mahukar v C.R. Bard, Inc., 79 F.3d 1572 (1996)
Vitronics Corp. v Conceptronic Inc., 90 F.3d 1576, 1582 (1996)
Regents of the University of California v Eli Lilly & Co., 119 F.3d 1559 (1997)
Warner-Jenkinson Co, Inc. v Hilton Davis Chemical Co., 520 US 17 (1997)
Al-Site Corp. v VSI Int'l, Inc., 174 F.3d 1308 (1999)
Enzo Biochem, Inc. v Calgene, Inc., 188 F.3d 1362 (1999)
Solomon v Kimberley-Clark Corp., 216 F.3d 1372 (2000)
McGingley v Franklin Sports, Inc., 262 F.3d 1339, 1351 (2001)
Enzo Biochem, Inc. v Gen-Probe Inc., 323 F.3d 956 (2002)
Festo Corp v Shoketsu Kinzoku Kogyo Kabushiki Co. (Festo II), 522 U.S. 735, 122 S.Ct. 1831 (2002)
KSR International Co. v Teleflex Inc., 127 S.Ct. 1727 (2007)
Pfizer v Apotex, 480 F.3d 1348 (2007)
Takeda Chemical Industries, Ltd. v Alphapharm Pty., 492 F.3d 1350 (2007)

About the author

Petra Ebermann is a fully qualified German lawyer and holds a LL.M. degree in mercantile law (University of Stellenbosch, South Africa). She completed her doctoral thesis while she was a research associate at the Institute of Law and Economics at the University of Hamburg. She currently works as a lawyer specialising in patent, trademark and unfair competition law.

European Studies in Law and Economics

The European Studies in Law and Economics Series is an initiative of the board of the European Doctorate in Law and Economics programme. It is a peer-reviewed book series for a wide audience, including policy makers, legislators, economists, lawyers and judges. The volumes cover a broad range of topics. Each volume is devoted to promote the understanding of the effects of laws on human behaviour, thus providing the tools for a better assessment of the impact of laws on the economic system.

The European Doctorate in Law and Economics (www.edle-phd.eu) is the academic response to the increasing importance of the economic analysis of law in Europe. It is an excellence programme offered by the Universities of Bologna, Hamburg and Rotterdam and sponsored by the European Commission under the Erasmus Mundus scheme. It offers the unique opportunity to study Law and Economics on a PhD level in three different countries. The programme prepares economists and lawyers of high promise for an academic career in a research field of growing importance or for responsible positions in government, research organizations and international consulting groups.

The editors also invite authors from outside the European Doctorate in Law and Economics to submit publishing proposals. Please contact Ann-Christin Maak (ac.maak@intersentia.co.uk) for further information.

www.ingramcontent.com/pod-product-compliance
Ingram Content Group UK Ltd.
Pitfield, Milton Keynes, MK11 3LW, UK
UKHW051922100926
8556IPUK00021B/1329

9 781780 6807